DATE DUE

17 '74	MAY 05 '90	
NOV 14 '76	MAR 24 1991	MAR 03 '95
DEC 6 '77	APR 03 '96	
APR 20 '78		
MAY 9 '80	RT'D MAR 20 '96	
MR 16 '81		
NOV 04 '87	MAY 4 '92	
OCT 1	MAY 27 '97	
	APR 30 '97	
	MAY 02 '93	
MAR 24 '89		
MAR 2	APR 21 '89	APR 07 '96
APR 10 '89		
APR 27 1989		
APR 26 '89		
MAY 01 '92		
MAR 29 '93		
GAYLORD		PRINTED IN U.S.A.

Wordsworth

AND THE ART
OF LANDSCAPE

Wordsworth

AND THE ART OF LANDSCAPE

The outward shows of sky and earth,
Of hill and valley, he has viewed;
And impulses of deeper birth
Have come to him in solitude.

RUSSELL NOYES

HASKELL HOUSE PUBLISHERS Lᴛᴅ.
Publishers of Scarce Scholarly Books
NEW YORK, N. Y. 10012
1973

393331

HASKELL HOUSE PUBLISHERS Ltd.

Publishers of Scarce Scholarly Books

280 LAFAYETTE STREET

NEW YORK. N. Y. 10012

Library of Congress Cataloging in Publication Data

Noyes, Russell.
    Wordsworth and the art of landscape.

    Reprint of the 1968 ed., which was issued as no. 65
of Indiana University humanities series.
    Includes bibliographical references.
    1. Wordsworth, William, 1770-1850. 2. Nature in
poetry. I. Title. II. Series: Indiana. University.
Indiana University humanities series, no. 65.
[PR5892.N2N67 1972]3   821'.7   72-6864
ISBN 0-8383-1660-3

Indiana University Humanities Series Number 65
Indiana University, Bloomington, Indiana

EDITOR: Edward D. Seeber
ASSISTANT EDITOR: David H. Dickason
ASSISTANT EDITOR: Hubert C. Heffner

The Indiana University Humanities Series was
founded in 1939 for the publication of occasional
papers and monographs by members of the faculty.

PREFACE

This book grew out of my love of landscape fostered in my youth spent among the White Mountains of New Hampshire. On summer evenings when the hermit thrush softly trilled his woodnotes, from the porch of our farmhouse I used to watch with increasing delight the long, creeping shadows advance across the meadow. Often I would linger at my station until the darkness came and the song of the thrush was taken over by the shouts of the whip-poor-will. Sometimes in these moments "a holy calm overspread my being," as Wordsworth so eloquently says under somewhat similar circumstances, and I felt

> A never-failing principle of joy,
> And purest passion.

I made no vows; but when the decision of choosing a major subject at college confronted me, I chose to study landscape architecture. Under the skilful guidance of Frank A. Waugh and his staff at the University of Massachusetts I became professionally prepared in this field. At the same time, in the classes of Frank Prentice Rand there came the dawning of another love, the love of "the great Nature that exists in the works/ Of mighty Poets." Hence, after graduation instead of making my way in the world as a landscape architect, as I was prepared to do, I went on to graduate school to study the English poets. Since then, for more than three decades I have been in the ranks of the college teachers of literature with Wordsworth above all others as my poet for special study. Still, landscape architecture has remained with me in a number of ways a lively and rewarding avocation. At long last in this present work I have brought these two lifelong devotions into one compass. Like Robert Frost, who spurned the pleas of the two tramps in mud time to yield to their separation,

> My object . . . is to unite
> My avocation and my vocation
> As my two eyes make one sight.

This work has been based upon a fresh and direct study of original texts, landscape paintings, gardens, and scenery that are involved in the art of landscape. Acknowledgment of my debt to published scholarship is made in the notes; but some books that have been of importance in building the historical background, or influential on points of interpretation, may be singled out for special mention. The chief begetter of this work is Christopher Hussey. In his spirited book, *The Picturesque,* he first revealed the extensive interchange among the arts concerned with the landscape in the eighteenth century and coined the term *the art of landscape* to describe the singleness of those arts. Although I cannot support all of Mr. Hussey's conclusions, I admire the gusto with which he has presented them. He roused me to challenge some of his findings and eventually to examine the art of landscape as a singly oriented art in all of Wordsworth's creative activities. For the history of taste in the eighteenth century I have found B. Sprague Allen's *Tides in English Taste* to be of inestimable value and for aesthetic theory Walter J. Hipple, Jr.'s *The Beautiful, the Sublime, and the Picturesque* of great help. C. V. Deane's *Aspects of Eighteenth-Century Nature Poetry* has been useful in emphasizing the originality of the English landscape poets. William D. Templeman has seemed much the best writer on William Gilpin, and Jean H. Hagstrum has been stimulating and helpful on the relationships between painting and poetry *(The Sister Arts)*. For the chapter on "Wordsworth and Landscape Painting" I have been inspired by Kenneth Clark's brilliant book, *Landscape into Art*, and guided through the year-by-year progress of Wordsworth as art critic by Martha H. Shackford's *Wordsworth's Interest in Painters and Pictures*. For Wordsworth's interpretation of landscape beyond what the poet himself tells us, I have been chiefly helped by C. C. Clarke's *Romantic Paradox*, wherein the author shows how images in the poetry carry the paradox of outer and inner worlds and contribute to rich and noble effects.

In making acknowledgments of personal assistance it is difficult to know where to begin. I owe much to the kindness of librarians, especially those at the Harvard College Library, the Newberry Library, the Indiana University Library, the British Museum, and the Wordsworth Library at Dove Cottage. For special help in the study of the landscape paintings and sketches of Constable I am indebted to the staff at the Victoria and Albert Museum. To my brother, Wilbur Fiske Noyes, with whom I climbed the mountains and camped by the lakes of New Hampshire while he captured their beauty in his canvases, I owe most of whatever critical awareness I may have of landscape painting. To many friends in England who opened their homes and gardens to me I am deeply indebted; among these I must name Dorothy Dixon, great-granddaughter of Wordsworth, who shared the treasures in her home at Stepping Stones, Ambleside; Mr. and Mrs. Hall, the present owners of Lancrigg, who invited me to partake of their sherry and with whom I sat before the open fire talking of Wordsworth and Lancrigg; and Mr. and Mrs. Gifford, residents at Rydal Mount, who graciously showed me about the house and grounds and asked me to come back to take pictures when the sun was right—which, of course, I did. To several authors of books on English gardening, I am indebted for personal kindnesses: to A. G. L. Hellyer, editor of *Amateur Gardening*, who generously shared his expert knowledge of English gardens over coffee in his London club; to H. F. Clark, author of *The English Landscape Garden*, who without prompting on my part sent me his ample and carefully compiled bibliographies; and to Christopher Hussey, already named above, who entertained me at his beautifully landscaped home in Kent, which features a twelfth-century ruined castle. Nor must I omit from mention, though not an author, William Capenor, head gardener at Coleorton Hall, who showed me all around the grounds of the Beaumont estate and pointed out the still distinguishable features of the Winter Garden designed by Wordsworth.

For kind permission to reproduce illustrations for the text I am obligated to the National Gallery, London, the Victoria and Albert Museum, and *Life* magazine. For expert help in taking original photographs I am indebted to my stepson, Ross Lockridge, whose pictures appear in the text along with my own.

My thanks are also due to Frank Prentice Rand, Edward D. Seeber, editor of the Indiana University Humanities Series, for his careful reading and criticism of my manuscript and to my Press editor Walter Albee and his assistant, Patricia Thomas, whose patience and skill have contributed immeasurably to the final form of this book.

To the President and Board of Trustees of Indiana University I am grateful for a sabbatical leave, which gave me freedom to work at the British Museum, to study at major art galleries at home and abroad, and to visit many English gardens.

The greatest obligation is to my wife, Vernice Lockridge Noyes, who has shared my enthusiasm and my wanderings in search of the art of landscape, has been a sympathetic and discerning critic of my labors, and has typed this manuscript.

RUSSELL NOYES

15 April 1966, Indiana University

CONTENTS

ILLUSTRATIONS

to Vernice

INTRODUCTION

William Wordsworth is England's supreme poet of Nature. But Wordsworth did not create his various, affectionate, and extraordinary interpretations of Nature in a vacuum. More than one hundred years of preparation were needed to establish the congenial climate that fostered and inspired him. In England at the beginning of the eighteenth century the world of Nature was conceived of as largely existing apart from man, to be reckoned merely as his servant or his foe. Representations of Nature were narrow and frequently based upon inaccurate observations of natural fact. Life in the country was considered dreary, monotonous, and difficult. There was a prevailing dislike of the grand or the terrible as revealed in mountains, the ocean, storms, and winter. A preference was held for a landscape ordered and made symmetrical by art. Gardens were laid out in geometric patterns, ornamented by trees and shrubs cut into cones, globes, and pyramids, and bounded by high walls that shut off the surrounding country. The small amount of landscape painting that was done (chiefly by painters of foreign extraction) was of foreign scenes or of local scenes made to look like landscapes of the Dutch or Italian masters. Poetical descriptions of landscape were meager and of a highly generalized sort, presented in a vocabulary restricted and limited, with almost no touches of local color. Travel over country roads by carriage, or on horseback, was so arduous, even dangerous, that little pleasure could be taken in viewing the land-

1

scape. Yet by the end of the century, when Wordsworth was well launched into his career, basic attitudes towards Nature had been momentously altered. There had developed a love of country life, a widespread appreciation of natural beauty, and an enthusiasm for landscape passionate in its intensity. Representations of Nature were distinguished by full and first-hand observation; by a rich, sensuous delight in form, color, sound, and motion; by a preference for the wilder forms of landscape; even by a recognition of divine life in Nature, and by a consciousness of the interpenetration of that life and the life of man.[1]

As the century moved from relative indifference towards landscape to an attitude of unrestrained enthusiasm, various art forms were irresistibly impelled towards new expressions—in poetry, in painting, in gardening, and in the art of travel. An entirely new kind of garden was created by the English (known on the continent as *le jardin anglais*) with winding paths and serpenting streams created to look like and to merge with the native countryside. Travel for the purpose of taking delight in viewing the landscape became, shortly after the mid-century, fashionable and widespread. At the century's close, though the sentimental excesses of picturesque travel were ridiculed, there was no abatement of country touring. English landscape painting, after the 1760's, had been put on a firm footing by such noteworthy artists as Wilson, Gainsborough, and Girtin; by 1800 the masters of landscape, Constable and Turner, were moving into their periods of greatest creativity. The poetry of Nature was auspiciously brought into favorable prominence as early as 1726 with the publication of Thomson's *Winter* and Dyer's *Grongar Hill*. By 1730 Thomson's *Seasons* was completed and thereafter became immensely popular and was widely imitated. By its example Thomson successfully challenged the ideal of artificiality in English poetry and inaugurated a new era in the attitude toward Nature. By the close of the third decade of the nineteenth century under the leadership of Wordsworth the poety of Nature had become one of the most prominent features and chief glories of the Romantic Age.

Initial manifestations of the new state of feeling about Nature appeared at different times during the century in the several art forms, but always there were remarkably close relationships among them and a good deal of cross-fertilization going on. So close, indeed, at moments were the poetry of Nature, landscape painting, landscape gardening, and the art of travel that they lost their isolation, as separate arts, and combined into *the art of landscape*. What brought the arts together, to begin with, was the artists themselves, who were as likely as not accomplished in more than one art: Pope was an expert gardener as well as poet; the poets Thomson and Dyer were also landscape painters and travelers of note; Shenstone was a layer-out of grounds and an admired versifier upon them; Gray was poet, critic of art *par excellence,* and distinguished traveler. More importantly, the art of landscape in the eighteenth century was oriented to the visual way of looking at the world. Scenes in Nature which were "eminently suitable for pictorial representation" were the ones chosen for representation on canvas or in words. Gardens were laid out to look like a series of painted pictures. Travelers sought views that composed in the way that the landscape painters had painted them. Picture-making in the art of landscape was called the picturesque,[2] but the picturesque was not the whole of the art; nor was the art of landscape even by strictest definition necessarily an imperfect art. Numbered among its practitioners were sentimental cultists, but there were also among them true artists and inspired originators. Wordsworth was a keen student of the picturesque and in the poetry of his formative

years fell under the spell of some of its more restricting practices, but in his maturity he moved far beyond the visual interpreters of the landscape.

Wordsworth was not only England's foremost poet of
Nature; he was also a knowledgeable critic of landscape painting, an expert gardener, and a master of the art of travel. In
short, Wordsworth was a rounded and eminent practitioner of
the art of landscape on its highest levels. He had much to say
not only about the theories and practice of poetry, but also
about all the related arts. It is my purpose in this study to examine Wordsworth's principles and practices in the art of landscape in painting, gardening, travel, and poetry, both as they
relate to his eighteenth-century predecessors and as they are
revealed in his own work.

ONE

The Art of Landscape
Before Wordsworth

The Beginnings of Natural Style
in English Gardening

Dissatisfaction with the standards of neoclassical art, and the desire to be emancipated from them, was first directed against the absurd extremes to which the art of formal gardening had lent itself. During the reign of Queen Anne, while the classical spirit was apparently still at its height, it became the fashion to condemn artificiality and to extol wild, uncultivated Nature. Cooper, third Earl of Shaftesbury, preferred the unspoiled naturalness of the wilderness to the formality of man-made gardens:

> I shall no longer resist the passion in me for things of a *natural* kind; where neither *Art,* nor the *Conceit* or *Caprice* of Man has spoiled their genuine *Order....* Even the rude *Rocks,* the mossy *Caverns,* the irregular unwrought *Grottoes,* and broken *Falls* of Waters, with all the horrid Graces of the *Wilderness* itself, as representing NATURE more, will be the more engaging, and appear with the Magnificence beyond the formal Mockery of princely Gardens.[1]

Addison was an even more outspoken advocate of naturalness in landscape than was Shaftesbury, as may be seen from his statement of preferences in *Spectator* 414:

There is something more bold and masterly in the rough careless strokes of nature than in the nice touches and embellishments of art. The beauties of the most stately garden or palace lie in a narrow compass, the imagination immediately runs them over, and requires something else to gratify her; but, in the wild fields of nature, the sight wanders up and down without confinement, and is fed with an infinite variety of images.

I do not know whether I am singular in my opinion, but, for my own part, I would rather look upon a tree in all its luxuriance and diffusion of boughs and branches, than when it is thus cut and trimmed into a mathematical figure; and can not but fancy that an orchard in flower looks infinitely more delightful than all the little labyrinths of the most finished parterre.

At Bilton, Warwickshire, Addison gave practical expression to his inclinations by making over his own estate into "a pretty Landskip . . . a confusion of Kitchin and Parterre, orchard and flower garden" (*Spectator* 477). Addison was in fact the pioneer of an entirely new style in the art of gardening. After him the garden was no longer to be regarded as a walled-in enclosure laid out and maintained along mathematical lines, but was to be a free and open landscape of the whole countryside. Pope, like Addison, was also an outspoken advocate of naturalness in gardening and scornful of people who think that is finest which is least natural. He sets forth his position in "Essay on Verdant Culture" (*Guardian* 173):

There is certainly something in the amiable symplicity of unadorned Nature that spreads over the mind a more noble sort of tranquillity, and a loftier sensation of pleasure, than can be raised from the nicer scenes of Art. . . . I believe it is no wrong observation that persons of genius, and those most capable of Art, are always most fond of Nature. On the contrary, people of the common level of understanding are principally delighted with the little niceties and fantastical operations of Art, and constantly think that finest which is least natural.

Pope offered a full statement of his principles of gardening in his famous "Epistle to Burlington" (1731). His basic precept was that gardens should be so planned as to conceal all traces of man's interference. He realized that in making improvements on the grounds the best effects could be obtained by adapting the natural contours to the design and by doing what is harmonious with Nature. He encouraged the designer to have an over-all plan and to work as a painter does in creating an idealized picture of the scene before him.

> To build, to plant, whatever you intend,
> To rear the Column, or the Arch to bend,
> To swell the Terras, or to sink the Grot;
> In all, let Nature never be forgot.

[vv. 47–50]

However, Pope was more of an innovator in theory than he proved to be in practice. His own five acres at Twickenham featured the formal design, except where his paths "twisted, twirled, rhymed, and harmonized" in rococo playfulness. Nevertheless, his influence upon his contemporaries in the formal-informal way of laying out a garden was considerable. Professional gardeners got hold of his ideas and began to publicize them. He was often consulted, especially by Bridgeman and Kent. Twickenham was probably the model for Kent's design for Lord Burlington's Chiswick, begun around 1727.

The first writer on practical gardening to place Addison's new point of view before the public was Stephen Switzer in *Ichnographia Rustica* (1718). Quoting *The Spectator,* Switzer agrees "that a little regularity is to be recommended near the building," but beyond it a designer "ought to pursue Nature . . . and by as many Twinings and Windings as the Villa will allow" make his design "more rural, natural, more easy." He wants to do away with imprisoning brick walls and to make "a whole estate appear as one great Garden." His own designs of a natural kind are laid out mathematically and the curves of his winding paths are tame. Yet he is significant as a transitional figure, one that repeatedly voiced the desire for variety and irregularity. Another fashionable designer of gardens of the transitional period (following the lead of Addison and Pope) was Charles Bridgeman. His designs were a compromise between the formal and natural styles, but he reached more daringly towards the natural than any of his contemporaries. His "straight walks with high clipped hedges" were only his "great lines." "The rest he diversified by wilderness, and with loose groves of oaks."[2] His most important innovation was the introduction of the sunken fence, the so-called ha-ha, which opened the garden view and merged it with the countryside. His principal layout was done for Bubb Doddington at Eastbury in Dorset. Thomson, in "Autumn," describes its "green, delightful walks":

> Oh lose me in the green delightful walks
> Of Dodington, thy seat, serene and plain;
> Where simple Nature reigns; and every view,
> Diffusive, spreads the pure Dorsetian downs,
> In boundless prospect.
>
> [vv. 653–57]

The ha-ha produced a vision of "boundless Prospect." In a relatively short time the use of the ha-ha was to lead to the abandonment of the formal garden for the winding path through the orchard.

Italian Landscape Painting and the English Landscape Poets

Soon after the Peace of Ryswick in 1697, the Grand Tour became a part of the fashionable English gentleman's preparation for life. The passage through the Alps, the journey through Italy, and the contact with Italian landscape painting opened up a whole new world of aesthetic appreciation for landscape. Enthusiasm ran high for Italian landscape art, which appealed to the English because it had the classic tinge, "the ruined fragments of antiquity" which Dutch and Flemish art did not have. The painters most admired were Claude Lorrain, Salvator Rosa, and Gaspard and Nicolas Poussin. Claude Lorrain minutely studied the actual features of natural forms and combined them into an ideally composed landscape. He excelled at depicting the wide and light-filled sky, and the sun, especially at rising and setting; also sea scenes with ships, rivers with waterfalls, bridges, and classic temples, commonly appearing in the middle distance; and in the foreground, peasants and cattle or characters out of Biblical or classical stories—yet always the landscape and the composition were predominant. Salvator Rosa generally chose to represent wild and grotesque places, precipices and great rock masses of fantastic form, cascades and torrents, desolate ruins, caves, trees of dense growth, or shattered boughs, and the whole peopled with banditti or uncouth characters, or with some classical or Biblical characters whose stories reflect horror or cruelty. Gaspard and Nicolas Poussin were noted for their renderings of classical themes and for their unity of design. English travelers in their enthusiasm for Italian art began collecting and carrying home "many-figur'd sculptures" and innumerable paintings with which to "deck their long galleries and winding groves," as Dyer said. In nearly all the great English collections, and in many a small one, the pictures of Claude Lorrain, Salvator Rosa, and Gaspard Poussin were conspicuous. Increased interest in painting in general and landscape painting in particular followed close upon the popularization of the Grand Tour. The pictures, prints, and drawings—originals and copies—which poured into England established patterns by which the landscape was to be viewed, and they familiarized the eyes of travelers with what they were to see. When Addison made his trip to Italy, he

PASTORAL LANDSCAPE

by Claude Lorrain (*Liber Veritatis* 85 British Museum)

found beauty in the sort of landscape—"elaborate, widespread, greatly diversified, and having classical associations"—made famous by Claude Lorrain. Later, the paintings of Salvator Rosa prepared young Walpole and Gray to enjoy the grandeur of mountain scenery. Italian landscape paintings were often copied or imitated by the English, and prints were made of them by engravers. In fact, according to Elizabeth Manwaring, the diffusion of Italian ideal landscape came chiefly through the engravers. The reproduction of Claude Lorrain's drawings, for example, by Richard Earlham (1742–1822), who combined etching with mezzotint in the *Liber Veritatis,* provided a reference book of masterpieces for the amateur artist or landscape gardener. The prints, as well as the paintings, gave entrance to a world almost as fanciful as that of Arcadia.

Enthusiasm for Claude's distances and Salvator's gloom preceded by several decades the first noteworthy attempts of eighteenth-century English poets to write about Nature.[3] When they did so, their great familiarity with Italian landscape painting (many of them were either keen students of or themselves practiced landscape painting) often led them to contrive a literary landscape that consciously or unconsciously had been subject to a pictorial transformation. James Thomson, foremost of these poets, gives us in *The Seasons* (1726–1730) a gallery of paintings. Thomson excelled in rendering the ever-varying light of the natural world and has offered us some of the richest imagery of natural light ever written: the dancing light and shade of the forest pathway, the rapid flight or slow march of clouds, the golden shadowy sweep of wind over ripened grain. "Summer" abounds in Claudian sunrises and sunsets, extended views, and Arcadian scenes of pastoral charm. In "Spring" there is a masterly word-picture of sunlight after vernal showers, which in its movement and glittering vitality seems to pass beyond Claude to something resembling Constable's more ambitious landscape style.[4]

Till in the Western sky, the downward sun
Looks out, effulgent, from amid the flush
Of broken clouds, gay-shifting to his beams.
The rapid radiance instantaneous strikes
Th' illumined mountain, thro' the forest streams,
Shakes on the floods, and in a yellow mist,
Far smoaking o'er th' interminable plain,
In twinkling myriads lights the dewy gems.
Moist, bright, and green the landskip laughs around.
[vv. 189–97]

Thomson rendered the colors of the natural scene with great richness and fidelity—especially the golden, ethereal light of the sky—and he achieved on his verbal canvas the grace and power of natural motion. He gloried in the large expansiveness and the titanic exuberance of Nature—the river flood, the windstorm, and the deluge—scenes which he vitalized with verbs of motion: rush, shoot, roll, burst, swell, and so on. At times in Thomson there are reminiscences of Salvator's dashing brush in dead or blasted trees, in precipices and lightning. Thomson attempted to idealize Nature as the painters had by humanizing or mythologizing the landscape. His chief, and very effective, instrument for doing this was a pictorial image evoked through natural personifications. At the same time he characteristically sets off the beauties of Nature as they were set off by the landscape painters of the previous century. Thomson was the first of the nature poets anticipating the "picturesque" mode of later poets and gardeners who looked at the landscape as a series of more or less well-composed pictures. Dyer, who was a landscape painter as well as a poet, likewise encouraged the picturesque vision. He is best known for "Grongar Hill" (1726), a delightful "prospect piece" of his native vale of Towy, describing not one single picture but a series of pictures—of rivers, woods, and hills—as they open in a wide expanse to the eye of a climber. Following Dyer's example, the "prospect poem," which satisfied the craving for pictorial "variety," especially "contrast," became widely popular.

The poets Gray and Collins tended to present natural scenes with pictorial details, but often these details were subordinated to moods or reflections. Gray's famous "Elegy Written in a Country Churchyard" consists of a series of alternating descriptions and meditations. The opening stanzas, descriptive of country life, give us a wide, peaceful evening landscape of Claudian mode. A number of single lines have the power to suggest whole pictures:

> The lowing herd wind slowly o'er the lea . . .
> Oft did the harvest to their sickle yield . . .
> How bow'd the woods beneath their sturdy stroke!

The middle section of the elegy is predominantly reflective, but the last section is again pictorial. Here the pictorialism combines with the elegiac theme, as Hagstrum has pointed out, much in the way that it does in Poussin's *The Shepherds of Arcady*.[5] In his later period Gray delighted in the wilder aspects of Nature and in those that would harmonize with Gothic ruins. He offers in "The Bard" the Salvatorial elements of mountain precipice, warring winds, and foaming torrents to serve as dramatic support for the bard's fierce and awesome song. Collins was a lover of Nature and a follower of Thomson, though he did not see Nature as pictorially as the author of *The Seasons*. For the most part Collins' nature pictures are of a shadowy quality and accompanied by fanciful personifications. Like Gray, he was attracted to the landscape not for itself alone but for the ideas and emotions that the landscape evoked. In "Ode to Evening," his finest lyric, he develops by means of selected twilight sights and sounds the mood of tender reverie conducive to meditative exploration of the "dim-discover'd Tracts of Mind." There is hardly any landscape in the ordinary sense in "Ode to Evening," though one commentator thinks it bears comparison to some pictures of the English water-colorist Girtin in his faithfulness to Nature and his subdued tones and pale lights.[6]

The Warton brothers show a strong perference for wild scenery—the unfrequented forest, the high cliff, the desolate seashore—Salvatorial elements that whet the appetite for violent deeds or melancholic musings. Joseph Warton in *The Enthusiast* (1740) proclaims the superiority of unspoiled Nature over man-made gardens with their pompous artificialities of "Marble-mimic Gods,/Parterres embroider'd, Obelisks, and Urns/Of high Relief." Thomas Warton in *The Pleasures of Melancholy* (1747) plays up the trappings of the "Il Penseroso" school—solitude, delight in darkness, ruined abbeys, "hollow charnels," and midnight haunts. The Wartons, though unoriginal poets, had a genuine love of Nature and did abet an enthusiasm for the picturesque both through their own writings and through their eulogizing of Thomson's *Seasons*.

William Cowper knew the country, lived there all his adult life, and rejoiced in the simplicity and serenity he found there. His poetry is filled with a loving appraisal of Nature's gifts, but his scope is limited. Because of ill health he did not range far. Mountains, torrential storms, and wild scenery he never describes and only occasionally mentions. But the scenes about Olney, which he knew literally by heart, he describes with minute and loving fidelity. His sympathetic rendering of visual detail is illustrated in his descriptions of trees. When he takes a walk, he observes with delight the overarching branches of the ash, the lime, and the beech and the distinct patterns of shadowy foliage cast on their trunks. The landscape painter Gainsborough shared Cowper's affection for trees and in his own medium was making a record of it. In Cowper's poetry there are many little pictures of Nature, complete in a few lines (as, for example, the redbreast in winter as he flits from twig to twig shaking the pendent drops of ice upon the withered leaves below). Cowper's relish of a fair prospect began when he was a boy and never left him. His finest example in this class of composition is his well-known description of the Ouse Valley as seen from an eminence (*The Task*, Book I). As he sets forth the features of the prospect before him he follows a rhythmical line such as may be found in the landscape compositions of any of the master painters. But he does not arrange, add, or select details for the purpose of idealizing the countryside as Claude would do. He reports realistically what he sees of an English landscape more as John Crome would report it. And he adds the joy in contemplating what he sees of the beauty and peace of English country life. For him the country is the place of physical as well as mental health. Rural sights and sounds exhilarate and restore the human body and spirit. Cowper is suspicious of cities and the products of civilization. The beauty of the countryside is lovelier to him than the adulterated works of art.

In James Beattie and William Lisle Bowles we have two sincere lovers of Nature with a moderate talent for descriptive verse. Beattie's chief poem is *The Minstrel* (1771) in which he casts himself in the role of Edwin, a poetically sensitive youth who roved the uplands and climbed the craggy cliffs to scan all Nature with "curious and romantic eye." He confronted storms, torrents, sunrises, sunsets, clouds, lakes, long vales, meadows, and groves in a wide variety of prospects in all seasons. The effect of these confrontations upon the plastic mind of young Edwin was to awaken a sense of the cleansing power of Nature's solitudes and of its purity and joy. *The Minstrel* was widely read in the last quarter of the century and helped to spread a love of mountain scenery. The poem found a ready home in the heart of young Wordsworth.

Bowles studied in Winchester School under Joseph Warton, who taught him to rejoice in "the fresh beauty of the trees" from the hilltop and to trace with joy "the prospects spread around." When disappointment in love came to Bowles as a young man, he went on a tour of England, Scotland, and the Continent in search of forgetfulness. His *Sonnets* (1789), which are a record of his wanderings, recount in sentimental vein how contemplation of the landscape awakened in him "the wonted sense of pure delight." Bowles tends to see the landscape as it corroborates the art gallery. Typical of his offering is the sonnet "At Tynemouth Priory," built upon such features as are characteristic of a painting by Claude Lorrain—a sea scene with sunset, ruined castle, quiet waters, and human figure:

> As slow I climb the cliff's ascending side,
>   Much musing on the track of terror past,
>   When o'er the dark wave rode the howling blast,
> Pleased I look back, and view the tranquil tide
> That laves the pebbled shore: and now the beam
>   Of evening smiles on the gray battlement,
>   And yon forsaken tower that time has rent:—
> The lifted oar far off with transient gleam
> Is touched, and hushed is all the billowy deep!
>   Soothed by the scene, thus on tired Nature's breast
>   A stillness slowly steals, and kindred rest;
> While sea-sounds lull her, as she sinks to sleep,
> Like melodies that mourn upon the lyre,
> Waked by the breeze, and, as they mourn, expire!

Bowles's sonnets lack depth of thought and poetic force; yet they do reveal a genuine appreciation for the beauty of Nature and a partial success, at least, in harmonizing the moods of Nature with those of the mind.

Le Jardin Anglais *and the Controversy between the Brownists and the School of the Picturesque*

As we have seen, the first step in the development of natural gardening was accomplished when the destruction of the garden wall and the adoption of the sunken fence opened up the countryside. Once the wall was down, it was no longer possible to ignore the strange and untidy landscape to be seen beyond it. The second step, then, was to create out of Nature in the raw state something pleasant to look at and to live with. This was done by studying the idealizations of Nature in the canvases of the Italian landscape painters and adapting their methods of composition to the medium of garden design. One studied Claude to compound effects that were idyllic, Salvator to produce those that were wild and horrendous. In either case the connoisseur sought not to represent Nature as she was but as she emerged from the selective process of the pictorial masters. Claude Lorrain's point of view, as described by Reynolds in his Fourth Discourse, is exactly that of the new fashion of garden design: "Claude Lorrain . . . was convinced, that taking nature as he found it seldom produced beauty. His pictures are a composition of the various draughts he had previously made from various beautiful scenes and prospects." Gardeners learned to construct Elysiums like those of the painters with arching trees framing the view, tree clumps balancing buildings, irregular bodies of water reflecting the golden evening light, and a herd of deer or flock of sheep to enliven the foreground.

William Kent, called by Walpole "the father of modern gardening," was the first to use the principles of painting in designing landscapes. He was himself an architect and painter and is said to have gained his inspiration for landscape gardening by working on illustrations for Thomson's *Seasons,* which are full of pictorial reminiscences of Italy. In designing gardens, Kent's fundamental idea was to make "natural pictures" by means of the principles of perspective, and the management of light and shade. He specialized in the gently undulating line, in the winding walk and naturally flowing stream. He used clumps of trees to screen what was unsightly, to vary what was monotonous, or to emphasize what was interesting. Where objects were wanting he added buildings, seats, and statuary and even had dead trees planted in Kensington Park to heighten the comparison with Salvator. Sometimes a too literal or indiscriminate application of the new theory of design led to artificial results and extravagances. At the same time Kent's natural use of water, woods, and meadows established a landscape style that was manageable and that resulted in some admirable gardens. Two of Kent's best designs, Chiswick Park in London and Rousham House near Oxford, are today well preserved and still retain much of their original charm.

One of the most perfect examples of picturesque landscape inspired by the Italian painters also survives in its original condition at Stourhead in Wiltshire. In the 1740's Henry Hoare skilfully made over his estate into a Claude landscape. He dammed up the head waters of the Stour River and formed an artificial lake of eighteen acres in a valley of the park. The steep and broken hillside around the lake he planted with beech, conifers, and rhododendrons; then he discreetly set amongst the luxuriant foliage a number of ornamental buildings and bridges to be seen picturesquely down glades, among trees, or across the lake. In early summer, when the rhododendrons are in bloom and the fragrance of the azaleas spices the air, a visitor to Stourhead who looks upon the white facade of the Pantheon thrown into relief against the dark greenery around it and sees its shimmering reflection in the lake may recapture a living vision of Arcadia first made real in the English landscape over two hundred years ago.

William Shenstone, poet, essayist, and man of taste, spread the idea of making pictures in landscape. He devoted his life and the whole of his slender resources to transforming his estate, the Leasowes, into a series of scenes of grandeur, beauty, or variety pleasing to the imagination. Shenstone set

STOURHEAD in Wiltshire

Photograph by the author

forth the artistic principles upon which he worked in an essay
entitled "Unconnected Thoughts on Gardening" (1764). He
acknowledged the dependence of the gardener upon the landscape painter. "The landskip," he wrote, "should contain variety enough to form a picture upon canvas: and this is no bad
test, as I think the landskip painter is the gardiner's best designer." Symmetry was to be preserved in the garden as the
painter preserves it, not by identical masses, but by subtler
means of allowing a wood or hill to balance a house or obelisk.
His aim was to heighten the peculiar charm of each scene, and
though the hand of art was not supposed to tamper with Nature—at any rate "other than clandestinely and by night" as
he observed—it did so extensively at the Leasowes with its
lovers' seats and its trophies or garlands placed at strategic
points about the grounds. In spite of some unnatural striving
after natural effects, visitor after visitor eulogized the skill
with which Shenstone hid the art of the gardener and crystallized the temper of well-bred charm and gentlemanly elegance.
The Leasowes became a shining example to its age of how well
a small domain could be transformed into an ideal of landscape combining the attractions of Arcadia, as found in the
paintings of Claude Lorrain, Gaspard Poussin, and Salvator
Rosa.

As the fashion for picturesque gardening was carried forward into the second half of the century the sentimental ma-
nipulation of Nature increased. In his desire to duplicate the
emotional tones of the Italian masters—the luminous brightness of Claude Lorrain, the pastoral dignity of Poussin, or the
romantic wildness of Salvator Rosa—the man of taste would
identify situations of varying emotional appeal by means of
ruins, cypress trees, obelisks, weeping willows, grottoes, and
sunny meadows. He also sought to increase pleasurable thrills
by creating dramatic contrasts in the successive scenes and by

having the promenade reveal them suddenly and unexpectedly. An exaggerated attachment to melancholic musings and solitude that was fashionable at the time led to an attempt to put gnarled oaks, ruined moss-grown fortresses, and mouldering ivy-hung abbeys into every landscape. Though the excesses of picturesque gardening were widely satirized, a sampling of garden books published in the 1770's reveals that the authors leaned towards approval of the picturesque approach.[7]

The challenge to picturesque gardening was initiated by "Capability" Brown (so-called because he saw "capabilities" in the laying out of grounds). Brown, who started out as a kitchen gardener at Stowe, aimed at creating landscapes that should arouse emotions by means of Burke's ideas of beauty —smoothness, gradual variation, and delicacy of form. His method in remodeling an estate was to remove all traces of old formal surroundings from the area around the house, demolish the stately avenues, and transport kitchen gardens, stables, and even whole villages to places where they could not be seen. He not infrequently did away with the ha-ha and allowed the rough grass to encroach to the very walls of the house on all sides so that the house would appear to be set down in the middle of a field. His landscapes resolved themselves into a few quite obvious elements—an encircling belt of woodland with the inner edge made irregular, open stretches of sweeping turf, and sloping contours accentuated with groups of trees or majestic single specimens. His speciality was the management of water, which he used to enliven the middle distance. His system did produce some of the finest parks ever created in England. His greatest success was at Blenheim, where he improved the lake and altered a meaningless canal to a natural winding stream. From mid-century until his death in 1783 "Capability" Brown was the most popular of all designers. But to the following generation he appeared as an unimaginative

BLENHEIM PALACE

View from across the lake. Photograph by the author

despoiler of many old attractive gardens rather than an improver to be admired.

After Brown's death the lead in landscape design was taken over by Humphrey Repton, who knew design and the importance of proportion, variety, harmony, and unity, but who as a practical gardener also appreciated the simple principle of utility. Repton thought that places were to be laid out primarily for their enjoyment in real life, not with a view to their appearance as a picture. For him utility must take precedence over beauty, and convenience be preferred to picturesque effect. When in 1794 Richard Knight in *The Landscape* lashed Repton and the practical improvers unmercifully, and Price followed with *Essays on the Picturesque* loudly championing the cause of picturesque gardening, Repton counterattacked in the following year with *Sketches and Hints on Landscape Gardening* to weaken the influence of painting on landscape gardening and to establish the preëminence of general utility. Though Repton staunchly supported Brown's position in opposition to the theories of Knight and Price, somehow the longer he lived the more open-minded he became towards different theories and styles. In practice he moved steadily away from Brown's principles to a "gardenesque" style, with some layouts even featuring terraces and parterres near the house and a multiplicity of gardens with picturesque effects.

The leading exponents of picturesque beauty were William Gilpin, Richard Payne Knight, and Uvedale Price. William Gilpin, called "the founder and master of the picturesque," was born and bred in Cumberland, a region which fostered in him, as it did in Wordsworth, a true and deep delight in landscape beauty. He earned his livelihood as a schoolmaster, but was talented as a painter of landscape as well as a gifted writer upon it. He expounded ideas of picturesque beauty according to a set of values which were easy to understand and to imitate. His *Three Essays: On Picturesque Beauty; On Pictur-*

esque Travel; On Sketching Landscape, published in 1792, contain the essentials of his aesthetic theories. But he had defined his terms as early as 1748 in *A Dialogue upon the Gardens . . . at Stow,* and expanded them in a widely influential work *Essay on Prints,* 1768. In a series of books on picturesque travel, appearing in 1782 and after, the picturesque ideal of roughness and intricacy in the landscape was analyzed and popularized. Gilpin defined "the picturesque" as "a term expressive of that peculiar kind of beauty, which is agreeable in a picture." Not all beauty, he explains, consists of *picturesque beauty*—i.e., beauty which would serve effectively in forming a picture. Neatness and smoothness may add to beauty, but they do not make for picturesqueness. Roughness is the most essential point of difference between the *beautiful* and the *picturesque.* To a painter roughness is a vital aid in successfully achieving effects in variety, light and shade, and coloring. For this reason a painter prefers ruins to perfect architecture, a cart horse to a polished Arabian. The objects of Nature *in themselves* by roughness of texture, by irregularity of outline, by variegated and graduated colors, and by contrasting *lights* and *shades* produce infinite variety. Nature fails only in composition. Examining the landscape by the *rules of the picturesque* may seem like a deviation from *Nature* to art. Yet, in fact, it is not so: "For the *rules of picturesque beauty,* we know, are drawn from *nature:* so that to examine the face of nature by these rules, is no more than to examine nature by her most beautiful exertions."[8] To Gilpin Nature was the ideal; only man had deformed her. Gilpin's writings were widely circulated, some of them—his illustrated manuscripts on the picturesque beauty of English landscape—for years before publication. He was an immensely popular author and taught a whole generation of Britishers the aesthetic appeal of natural and man-made scenery.

In his many observations on landscape gardening scattered

throughout his works, Gilpin constantly extols Nature above art. His picturesque eye is seldom pleased with artificial attempts to please, that is, with the creation or embellishment of ruins or simulation of rustic effects. He thinks there is something awkward and incongruous about restoring ruins, especially when ornaments are added:

A monk's *garden* is turned into a trim parterre, and planted with flowering shrubs: a view is opened to some ridiculous figure . . . that is placed in the valley, and [on] a circular pedestal of the abbey-church . . . is erected a mutilated heathen statue!! . . . A ruin is a sacred thing. Rooted for ages to the soil; assimilated to it; and become as it were, a part of it; we consider it as a work of nature, rather than of art. . . . the *magnificence* of ruin was never attained by any modern attempt.[9]

The artificial plantings of shrubbery around the castle and abbey at Chepstow on the River Wye seemed paltry and out of place:

As the embellishments of a house, or as the ornaments of little scenes which have nothing better to recommend them, a few flowering shrubs artfully composed may have their elegance and beauty; but in scenes like this, they are only splendid patches, which injure the grandeur and simplicity of the whole.[10]

He did not think the scenery of Blenheim was in any way improved by patches of flowers and flowering shrubs artificially disposed and introduced where the imagination wished "to be engrossed by the grand exhibition of simplicity and nature." He did not object to knots of flowers and flowering shrubs around a house, which, being an artificial object, must in some degree partake of art. But he insisted that where these adornments were planted they should blend with clumps of forest trees which connect them with the park so as to partake of Nature.[11] He was pleased with the cottage found in woody scenes of the forest not only "as an embellishment of a scene but as it shows a dwelling where happiness may reside unsupported by wealth."[12] Space does not permit a recording of Gilpin's ideas on park grounds, farm lands, ornamental buildings, kitchen gardens, gravel walks, bridges, canals, and so on. His general principle seems to be that everywhere "amidst the grand objects of nature, it would be absurd to catch the eye with the *affected* decorations of art."[13] Of Gilpin's observations on trees, however, which are knowledgeable and enthusiastic, some account must be given. In his *Remarks on Forest Scenery* (1791) he says it is "no exaggerated praise to call a tree the *grandest,* and most *beautiful* of all the productions of the earth." The minuter flowers and shrubs, though "beautiful as *individuals,* . . . are not adapted to form the arrangement of *composition in landscape;* nor to receive the *effects of light and shade;* they must give place in point of *beauty*—of *picturesque beauty* at least . . . to the form and foliage, and ramification of the tree."[14] Lightness and balance are characteristic beauties in a tree. A withered top or a curtailed trunk in a grand old tree speaks in a style of eloquence. Colored mosses, or ivy, or roots raised above the soil can add picturesque beauty to a forest tree. The motion of trees and the pleasing patterns of checkered shade formed under them add to the observer's delight. The oak is the most picturesque and the most accommodating in composition. The beech, the sycamore, the weeping willow, the cedar of Lebanon, the yew, and the holly are all worthy of praise. But no trees should be unnaturally shaped: "Clipped yews, line hedges, and pollards . . . are disagreeable." Price acclaimed Gilpin's originality, and Wordsworth sympathized with many of Gilpin's ideas on gardening. These ideas, filtered through succeeding generations, were influential in establishing sound taste in modern landscape gardening.

The most spirited defender of the picturesque style in gardening and a leader of the attack upon the practical improvers of grounds was William Payne Knight, scholar, connoisseur, and designer of Downton Castle and of the still surviving beautiful park along the Teme River in Shropshire. Knight set forth his ideas in a popular and entertaining work entitled *The Landscape, A Didactic Poem in Three Books. Addressed to Uvedale Price, Esq.* (1794). What we require in garden design, he says in this work, is the same as what we require in painting—congruity of all the parts:

> 'Tis still one principle through all extends,
> And leads through diff'rent ways to diff'rent ends.
>
> * * *
>
> 'Tis just congruity of parts combin'd
> To please the sense and satisfy the mind.
>
> [Book I, vv. 35–36, 39–40]

For violation of the principle of congruity Knight censures Repton in his plan for improving Tatton Park, in Cheshire, for recommending a tedious, roundabout approach to the manor house in order to show off the extent of the property. The approach should rather be, he says, in careless, easy curves following a line such as would be taken by a person going naturally from point to point.

> First fix the points to which you wish to go;
> Then let your easy path spontaneous flow.
>
> [Book I, vv. 154–55]

When the mansion does at last come into view, it should be "well-mix'd and blended with the scene"; it should not stand lonely in solitary pride, as the improvers would place it, a lump or excresence amid shaven lawns spreading around it. The landscape should be planned in component parts, says Knight, with foreground, middle distance, and background in three marked divisions such as are always found in the landscape paintings of Claude, Hobbema, Salvator, or Ruysdael. The foreground is of most importance and in treating it we must again follow the lead of the landscape painters. But behold, he sarcastically notes, what the improvers are doing!

> See yon fantastic band,
> With charts, pedometers, and rules in hand
> Advance triumphant, and alike lay waste
> The forms of nature, and the works of taste!
> T'improve, adorn, and polish, they profess;
> But shave the goddess, whom they come to dress.
>   [Book I, vv. 261–66]

Rather than the barren smoothness of the improvers, Knight would have back again the old formal terraces.

> Oft when I've seen some lovely mansion stand,
> Fresh from th' emprover's desolating hand,
> 'Midst shaven lawns, that far around it creep
> In one eternal undulating sweep;
> And scatter'd clumps, that nod at one another,
> Each stiffly waving to its formal brother;
> Tir'd with th' extensive scene, so dull and bare,
> To Heav'n devoutly I've address'd my pray'r,—
> Again the moss-grown terraces to raise,
> And spread the labyrinth's perplexing maze;
> Replace in even lines the ductile yew
> And plant again the ancient avenue.
>   [Book II, vv. 1–12]

Knight approves of arched and flagged bridges such as are to be found in the drawings of Claude Lorrain's *Liber Veritatis*, where a great variety of forms is introduced, and he likes the large, gnarly trees such as are featured by Claude. A man is especially blessed, Knight thinks, who has an ancient ruined abbey on his place, or castle, or even an old cottage overgrown with honeysuckle and ivy. He is especially to be envied if he has on his grounds a ruined temple with broken columns and sculptured fragments; but let us not have any reconstructed ruins or trick church steeples. In discussing trees, Knight pleads for keeping all old, picturesque specimens and for the planting of them as they would be found in Nature, not set out in quaint varieties of patterns to cause surprise (as, for example, blue Scotch firs placed in alternate, checkered squares with yellow plane trees). Let your oak be your tree for general masses (the beech for chalky or light soils), and let variety be achieved with the intermixture of lime-tree, willow, and ash.

When, in 1795, a second edition of *The Landscape* was published, Knight added a note curtly admonishing Repton for his *Letter to Price*. Knight thought that Repton had taken unfair advantage of a supposed distinction between the picturesque and the beautiful. The distinction ingeniously made by Repton, Knight declares, is "an imaginary one. . . . The picturesque is merely that kind of beauty which belongs exclusively to the sense of vision; or to the imagination, guided by that sense."[15] This thesis wherein he grounds the picturesque in the visual sense Knight elaborated in the *Analytical Inquiry into the Principles of Taste* a decade later. Landscape, he says there, must bring direct pleasure to the sense of sight—in tints that affect the eye in a fashion at once "harmonious," "pleasing," and "picturesque." That which delights the eye with its irregularity in broken and graduated light and color is picturesque (as shaggy animals, irregular trees, and mouldering ruins). Picturesque beauty, he explains, exists independent of painting, though painting separates the irregularity of visible things from all other aspects, draws our attention to it, and cultivates our sensibility. In gardening, as in painting, Knight says, there must be consistency and propriety. Near the house he preferred a formal garden, picturesque in its varied and intricate textures; at some remove there could spread a wilder forest-park with an open park between.

COMPARATIVE SCENES

from Richard Payne Knight's *The Landscape* (engravings by Thomas Hearne)

THE SAME HOUSE, "IMPROVED"

GOTHIC HOUSE LANDSCAPED IN THE PICTURESQUE MANNER

Uvedale Price joined Knight, his neighbor and friend, in an ardent crusade for the picturesque style in gardening and laid out Foxley, his Herefordshire estate, on picturesque principles. Price was the friend of Sir George Beaumont and of Wordsworth, who visited him in 1810 and 1824. His works on the picturesque remain the dominant ones and had a wide vogue. His *Essay on the Picturesque*, which first appeared in 1794, was republished in 1795 and 1796, and a second volume was added in 1798. Price applies the term *picturesque* "to every object, and every kind of scenery, which has been, or might be represented with good effect in painting." Picturesque principles, he asserts, are founded in Nature but can be most easily studied in painting, for painters see effects in Nature which men in general do not see. The most effective means of evoking the picturesque are roughness and sudden variation, joined to irregularity. These features are most often to be found in Gothic cathedrals, old mills, gnarled oak trees, worn-out cart horses, shaggy goats, wandering gypsies, and other objects of the same kind. Price did not mean to insist that an object to be picturesque must be old and decayed, but he did point out that beautiful objects will become picturesque by the operation of time. Beech trees as they age, for example, will have twisted and broken branches, their trunks will be intricately patterned by mosses and stained by weather, and they will develop fantastic roots that seem to fasten upon the earth with their dragon claws. Thus the picturesque renders beauty more captivating, yet has at the same time a distinct and separate character from both the beautiful and the sublime. With respect to the art of laying out grounds, Price recommended the studying of pictures "not merely to make us acquainted with the combinations and effects that are contained in them, but to guide us by means of those general heads of composition, in our search for the numberless and untouched varieties and beauties of nature."[16] He did not mean that the gardener was

to imitate particular pictures, or even to reproduce the same
kinds of scenes as are found in pictures; rather the improver of
grounds was to be guided by the universal *principles* of painting. In the art of landscaping Price noted a great affinity between the landscape painter and the landscape gardener. "The
landscape gardener would prepare his colours, would mix and
break them, just like the painter. . . . Every aim of the painter,
with respect to form, and light and shadow, would likewise be
equally that of the gardener."[17] It was the failure of the
"Brownists," owing to their exclusive attention to smoothness
and flowing lines, to neglect the charms of two of the most universal sources of pleasure, variety and intricacy, that aroused
Price's opposition to them. He dwelt upon the monotony of
Brown's lay-outs and suggested that he would have found
inspiration if he had studied the canvases of the landscape
artists. Price lamented that the improvers isolate and separate
everything and "make all insipid by dotting with clumps one
uniform, green surface." "The sprinkling of a few, scattered
trees on the edges of banks will not do; there must be masses,
and groups, and various degrees of openings, and concealment;
and by such means, some little variety may be given to these
tame banks."[18] There was more charm, Price said, in the intricacy and suspense around the old formal gardens with their
terraces, summer houses, and iron gates, which the improvers
have wantonly swept away. In his ideal estate Price would
have a formal garden adjacent to the house; beyond the last
terrace there would be a pleasure ground with gravel walks
sweeping among the ornamental trees and at a distance the
wooded park. The country house must be given a picturesque
appearance from many viewpoints. The outline against the sky
must be "broad," with the sweep to hill or wood broken by the
irregular planting of trees to give intricacy. The surroundings
of houses must give the impression of having been arranged by
no other hand than that of Nature. And Nature must give the

finishing roughness to the gardener's work, but unadulterated Nature is not sufficient as a model in the laying out of a landscape. Price saw as the chief defect in modern gardening an affectation for the simplicity of mere Nature, whereas art ought to be employed and even in some degree displayed. The great lesson that Price taught his contemporaries was the study of basic artistic principles. Uppermost in the designer's mind must be the over-all unity of the separate parts. Price summed up in the last sentence of his essay "On Decorations Near the House" the *summum bonum* of picturesque garden design:

The difficulties in gardening, as in other arts, do not lie in forming the separate parts, in making upright terraces and fountains, or serpentine walks, plantations and rivers, but in producing a variety of compositions and effects by means of those parts, and in combining them, whatever they may be, or however mixed, into one striking and well connected whole.

The Art of Scenic Travel

The beginnings of travel in England for the purpose of viewing scenery can be traced to experiences among English travelers on the Grand Tour. The sojourn in Rome acquainted them with the paintings of Claude and Salvator through which they learned to identify the pictorial elements in the landscape. Thereafter they spoke knowingly of "broken and interrupted scenes," of "infinite variety of Inequalities and Shadowings," and of the amphitheatrical form of the Bay of Naples, which proclaimed itself a unified, perfectly composed Ideal Landscape. But the supreme experience of the tour was the crossing of the Alps, which awakened a taste for grand and mountainous scenery. Before the eighteenth century, men were conditioned by their classical and Christian heritage to look upon mountains as "unnatural Protuberances upon the Face of the Earth" with little meaning and less charm. But the way was

made ready by seventeenth and early eighteenth-century the-
ologians and by men of letters for the aesthetics of the infinite.
When Thomas Burnet crossed the Alps in 1671, he was re-
pulsed by the "wild and multifarious confusion," but he was
also awed and delighted by the vastness and majesty he beheld. To John Dennis the sight of the Alps in 1688 gave a
"transporting Pleasure" mingled with "a delightful Horrour" and
"a terrible Joy," ingredients that the Sublime is made of and
that prepared a man to enjoy Salvator on reaching Rome. The
third Earl of Shaftesbury made his crossing in 1686, two years
earlier than Dennis but did not report his reactions until 1709,
when they were worked into *The Moralists*. The travelers in
this essay make their way over "Mighty Atlas" but are confronted with the same vast and wild Nature that confounded
Shaftesbury in his passage through the Alps. They are seized
with the same giddy horror; yet, like Shaftesbury, their imagination is lost in sublime serenity while they contemplate the
immensity and wildness spread out before them. Addison was
ill at ease when he crossed the Alps in 1699 on his way to Italy,
but after he had "done" Rome and its galleries and assimilated
the point of view of Claude and Salvator, he saw the Alps on
his journey home with a reformed eye. He felt his imagination
expand with "hugh Precipices of naked Rocks . . . cleft in some
places so as to discover high mountains of snow." He learned
to love a prospect and the majestic aspects of mountains and
ocean. In *Spectator* 412 he dilates upon the pleasure of the
imagination in greatness, such as "the prospects of an open
champaign country, a vast uncultivated desert, of huge heaps
of mountains, high rocks and precipices, or a wide expanse of
water." James Thomson never left his homeland, but he was
acquainted with the aesthetics of wild Nature as set forth by
Shaftesbury and Addison. He has many authentic passages in
The Seasons describing first hand his native Scottish mountains, the most realistic being those in "Winter"—the "loose

disjointed cliffs and fractured mountains wild" when the "father of the tempest" comes down upon the north and "joyless rains . . . dash on the mountain's brow and shake the woods."

When in 1739 Horace Walpole and Thomas Gray set out on the Grand Tour, they were self-consciously prepared by their reading of Burnet, Dennis, Shaftesbury, and Addison, and by their admiration of Thomson's *Seasons*, directly to experience the sublimities of vastness and grandeur in the Alps. Gray set down his first impressions briefly in his journal: "Magnificent rudeness, and steep precipices. . . . You here meet with all the beauties so savage and horrid a place can present you with; Rocks of various and uncouth figures, Cascades pouring down from immense height out of hanging Groves of Pine-Trees, & the solemn Sound of the Stream, that roars below, all concur to form one of the most poetical scenes imaginable."[19] The ascent to the Grande Chartreuse remained with Gray the most memorable of his Alpine experiences. He described to Richard West his feelings on that occasion: "In our little journey up to the Grande Chartreuse, I do not remember to have gone ten paces without an exclamation, that there was no restraining. Not a precipice, not a torrent, not a cliff, but what was pregnant with religion and poetry."[20] Throughout the remainder of his life Gray continued to feel the enthrallment of the vast, the wild, and the mountainous. Nearly thirty years later, when he came back from Scotland in 1765, he extolled the wild beauty of the Scottish Highlands in a letter to William Mason: "A fig for your poets, painters, gardeners, and clergymen, that have not been among them; their imagination can be made up of nothing but bowling-greens, flowering shrubs, horse-ponds, Fleet ditches, shell grottoes, and Chinese rails."[21]

During the interval between Gray's crossing of the Alps in 1739 and his visit to Scotland in 1765 interest had been increasing among travelers for viewing the English landscape picturesquely. The accounts of those persons who had made the Grand Tour, the pictorial descriptions of Thomson and other nature poets, the idealized representations of the landscape in the paintings of Claude, Salvator, and Poussin and of certain English landscape painters, and the numerous gardens laid out along picturesque lines—all these resources offered to the traveler a composite of idealized Nature for his mind's eye which he sought to discover in his travels through the real world of existence. Burke's *Inquiry....Ideas on the Sublime and the Beautiful* (1756) aided in arousing the aesthetic appreciation of scenery. In the 1760's the popularity of the Ossianic poems, reënforced by the popularity of Salvator and the growing acceptance in general of wild and mountainous scenery, led to the widespread favor among travelers of gloomy forests, lonely heaths, mossy rocks, plunging torrents, and storm-bent trees. Women were among the first to succumb to the lure of the picturesque (possibly because so many of them copied prints, sketched, or painted), and the new turnpike roads offered them safer and more comfortable travel to more remote districts.

In the 1770's enthusiasm for picturesque travel, especially to the mountainous regions, came suddenly and powerfully into fashion. What seems to have precipitated the popular response was a letter first published in 1767 but written possibly as early as 1756 by John Brown, D.D., to Lord Lyttleton about the aesthetic appeal of the Lake District. The immediate effect of the publication was to send Arthur Young and Thomas Gray to the Lakes. The long-range effect was to establish a cult for picturesque travel to all parts of Great Britain that did not subside for many years. The same year that Brown's letter appeared, Young brought out a travel book, *Six Weeks Tour in the South Counties of England and Wales,* and after his visit to the Lake Country he followed it in 1768 with *Six Months Tour in the North of England.* The professed design of Young's books was to report on farming conditions, but the author had an eye as well for the picturesque as he passed through the countryside and as he visited various gentlemen's estates. He was indefatigable in the pursuit of fine views. Even from Mr. Tucker's cabbage-field, situated on the top of a hill, he saw a "bewitching" landscape such that he "would at any time, with the utmost pleasure, ride forty miles to view such another." He carefully notes and admiringly sets down the artistic elegance with which estate owners' imitate and ornament Nature. At Fountains Abbey the extensive grounds with statues, Gothic tower, obelisk, Roman monument, and Chinese temple are "all truly beautiful and picturesque." Hackfall Place is more picturesque and full of coloring than "the painting of a Claude." Young liked to compare the real landscape to landscape paintings and to view as through an imaginary picture frame the idealized Arcadian landscape of the estates he visited. But he reserves his unrestrained enthusiasm for the scenery of the Lake Country. Lake Windermere is "gloriously environed; spotted with islands more beautiful than would have issued from the pencil of the happiest painter, [surrounded by] mountains rearing their majestic heads with native sublimity."[22] He rhapsodizes upon the varied, romantic features of Keswick Lake and the view from the top of Skiddaw:

> *Keswick,* upon the whole, contains a variety that cannot fail of astonishing the spectator: The lake, the islands, the hanging woods, the waving inclosures, and the cascades are all most superlatively elegant and beautiful; while the rocks, clifts, crags, and mountains are equally terrifying and sublime. . . . What [he scornfully asks] are the effects of *Louis's* magnificence [the formal layout at Versailles] to the sportive play of nature in the vale of Keswick?[23]

Gray made a fortnight walking tour through the Lake Country in 1769 and published his observations in *Journal in the Lakes,* 1775. His notes were read by every person of taste and played no small part in making the Lakes a popular touring ground. Gray carried a "Claude Glass"[24] with him and went to the hilltops to capture the view. There he beheld the "most amazing and most superlative prospects." Gray thought that a mountainous country was the only one that could furnish truly picturesque scenery. Gray's descriptions are quiet and controlled but aesthetically penetrating, as in his word picture of Grasmere Vale seen from the high point on Dunmail Raise:

Just beyond it [*Helm-crag*] opens one of the sweetest landscapes that art ever attempted to imitate. The bosom of the mountains spreading here into a broad basin discovers in the midst *Grasmere-water;* its margin is hollowed into small bays with bold eminences: some of them rocks, some of soft turf that half conceal and vary the figure of the little lake they command. From the shore a low promontory pushes itself far into the water, and on it stands a white village with the parish-church rising in the midst of it, hanging enclosures, corn-fields, and meadows green as an emerald, with their trees and hedges, and cattle to fill up the whole space from the edge of the water. Just opposite to you is a large farm-house at the bottom of a steep smooth lawn embosomed in old woods, which climb half-way up the mountain's side, and discover above them a broken line of crags, that crown the scene. Not a single red tile, no flaming Gentlemen's house, or garden walls break in upon the repose of this little unsuspected paradise, but all is peace, rusticity, and happy poverty in its neatest, most becoming attire.[25]

Gray sees the scene before him with the eyes of a painter as well as with those of a poet. By reason of the truthfulness and sensitivity of his *Journal in the Lakes* Gray became an admired pioneer in the literature of picturesque travel.

As contagion for picturesque touring spread in the last quarter of the century, tourbooks and guides multiplied. Besides the works of Young and Gray already mentioned there were worthy of note Thomas Pennant's *Tour of Scotland,* 1771 (and *Second Tour of Scotland and the Hebrides,* 1776); William

Hutchinson's *An Excursion to the Lakes,* 1774, good on the artistic effects of changing lights and shades in the landscape; Henry Wyndham's *A Gentleman's Tour through Monmouthshire and Wales in ... 1774, 1775,* that opened eyes to the strangely neglected "grand scenery of Wales"; and Thomas West's *Guide to the Lakes,* 1778, which particularized the routes to be taken by the traveler and identified various stations for viewing the landscape to advantage. Wyndham's book evidently met a need, for it was republished in 1794, 1798, and 1809; West's *Guide* was useful and popular, and went into a seventh edition in 1799. But among all the travel books none matched the originality and influence of those by William Gilpin. In an earlier section we took note of the importance of Gilpin's pioneering work in connection with picturesque gardening. But he is a far more significant figure in the history of picturesque travel. He made many tours and gave fascinating accounts of them in a series of publications.[26]

According to Gilpin the picturesque traveler seeks in Nature the kind of beauty that would be suitable for inclusion in a picture. He also seeks picturesque beauty in animate and inanimate objects: birds, animals, and people; pictures, statues, gardens, ancient buildings, and ruined castles and abbeys. As the pictorial qualities are always in the traveler's mind, the pursuit after picturesque beauty involves the state of expectancy. The traveler moves forward as if he were in an unexplored country where every new discovery is an agreeable surprise and the source of a new pleasure. After the first pleasure of discovery there comes to the traveler the intellectual pleasure of testing the new scenes appreciatively; and sometimes this is followed by the highest pleasure, the emotional response of delight when a grand scene strikes the traveler overwhelmingly. Gilpin was no mere technical analyzer of landscape by the rules of art; he reveals himself to be capable of responding at times to the scene before him in a nonintellectual, almost mystic, manner. In his *Essay on Picturesque Travel* Gilpin writes:

We are most delighted when some grand scene, though perhaps of incorrect composition, rising before the eye, strikes us beyond the power of thought—when the *vox faucibus haeret;* and every mental operation is suspended. In this pause of intellect, this *deliquium* of soul, an enthusiastic sensation of pleasure overspreads it. . . . We rather *feel* than *survey* [the scene].[27]

One thinks of Wordsworth's response to Nature's beauty when "Thought was not; in enjoyment it expired." Like Wordsworth, Gilpin also found pleasure in the visions of Nature that fancy recreated. "Often," he says, "when slumber has half-closed the eye, and shut out all the objects of sense, especially after the enjoyment of some splendid scene; the imagination active and alert, collects its scattered ideas, transposes, combines, and shifts them into a thousand forms, producing . . . exquisite scenes."[28]

Gilpin has a fine sense of form; also sensitiveness to color, and to the varieties of light and shade. He draws pictures of mountains to show whether or not they have a good sky-line. Some are too regular, some are grotesque, some look deformed. He minutely examines the picturesque ingredients in the scenes before him—the stillness of the air, the strong light and shades, the tints upon the mountain, the polish of the lake. He finds magnificence and beauty in mountain scenery, but he says it must not be supposed that every scene is *correctly picturesque.* Wherever Nature fails in composition, it is up to the traveler to compose the landscape by selecting and combining objects so as to make a picture. The imagination will reshape those scenes which contain deformities. It will correct one part of Nature by another and compose a landscape, as the artist composed his celebrated Venus. But the power "which imagination has over these scenes is not greater than these

scenes have over imagination." The impressive calm from an
extended mirror of a quiet lake, the gray obscurity of a summer evening, the rough blast of a tempest, and sometimes in
the midst of tempest the sudden breakthrough of bright sunbeams to light up the storm—each may impose its power over
the imagination. Nothing is more impressively picturesque
than the dramatic play of light and shade in a mountainous
country. Gilpin singles out one such astonishing effect in an
extensive view of the Keswick region seen from the high road
where a sunset flood of splendor was contrasted by the fullest
depth of shade: "The whole was a scene of glory—but a scene
of glory painted by the hand of nature."[29]

An ideally picturesque view, according to Gilpin, should
contain distant mountains for the background, lakes in the
middle distance, and a foreground of rocks, woods, broken
grounds, cascades, or ruins. "An ancient oak," Gilpin suggests,
"will provide magnificence to mantle over a vacant corner of
the landscape, or to scatter a few loose branches over some ill-
shaped line." (How many sketchers, Mr. Hussey reminds us,
have "called upon" this invaluable tree!) In the far or middle
distance "the ruling character is *tenderness*," which in a foreground "gives way to what the painter calls *force* and *richness*." It is in the foreground that the picturesque qualities of
irregularity and roughness are best displayed. Here the shaggy
animals of wild regions show themselves to excellent advantage. In the Scottish Highlands, Gilpin says, the flocks and
herds are picturesque wherever found. Cattle and sheep mix
well together, and human figures combine agreeably with animals; indeed they "give a grace to a group, as they draw it to
an apex." The rougher animals, being better adapted to receive the beauties of light, are more picturesque than the
sleeker ones; hence the tattered sheep and the rough cow are
more picturesque than the trim horse. In a mountainous and
rocky country no ornament can surpass goats in picturesque-

ness. Their colors and shagginess are pleasing and their actions still more so. It would add "new terrors to a scene, to see an animal browsing on the steep of a perpendicular rock." In grand scenes the works of Salvator Rosa are a model when it comes to adornment. The barren craggy amphitheatre that opens out from Dunmail Raise (the mountain pass which leads from Grasmere) is a view of the horrid kind such as, if one were composing it, could best be completed with a group of banditti.

Gilpin insists that the picturesque traveler will test his powers in the presence of the scene with his eyes on the objects before him and emphasizes again and again the essential value of direct observation of Nature. This was Gilpin's aim and this, too, was his achievement. He was an experienced guide who knew that to capture the picturesque scenes of Keswick Lake, for example, one must not climb to "some garish stand where the eye may range far and wide" but must "travel along the rough side-skreens that adorn it; and catch its beauties, as they arise in smaller portions—its little bays, and winding shores—its deep recesses and hanging promontories—its garnished rocks and distant mountains."[30]

In picturesque description Gilpin's object was to bring "the images of nature as forcibly and as closely to the eye as it can by high colouring." He achieves his objective not through any blurring or distortion of the facts, but by a dramatic heightening of them, as in his pursuit of the River Derwent into Borrowdale:

On passing this river, and turning the first great promontory on our left, we found ourselves in a vast recess of mountains. We had seen them at a distance, from the northern extremity of the lake. They were then objects of grandeur. But now they had assumed their full majestic form; surrounding us on every side with their lofty barriers; and shutting out, in appearance, every idea of escape. Wild and various beyond conception were their shapes: but they partici-

LAKE DISTRICT SCENERY

by William Gilpin from *Observations on Several
Parts of England, Particularly the Mountains and
Lakes of Cumberland and Westmoreland*

pated rather of the desolate, than of the fantastic idea. . . . The summits receded far behind; and we only saw the bursting rocks, and bold protuberances, with which the sides of these enormous masses of solid earth are charged.[31]

Gilpin had a rare talent for isolating picturesque effects and a gusto in describing them. Among writers of travel books of that era he is surpassed only by Wordsworth.

Gilpin's zestful books of picturesque travel heightened people's interest in "the new science" and sent them in droves to the countryside to analyze Nature for themselves. Wordsworth grew to manhood when the rage for picturesque travel was at its peak. He made his first visit to the Wye valley in 1793 under the spell of the picturesque. And Coleridge made a walking tour in Wales in 1794 to indulge his sensibilities in wild and romantic scenery. By 1800, although there seems to be no let-up in country touring, the picturesque was becoming a little obvious, and persons indulging excessively in raptures over the grand irregularities of mountains were looked upon as fadists deserving of satire. Jane Austen amusingly depicts in *Love and Friendship* the folly of Augusta, who had a "considerable taste for the Beauties of Nature," as lured to Scotland after reading Gilpin's account of his tour in the Highlands. She also gives a witty account in the *Tour through Wales in a Letter from a Young Lady* of Fanny making "very beautiful" sketches, though they did not closely resemble the original scenes because she had to do all her sketching while she ran along the road to keep up with her mother's horse. Probably the most ludicrous satire on travel for the sake of seeing wild scenery was *The Tour of Doctor Syntax in Search of the Picturesque* (1809). It was written by William Combe to provide a text for Rowlandson's drawings of the schoolmaster Syntax, who was smitten with the idea of touring the Lakes to replenish his empty purse:

> I'll make a TOUR—and then I'll WRITE IT. . . .
> I'll prose it here, I'll verse it there
> And picturesque it everywhere.
>
> [Canto I, vv. 122, 127–28]

At one point in his wanderings he loses his way, but to make the most of a bad situation he creates an imaginary landscape out of an undecipherable guide post.

> I'll make a drawing of the post;
> And tho' your flimsy taste may flout it,
> There's something picturesque about it.
>
> [Canto II, vv. 126–28]

He changes a pond to a stream; over a flat he throws a bridge; and so on:

> Whoe'er from nature takes a view,
> Must copy and improve it too.
>
> [Canto II, vv. 151–52]

Combe makes his most effective hits when he ridicules the artistic fanaticism of the Doctor refusing an invitation to join in a hunt for these characteristic reasons:

> Your sport, my Lord, I cannot take,
> For I must go and hunt a lake;
> And while you chase the flying deer,
> I must fly off to Windermere.
> Instead of hallowing to a fox,
> I must catch echoes from the rocks.
> With curious eye and active scent,
> I on the picturesque am bent.
> This is my game; I must pursue it,
> And make it where I cannot view it.
>
> [Canto XIII, vv. 125–34]

The *Tour* is a miserable thing, but Syntax gets it published anyway and prospers.

DR. SYNTAX SETTING OUT IN
SEARCH OF THE PICTURESQUE
by Thomas Rowlandson

The satires of Jane Austen, Combe, and others upon picturesque travel serve to underscore the wide acceptance of its
vogue. Even Dr. Johnson was subject to the contagion of the
picturesque. He went to Scotland very much in a picturesque
mood, and his journey into Wales contains much talk of scenery. Mrs. Radcliffe created the scenes in her fiction from a composite of Thomson's *Seasons*, prints of the Italian landscape
painters, and Gilpin's travel books. Scott accepted the picturesque mode and based the scenic descriptions in his romances
upon the principles of Gilpin's and Price's analyses. In time,
picture-hunting in the landscape according to formulated rules
passed out of fashion. But while it endured, an entire generation of travelers made discoveries for themselves about a new
world of beauty before them. And as it was passing, England's
poets, chief among whom was Wordsworth, transcended the
limitations of the picturesque and offered to the quickened
sensibilities of their readers various, intimate, and subtle interpretations of the natural world.

The English School of Landscape Painting

Many factors had long been preparing for a school of landscape painting in England. Yet it was not until the sixth decade
of the century, when interest in gardens was high and a taste
for natural landscape was becoming fashionable, that the
painting of English scenery by English painters properly began. Before 1755 native-born artists generally had been con-
tent to paint foreign scenes or to make local scenes look like
those of the Dutch or Italian masters. Around mid-century,
however, a trend towards the first-hand portrayal of English
scenery is observable in some of the work of George Lambert
(1710–1765), in which he depicts his native countryside with
sincere appreciation of its quiet charm; and in the work of the
three Smiths of Chichester (William, George, and John), who

often closely observed the individual details of the landscape, though they rearranged them to conform to the theatrical grandeur of Salvator Rosa. The break from foreign art was at last cleanly made by Richard Wilson (1713–1782), who, without impairing the national character of English painting, succeeded in grafting on to it certain elements derived from Italian classical art, which gave it sufficient vitality to establish a tradition of its own. Wilson, a native of Wales, early in his career acquired a certain reputation as a portrait painter, then went to Italy to study where he remained for some seven years. There he learned to paint Italian scenes or academic landscapes fused in mellow light after the manner of Claude Lorrain. The best of these, *The Death of Niobe's Children* (1755), was exhibited in London in 1760 and established his reputation as a landscape painter of the first order. In 1755, when he returned from Italy and settled in Wales, he began to break away from the picturesque formula. He undertook to paint his native mountains and glens in their natural beauty and with more vivid colors than he had formerly used. The result was that he turned out many fresh and original landscapes. Among the finest are the lovely *Landscape with Bathers* and the solemn and beautiful *The Convent-Twilight;* also the sunny, spacious *De Tabley House,* which has a glow of color and a richness of pigment we do not have again until we come to John Crome. It was probably with this latter picture in mind that Constable wrote: "I recollect nothing so much as a large, solemn, bright, warm fresh landscape by Wilson, which still swims in my brain like a delicious dream." A note of calm serenity often associated with Wilson's work is to be found in his river scenes: especially fine are *The River Wye* and *The Thames near Twickenham.* Among the noblest are his mountain pictures. Very impressive are *Summit of Cader Idris* (the tarn at the summit) and *Snowdon,* a superb example of Wilson's temperamental response to the landscape. Wilson had the poet's feeling and the poet's eye and went directly to Nature for his inspiration.

Richard Wilson can truly be called the father of English landscape painting. Ruskin described him as an apostle of "sincere landscape art, founded upon meditative love of nature." He was before his time and therefore at the mercy of patrons who were wedded to the "brown tree" and the classical tradition. Had he not been so encumbered, he might have forced the public to applaud his glowing natural landscapes sparkling in color, radiant with air and space. He was the master of light, surpassing Claude; characteristically the whole of his landscape is fused with light. He had a largeness of design, a serenity of style, and a power of expressing sunlight and atmosphere that put him far ahead of his contemporaries. He was a member of the Royal Academy, but landscape was not popular in his time, and he suffered financially. Constable said of him, "Poor Wilson! Think of his fate, think of his magnificence!" But with the glowing visions of Richard Wilson, England began her contribution to landscape art.

Thomas Gainsborough (1727–1788), Wilson's contemporary, made his fortune at portrait painting but "landscape had his heart." He was restless to escape from his work "in the Face way" (his own phrase) and go into the country where he could enjoy painting "Landskips." He felt that landscape could be studied only from Nature herself and that the canvas should not be "thrust between the artist and the sky." His models were the Dutch painters, Ruysdael and Hobbema, and later Rubens and Van Dyck. But he studied closely his native countryside and gave a faithful rendering of "this blessed plot, this earth, this realm, this England" that he so devoutly loved. He was fond of catching the romantic aspects of rural life—picturesque gypsies, farm groups with animals, or peasants at the cottage door. He enlivened all with grace and shimmering freshness. Constable pays tribute to Gainsborough's sensitive and poetical renderings of nature:

The landscape of Gainsborough is soothing, tender, and affecting. The stillness of noon, the depths of twilight, and the dews and pearls of morning, are all to be found on the canvases of this most benevolent and kind-hearted man. On looking at them, we find tears in our eyes, and know not what brings them. The lonely haunts of the solitary shepherd, the return of the rustic with his bill and bundle of wood, the darksome land or dell, the sweet little cottage girl at the spring with her pitcher, were the things he delighted to paint, and which he painted with exquisite refinement, yet not a refinement beyond nature.[32]

Among his best landscapes is the ever-enchanting *Mr. and Mrs. Robert Andrews,* a portrait painted in his youth with his subjects sitting in a wheat field—an ingenuous picture, fresh as the morning dew. Other masterpieces include *The Cottage Door,* a glowing vision of simple rural life; *Pastoral Landscape with Figures and Cattle,* luminous and vivacious; and the superb *Morning Walk.* On the realistic side were *Shepherd Boys with Fighting Dogs* and *The Woodman,* anticipating Simon Lee of Wordsworth. Gainsborough had a more marked and more original artistic temperament than Wilson. By his richness of color and lyrical delicacy of handling he helped landscape painting to become more nearly a serious and esteemed branch of art.

English landscape painting after Wilson and Gainsborough relapsed in the hands of their successors. The forward movement was re-initiated at the close of the century by the water colorists. The pioneer in water color was Alexander Cozens (c. 1700–1786) and after him his son John Robert Cozens (1752–1799), who to a greater degree than his father achieved tone, atmosphere, and color. The son developed a close observation of Nature and the expression of personal feeling. Unfortunately, there was a limited range of color at the disposal of Cozens; nevertheless, he produced effects of sunlight and veiling atmosphere never before attempted. His *Valley with Winding Streams* and his *Lake Scene* feature a dim blue— Cozens' favorite color—with great atmospheric distances, and a luminous arching sky flecked with gold. His genius was essentially poetic and imaginative. Generous John Constable said of him: "His works are all poetry." Turner was also an admirer of Cozens and praised him with gusto. Cozens prepared the way for Thomas Girtin (1775–1802), who in his short life suggested almost all the possibilities of water color as a medium for landscape painting. He had a feeling for the living presences in Nature which is akin to that found in Wordsworth's poetry; and he had largeness of mind and felicity of expression. Unfortunately Girtin died at the early age of twenty-seven, just when, after mastering the capabilities of his medium, he was in a position to exploit his knowledge to full advantage.

In his day Horace Walpole had looked hopefully forward to the time when there would be a great school of English landscape painters: "How rich, how gay, how picturesque the face of the country. . . . Every journey is made through a succession of pictures." By the end of the century his hopes were on the point of being realized; for three giants, Constable, Turner, and John (Old) Crome, who were to make the succeeding era notable, were launched into their careers.

T W O

Wordsworth and Landscape Painting

~つ⌒

Wordsworth Becomes a Critic of Art

Wordsworth developed a competence in art criticism in his maturity, but he got off to a slow start. In his formative years in Cumberland and Westmoreland he had not been much exposed to works of art. There is a playful reference to Wordsworth, as a boy, striking a whip through his grandfather's portrait. In one of his schoolboy poems ("Ode," 1786) he invokes Reynolds to paint the picture of his beloved. We do not know what works of art interested him as a college student at Cambridge. During his student days he probably became acquainted with the masterworks of Claude Lorrain and Salvator Rosa through the widely distributed volumes of their etchings, which were copied by English engravers. In *The Prelude* (Book VII) he spoke of visiting in London "spectacles within doors" and mentions in passing "The Painter fashioning a work/To Nature's circumambient scenery." When he was in Paris, in 1791, he sought out Charles Le Brun's *Magdalene,* a second-rate painting but one of the "sights" of the day, which at the time moved him more than did the Bastille.[1] As a schoolboy through his reading of eighteenth-century authors Wordsworth had become familiar with the tradition of poetical land-

HAGAR AND THE ANGEL

by Claude Lorrain (The National Gallery, London)

scape description and of topographical poetry, which he turned
to good account in *Evening Walk* (1787–93), and by the time
he composed *Descriptive Sketches* (1791–92) he seems to have
become well versed in the standards of taste in landscape
painting and in the picturesque and the sublime. In the spring
of 1794, when Wordsworth was contemplating setting up a
monthly miscellany with William Mathews, he wrote to his
friend that he could handle, besides essays on Morals and Poli-
tics, "critical remarks upon Poetry, and upon the arts of Painting and Gardening."[2] Although we have only a meager record
of his activities in the arts of painting and gardening during
the early years, we must assume from his statement to
Mathews that he had done some reading in the aesthetics of
art and that he had critically viewed certain gardens and paintings. He doubtless was well acquainted with William Gilpin's
illustrations in aquatint in his various books on the picturesque,
for two of Gilpin's works were owned by Wordsworth as a
young man.[3] And he seems to have made an early acquaintance with the life and writings of Joshua Reynolds. Besides his
mention of Reynolds in the schoolboy poem, already noted,
Wordsworth quoted Sir Joshua's *Discourses* towards the close
of the *Preface* of 1800 in speaking of taste as an "acquired
talent."

In 1803 Wordsworth made the acquaintanceship of Sir
George Beaumont (1753–1827), who became a close friend and
a foremost influence in opening up the cultural value of art.
Sir George was held in high repute at the turn of the century
as a landscape painter, an eager connoisseur, and a generous
patron. His large circle of artist friends included those who
had achieved eminence—Reynolds, Gainsborough, Romney,
Wilson, and West—and those of the younger generation—
Thomas Girtin, James Cozens, David Willkie, Haydon, Constable, and Edwin Landseer—many of whom he generously
helped with his great wealth when they were in need. His pri-

vate collection was a notable one, sixteen pictures of which he gave to the National Gallery when it opened in 1824. It included among the landscapes, four Claudes (*Narcissus and Echo, A Study of Trees, The Death of Procris, Hagar and the Angel*), a Nicolas Poussin (*Phocion,* washing his feet), a Canaletto (*View of Venice,* one of the chief inspirations to Thomas Girtin), a Rubens (*Landscape,* with the Castle Steen), an S. Bourdon (*Return of the Ark,* bequeathed to Beaumont by Reynolds, because "in it the poetical style of landscape may be seen happily executed"), and two Richard Wilsons (*Ruins of the Villa of Maecenas at Tivoli* and *Landscape with Figures Representing the Destruction of the Children of Niobe,* both commissioned by Beaumont). There were monochrome landscapes by William Gilpin, topographical and antiquarian watercolors by Thomas Hearne, watercolors by John Robert Cozens, and about thirty drawings in watercolor by Thomas Girtin. To Wordsworth, who early in their acquaintanceship expressed regret that he had had "so little opportunity for studying pictures to discover the finer and peculiar beauties of painting," all of Sir George's collection was a great delight. On the walls as a part of it were Sir George's own paintings. Those well known to Wordsworth included two now in the National Gallery (*A Landscape with Jacques and the Stag* and *The Cynical Philosopher*), *The Entrance to Conway Castle, Peele Castle,* and other landscapes at Coleorton Hall. Whenever Wordsworth visited Beaumont's home at Grosvenor Square, there was always much talk of painting, followed by close study of the pictures in Sir George's collection and frequent visits under his host's guidance to other galleries. Joseph Farington, an intimate of Beaumont's and an accomplished painter of landscapes, gives many glimpses in his diary of the doings of Sir George, Wordsworth, and the London world of painters.

It cannot be claimed that Beaumont's own paintings have

much standing today as works of art or that his tastes were progressive. He was a traditionalist who saw and thought in terms of the old masters then in vogue. His special favorite was Claude Lorrain, whose harmonious landscapes he tried to match in his own canvases. Beaumont's works also show a close study of Ruysdael and Nicolas Poussin, painters who offered a wealth of ideas in composition, but whose colors were somewhat heavy and opaque. Sir George clung to the dull coloring of his predecessors and once amused Constable by asking him, "Where is your brown tree?" Constable answered that he never had one. Throughout his life Beaumont was too closely wedded to tradition to direct Wordsworth to the exciting advances in painting going on around them. But in spite of limitations in taste, Sir George widely opened the world of art to the poet with the result that in the years of their friendship Wordsworth made a steady advance in his knowledge of painting. In the first year of their acquaintanceship Sir George presented Wordsworth with Sir Joshua Reynolds' *Works,* which Wordsworth reported in a short time he had nearly read through. He expressed an admiration for Sir Joshua's "sound judgement universally displayed" in the *Discourses* and "the comprehensive and unexclusive character of his taste." Sir George sent Wordsworth pictures and drawings from time to time. His own *Conway Castle* was hung in Dorothy's bedroom, and *Applethwaite Dell* was placed above the chimney piece. Wordsworth often came to look at landscapes as though he were seeing them through Sir George's eyes. In letters he described scenes that he would like to see taking their shape on canvas under his friend's patient hand. He dedicated the *Poems* of 1815 to Sir George and told him that "some of the best poems were composed under the shade of your own groves . . . inspired or colored by the beautiful country of Coleorton." Miss Shackford notes that in the essays prefixed to these volumes there appear to be close parallels to Reynolds' *Discourses of Paint-*

ing. Both writings define *genius, taste, imagination, imitation, nature,* and the *laws* governing the artist. In a grove of lime trees Beaumont placed a cenotaph to the memory of Sir Joshua Reynolds, with an inscription by Wordsworth.

Wordsworth became interested in the English Watercolor School when Henry Edridge, in September, 1804, probably at the urging of Sir George Beaumont, called at Dove Cottage. In 1806, at Sir George's in London, Edridge drew a tinted pencil picture of Wordsworth that is one of the best portraits ever done of him. The poet rapidly extended his knowledge of watercolor through Sir George's own work and through the paintings in his collection by Thomas Hearne, John R. Cozens, and Thomas Girtin. Wordsworth's instinct for color led him to enjoy these paintings which displayed a clarity and radiance not possible in oils. Girtin, who was well represented in Beaumont's collection, must have had a special attraction for Wordsworth because, as Laurence Binyon points out, Girtin responded to the wild hills and valleys of Yorkshire and the North of England very much as Wordsworth did: "The mountains for him were no mere background but living presences."[4] In 1808 William Havill, a distinguished watercolorist, painted in Wordsworth's neighborhood. "He has done," Wordsworth wrote to Sir George, "a view of Rydale Water, looking down upon it from Rydale Park, of which I should like to know your opinion."[5]

As Wordsworth's contacts with art in all its forms became more frequent, his judgment of pictures grew more confident. Farington records the poet's judicious remarks on Wilson's *Villa Madama:*

Wordsworth said, He thought Historical subjects should never be introduced into Landscape but where the Landscape was to be subservient to them.—Where the Landscape was intended principally to impress the mind, figures, other than such as are general, such as

may a thousand times appear, and seem accidental, and not particularly to draw the attention, are injurious to the effect which the
Landscape should produce as a scene founded on an observation of
nature.—He thought this picture by Wilson excellent, but objected
to the foreground dark trees on the left hand which seemed to Him
like a *skreen,* put before the more distant parts.[6]

From time to time he even bought an original for himself. He
wrote to Sir George of his purchase of a pencil sketch by Mr.
Green of Ambleside which he thinks "has great merit, the
materials being uncommonly picturesque and well put together."[7] In the spring of 1808 he and Coleridge visited the picture gallery where Mr. Angerstein's famous collection was displayed. They saw there many pictures by Rembrandt, among
them that masterpiece *The Mill.* Through Coleridge he became
acquainted with Allston in 1812 and visited his studio. Wordsworth acknowledged his debt to Allston's *Jacob's Dream* in his
Evening Voluntaries (1818). The poet of course was broadly
exposed during his London visit to Coleridge's ideas on art.
(They appeared in printed form in *Farley's Bristol Journal,*
autumn, 1814, under the title *On the Principles of General
Criticism Concerning the Fine Arts.*) Wordsworth's steady advance in the appreciation of the technique of painting may be
observed in his analysis (given an assist by Sir George Beaumont) of how Rubens achieved the magnificent breadth of
view in *Steen Castle:*

I heard the other day of two artists who thus expressed themselves
upon the subject of a scene among our Lakes. "Plague upon those
vile Enclosures!" said One; "they spoil everything." "O," said the
Other, "I never *see* them." . . . Now, for my part, I should not wish
to be either of these Gentlemen, but to have in my own mind the
power of turning to advantage, wherever it is possible, every object of Art and Nature as they appear before me. What a noble
instance, as you have often pointed out to me, has Reubens given
of this in that picture in your possession, where he has brought, as

it were, a whole County into one Landscape, and made the most formal partitions of cultivation; hedge-rows of pollard willows conduct the eye with the depths and distances of his picture; and thus, more than by any other means, has given it that appearance of immensity which is so striking.[8]

Although Wordsworth developed a competence in judging the techniques of painting, he was less interested in them than he was in the basic principles of art. There are certain elemental laws, he believed, which apply to all the arts generally, whether to poetry, architecture, gardening, or painting. His fundamental principle—the *prima philosophia*, as he called it— is that "the invisible hand of art should everywhere work in the spirit of Nature" and of "Antiquity, her sister and co-partner."[9] Art can never succeed, he was convinced, until it learned the lesson of freedom which Nature has to teach, in so far as Nature is the art of God. Wordsworth is scornful of the poet who would timorously follow man-made rules of art. He calls upon him to let

> Thy Art be Nature; the live current quaff,
> And let the groveller sip his stagnant pool,
> In fear that else, when Critics grave and cool
> Have killed him, Scorn should write his epitaph.
> How does the Meadow-flower its bloom unfold?
> Because the lovely little flower is free
> Down to its root, and, in that freedom, bold;
> And so the grandeur of the Forest-tree
> Comes not by casting in a formal mould,
> But from its *own* divine vitality.
>
> ["A Poet," vv. 5–14]

To demonstrate the divine origin of art, the poet conducted his daughter Dora on an early morning walk "through woods and spacious forests" there to behold how

the Original of human art,
Heaven-prompted Nature, measures and erects
Her temples.

["A Little Onward," vv. 35–37]

Wordsworth wrote in a letter to Fletcher (25 February 1825) that "he felt inclined to do a dialogue upon nature, poetry, and painting to be illustrated by the scenery surrounding Mt. Snowdon." Such a work would have been immensely revealing; but since Wordsworth did not write this dialogue, we shall have to fill in its outline from his scattered comments upon the subject. Added together, though they are far from complete, his remarks make an advance upon Dryden's *Parallel between Poetry and Painting*. To begin with, Wordsworth recognizes that for either the poet or the painter to achieve distinction, "the strife is hard." This is the thought he expresses in his well-known sonnet to Haydon:

High is our calling, Friend!—Creative Art
(Whether the instrument of words she use,
Or pencil pregnant with ethereal hues,)
Demands the service of a mind and heart,
Though sensitive, yet, in their weakest part,
Heroically fashioned—to infuse
Faith in the whispers of the lonely Muse,
While the whole world seems adverse to desert.
And, oh! when Nature sinks, as oft she may,
Through long-lived pressure of obscure distress,
Still to be strenuous for the bright reward,
And in the soul admit of no decay,
Brook no continuance of weak-mindedness—
Great is the glory, for the strife is hard!

When the painter or the poet is confronted with the objects before him, Wordsworth cautioned, they should not be allowed to overwhelm him, but should be controlled by his imaginative purpose. Wordsworth is quoted by Aubrey de Vere as deploring Scott's rather mechanical fashion of jotting down in his notebook various items that struck him as he took a walk. "He should have left his pencil and note-book at home, fixed his eye as he walked with reverent attention on all that surrounded him, and taken all into a heart that could understand and enjoy." Then after several days the picture surviving in his mind would have presented "the ideal and essential truth of the scene."[10] The painter or the poet must seize the essentials of a scene through his imagination, which modifies the objects of his observation, both in form and color, and blend them into one harmonious whole.

S——, . . . confounds *imagery* and *imagination*. Sensible objects really existing, and felt to exist, are *imagery;* and they may form the materials of a descriptive poem, when objects are delineated as they are. Imagination is a subjective term: it deals with objects not as they are, but as they appear to the mind of the poet.

The imagination is that intellectual lens through the medium of which the poetical observer sees the objects of his observation, modified both in form and colour; or it is that inventive dresser of dramatic *tableaux,* by which the persons of the play are invested with new drapery, or placed in new attitudes, or it is that chemical faculty by which elements of the most different nature and distant origin are blended together into one harmonious and homogeneous whole.[11]

Wordsworth's sonnet on a picture of Sir George Beaumont's Coleorton landscape, which his friend presented to him, shows how the poet used his imagination to "abstract," "confer," and "modify" the details of a scene in order to create a poem of his own. The images of the smoke and the travelers, Wordsworth tells us, are the only portions taken from Beaumont's painting. The rest were added "for the sake of variety."

> Praised be the Art whose subtle power could stay
> Yon cloud, and fix it in that glorious shape;

Nor would permit the thin smoke to escape,
Nor those bright sunbeams to forsake the day;
Which stopped that band of travellers on their way,
Ere they were lost within the shady wood;
And showed the Bark upon the glassy flood
For ever anchored in her sheltering bay.
Soul-soothing Art! whom Morning, Noontide, Even,
Do serve with all their changeful pageantry;
Thou, with ambition modest yet sublime,
Here, for the sight of mortal man, hast given
To one brief moment caught from fleeting time
The appropriate calm of blest eternity.[12]

Wordsworth's praise in this sonnet of the power of painting to
seize and hold a scene unchanged, to perpetuate "one brief
moment caught from fleeting time," is an observation he often
repeated. Landscape paintings, he thought, should fix a mood,
a condition, a moment soon to be lost and changed in the
eternal flux of Nature. Again and again he calls painting the
"silent Art" and emphasizes silence, permanence, and dynamic
expression as its essential traits.

Wordsworth insists that the true artist, whether painter or
poet, must always be free to record his own imaginative reactions and conceptions (if need be, to add "the light that never
was on land or sea"), yet at the same time he must render the
essential truth of a given scene. More than anything, a painting
must, like all works of art, possess an idea, a thematic mood, a
judgment relating it to the inner life. He stressed the need for
the intellectual preparation of the artist. He believed that the
idea and feeling communicated by the artist were more important than the color and form. Wordsworth stated his opinion
to Beaumont that an artist's mind should be fed from books;
and respecting a painter of their acquaintance, he wrote: "Ar-
nald would have been a better painter, if his genius had led
him to *read* more in the early part of his life." He added, "I

do not think it possible to *excel* in *landscape* painting without a strong tincture of the Poetic Spirit."[13] Joshua Reynolds in *Discourse VII* gives Wordsworth support on this latter point: "Every painter whose business is description, ought to be tolerably conversant with the poets, in some language or other; that he may imbibe the pictorial spirit, and enlarge his stock of ideas." Wordsworth praises Beaumont as a painter who infused his work with the poetic spirit. In "Elegiac Musings on Sir George Beaumont," the poet remembered his old friend as one who "portrayed with happiest pencil . . . this world of earth, air, sea, and sky,/ . . . all its spirit-moving imagery,/Intensely studied with a painter's eye,/A poet's heart."

Constable and Wordsworth

John Constable (1776–1837) was a landscape painter more richly endowed with the poetic spirit than Beaumont ever was; more than that, he was an enthusiastic practitioner of Wordsworth's artistic principles. He shared Wordsworth's view that trees, flowers, meadows, and mountains were full of the divine spirit and that if contemplated with sufficient devotion they would reveal moral and spiritual essences of their own. Both the painter and the poet believed that the beautiful objects of Nature can quicken our joys, humanize our attitude towards men, and enable us to "see into the life of things."

Constable was born and grew up in Suffolk, a quiet pastoral region with wide expanses of meadow land, farm houses and churches, winding streams, small country mills, and barges moving along canals. The country of the Stour valley did not offer dramatic scenery such as in the Lake Country fostered the poetic spirit in the schoolboy Wordsworth; yet the miller's son found delight in the sound of water escaping from the mill-dams, in willows, rotten planks, slimy posts and brick work, sheep-cotes, water plants, old nets, and always the sky "very bright and fresh, with gray clouds running fast." These were the objects and scenes that made him a painter. "I shall never cease to paint such places," he wrote. "Painting is for me but another word for feeling, and I associate all 'my careless boyhood' with all that lies on the banks of the Stour." But there were many years of disheartening struggle before Constable was able to capture on canvas something of the primal impulses of Nature in shapes and colors "fresh with points of morning dew."

Constable was, like Wordsworth, a late starter. Up to his twenty-fourth year he was capable of nothing more than amateurish work. He went to London in 1799 to study at the Royal Academy, where he hoped to discover the ways of putting down his own personal experiences with Nature on canvas. He learned how to use paint and brushes, and how to construct a picture. He studied the art of Italy, of the Netherlands, and of his own countrymen, Girtin and Gainsborough, and he copied their landscapes. But he soon became dissatisfied with being an imitator. "I have been running after pictures and seeking truth at secondhand," he wrote in 1802. "I have . . . endeavoured to make my performances look as if really *executed* by other men . . . I shall shortly return to Bergholt where I shall make some laborious studies from nature—and I shall endeavour to get a pure and unaffected representation of scenes that may employ me with respect to Colour particularly and anything else—drawing I am pretty well master of.—There is little or nothing in the [Royal Academy] exhibition worth looking up to. *There is room enough for a natural painter*" (by which Constable meant a painter of Nature).[14] He returned to his homeland in 1802 where the emotional ties that first nurtured him were still true and strong. There he sought among the well-loved scenes of his early life subjects for his "natural" pictures. He believed, with Wordsworth, that the simple scenes

and situations of rustic life were often "more consonant to nature, that is, to eternal nature and the great moving spirit of
things." He loved to paint humble life because, to quote
Wordsworth, "in that condition our elementary feelings co-
exist in a state of greater simplicity, and consequently may be
more accurately contemplated and more forcibly communicated"; and further, because in them "the passions of men are
incorporated with the beautiful and permanent forces of nature."[15] The subject to Constable, as to Wordsworth, was not
the important thing; he was satisfied with the smaller beauties
of Nature, which, he said, were to be found "under every
hedge." What he sought was to present, as Wordsworth did,
"ordinary things in an unusual aspect." Constable, again like
Wordsworth, put his trust in the senses as the instrument of
knowledge. Wordsworth's lines in "Tintern Abbey" fit Constable absolutely:

> . . . colours and their forms, were then to me
> An appetite; a feeling and a love,
> That had no need of a remoter charm,
> By thought supplied, nor any interest
> Unborrowed from the eye.
> . . . well pleased to recognize
> In nature and the language of the sense,
> The anchor of my purest thoughts, the nurse,
> The guide, the guardian of my heart, and soul
> Of all my moral being.
>
> [vv. 79–83, 107–111]

Constable went to great lengths to achieve, as did Wordsworth, "a faithful adherence to the truth of nature." "The great
vice of the present day is *bravura*," he wrote, "an attempt to do
something beyond the truth. Fashion always had, and will
have, its day; but truth in all things only will last, and can
only have just claims on posterity."[16] As a windmiller with a

keen eye for changes in weather, he learned to watch and study details in Nature in a way personal to himself.

After his return from London, Constable worked in the open air face to face with his subject and experimented with many features of technique that he later adopted and perfected. His greatest strides forward in maturing his medium seem to have come during a sketching trip to the Lake District in the fall of 1806. During his visit he met Wordsworth, probably at the home of Charles and Sophia Lloyd on Lake Windermere. What they had to say to each other about poetry and painting we have no way of knowing. We do know that Constable in his early years was fond of reading poetry. It is highly probable, therefore, that he was well acquainted with the poetry of Wordsworth at the time of their meeting. Sir George Beaumont, who helped Constable get started in his professional training and who befriended him throughout his life, would have seen to that. Beaumont told Farington he had read "Tintern Abbey" a hundred times; and he was always singing Wordsworth's praises to Constable.[17] Morse Peckham conjectures that on the occasion of their meeting Constable was much impressed with Wordsworth and that his exchanges with the poet (reënforced by his reading of the preface to *Lyrical Ballads,* even perhaps by his knowledge of the then unpublished *Prelude,* which Beaumont at that time had in bound manuscript) directly stimulated him to free his style by means of a poetic rendering of the truth of Nature.[18] This does indeed seem to be what happened. For though Farington reports Constable as amused at Wordsworth's strong-mindedness and his high opinion of himself,[19] Constable's Lake Country sketches do show a poetic splendor and a new daring in style.

The steps that Constable took in maturing his art after his meeting with Wordsworth will be given in some detail in the next several pages, and similarities between the creations of the poet and the artist will be noted. It should be kept in mind, however, that the influence (an important one, as will be seen) was from the poet to the painter and not at all the other way around.

In the Lake Country, Constable felt no personal attachment or affectionate response to the mountains as Wordsworth did (he told Leslie later in life that "the solitude of mountains oppressed his spirits"); yet he was excited by the grand and solemn effects of light, shade, and color among the mountains. In these sketches he indulges fully for the first time his interest in atmospheric effects—the shafts of sunlight and the lowering mists. He also started writing inscriptions, often enthusiastic, on the backs of his drawings: "*Helvellyn 21st Sepr. 1806—evening—stormy with slight rain. 25 Sepr. 1806—Borrowdale—fine cloudy day tone very mellow like. Borrowdale Oct. 2 1806—twylight after a very fine day. Borrowdale 4 Octr. 1806 Noon clouds breaking away after Rain. Borrowdale 4 Oct 1806—Dark Autumnal day at noon—tone more blooming this . . . the effect exceeding terrific—and much like the beautiful Gaspar I saw in Margaret St.*" To these inscriptions in Constable's own hand on drawings and watercolors in the Victoria and Albert Collection may be added another inscription from Constable's drawing of 12 October owned by Sir T. Gibson Carmichael: "The finest scenery that ever was." What Constable was after in these sketches was absolute truth. The simple shapes of the mountains prompted him to abandon the detailed rendering of form he had learned from Gainsborough and to turn to Girtin for breadth and simplicity. He sought most of all to capture the moment of reality (the "spot of time") that exists in the constant change in light and weather. He had come to realize that the world is seen as light and shade, never as line. In his watercolor sketches he followed the spacious planning and simplicity of Girtin but captured in his own individual way the vibrations of light with sharp, nervous edges; and he fixed the highlights, conveying light shattering into splinters on an uneven hillside, an effect that he sometimes obtained (as in *Borrowdale,* a watercolor) by scraping the paper vigorously with a knife. In the oil sketches he freely used the palette knife to lay on splashes of color. Although the Lake Country sketches are not characteristic of Constable's mature works (he forced the color in them as he never did when painting the scenery of the Stour valley), they show for the first time his new method for expressing light in motion. They also show a new freedom in draughtmanship—grand and solemn effects of light, shade, and color, and realism passing beyond the experimental stage. Indeed, they represent the poetic moment captured imaginatively with sweep and vigor and absolute truth.

After his return from the Lakes, Constable took serious counsel with himself and prepared a number of sketches in oils for exhibition in which, so he told Farington, he thought he had got something original.[20] In 1808, still ardently pursuing the leads of experimentation initiated in the Lake Country, Constable did a series of oil sketches of the Stour valley which have freshness and poetic vitality. By 1809 he had overcome all the technical difficulties of painting the landscape in oil, at least in a personal rendering of it. Two pictures of this year in the Tate Gallery, *View at Epsom* and *Lane near East Bergholt with a Resting Man,* show an assured mastery of breadth combined with a natural richness in color. By 1811 he had entered into the full possession of his powers as a painter in oils, with a completely personal style that was "fresh, delicate, and intimate." Graham Reynolds sums up Constable's accomplishments at that time:

His command of effects of light ranges from the brilliantly colourful buildings and trees of *Flatford Mill* seen under a bright cloudy summer sky to the subtle misty tones of storm in *Barges on the Stour.* The

immediacy of his apprehension of all the features of the landscape . . .
is conveyed by the dashing slashes of his fully charged brush, which
encompass detail without losing breadth.[21]

But Constable's art did not develop to full maturity until he
had learned to combine the fresh coloring of the emotion-
charged sketches done out-of-doors with the art of making the
large studio pictures for exhibition. In this undertaking he set
himself against the theory of color harmonization then in
vogue and also against what the academicians called "gallery
tone," the fashionable rich yellowish brown with which it was
wrongly assumed the old masters glazed their pictures. Constable was determined to preserve in the worked-up paintings
the freshness and vividness of color in the sketches. Next he
had to retain the sparkle—the sparkle of sunlight on grass, on
leaves, on water, on clouds. This he did with touches of white,
which his contemporaries ridiculed as "Constable's snow."
Most of all he aimed to keep the spontaneity of the sketches by
sweeping brush work and colors laid on with a palette knife.
In addition to re-creating these stylistic essentials from the
sketches, he had to fix a poetic vision of experience on the exhibition canvas in a picture constructed according to the laws
of composition. Disavowing historical subjects, the area of
greatest popular appeal, and working from Nature, he imaginatively created something almost out of nothing. In order to
plan the composition and hit upon the tonal scale of the exhibition picture, Constable would first execute a large-sized
sketch with boldness and freedom of touch—a surcharged expression of emotion recollected in the studio. For the exhibition picture copied from the studio sketch he would alter some
features of the composition and patiently subdue the agitated
impasto to a smoother finish more nearly like what the Academy approved. Today art critics almost invariably consider
Constable's large studio sketches superior in expressive power
to the exhibition pictures, but his contemporaries, to whom

even his finished versions looked rough, would never have tolerated these first studies. His artist friends constantly reminded him that he should be more concerned about finish. Farington writes in his Diary entry for July 23, 1814: "Constable called upon me.—We talked about filling the vacancies of Associates in November next. I told him the objection made to His pictures was their being unfinished; that Thomson gave him great credit for the taste of His design in His larger picture last exhibited, & for the indication shown in the colouring, but He had not carried His finishing far enough."[22] Constable thanked his friends for their advice but kept stubbornly on his independent way.[23]

In pursuing a fresh, original reading of Nature, Constable turned to the concrete and away from Reynolds' generalizing of the abstract. His sketches of trees show strikingly the extent of his break with the art theories of the eighteenth century. Whereas Reynolds would abstract the ideal tree from a variety of individual instances, Constable concentrated on depicting a particular tree that was known to him almost as a personal thing. Some of the great oaks and elm trees in his neighborhood were old friends that he spoke of with eloquence. His studies of them penetrate into their life and depict their individual characteristics with truthfulness and skill. Constable looked upon painting as a science that should be pursued as an inquiry into the laws of Nature. Like Wordsworth, who saw the poet "ready to follow the steps of the Man of Science" in his search for truth, he recognized that the first power requisite for the production of painting, as for poetry, was "the ability to observe with accuracy things as they are in themselves and with fidelity to describe them."[24] The scientist in Constable penetrated through the outer layer of reality to the inner core. This feature of his creed is revealed with special force in his rigorous studies of cloud formations. He learned the scientific classification of cloud forms into cumulus, cirrus,

FIR TREES AT HAMPSTEAD

by John Constable (Pencil drawing reproduced with
the permission of the Victoria and Albert Museum)

and stratus—what produces them, what they portend—so that by complete knowledge he could better portray them on canvas. Constable considered sky as the essential part of the composition, "the standard of scale and the chief organ of sentiment." In 1822 he painted about fifty sky studies (all have exact indications with regard to date, time of day, and state of the atmosphere), and in them he captured "with consummate skill in all their varied beauty our complex and changeful English summer skies."[25] There are no more truthful images of clouds than those painted by Constable.

But it was the business of the painter, Constable believed, to transmit not merely a visual pattern embodying scientific fact but to render the totality of human experience enhanced by a multitude of associations, past and present, in which human emotion plays a leading part. The quotations from the poets in the Prospectus to *English Landscape* (the volume of engravings prepared by David Lucas from Constable's paintings) are no mere literary embellishment. Constable saw an intimate relationship between the aims of poetry and painting. "A painter should be able to suggest," he wrote, "something more than an outward resemblance of his subject, as a poet can bring forth the scent of flowers." The artist must, like the poet, contrive to instill the "sentiment." To Fisher he said: "It is the business of the painter not to contend with nature, and put a valley filled with imagery 50 miles long on a canvas of a few inches, but to attempt to make something out of nothing, in attempting which he must almost of necessity become poetical."[26] It was Constable's close and loving communion with Nature that unlocked the poetry of it that we admire in his work. At times he who "never saw an ugly thing" in all his life found in created things a holy rapture that unites him with Wordsworth and both of them to the spirit of Traherne, who wrote: "You never enjoy the world aright, till the sea itself floweth in your veins, till you are clothed with the heavens, and crowned with the stars . . . yet further, and you never enjoy the world aright, till you so love the beauty of enjoying it that you are coveteous and earnest to persuade others to enjoy it."[27] By such rapture Constable enshrined his revelations of Nature from simple scenes (seemingly created out of nothing) such as the *Willows by a Stream* or *The Cottage in a Cornfield*. The descriptive element in them is dissolved into a "poetic" harmony, and reality is transformed by imaginative power into something that makes a direct impact on the feelings. Constable insisted upon being authentic; but he was not a realist, any more than Wordsworth was. What he meant by authentic was getting the authentic spirit rather than the letter. He gave a few telling details by means of which we can proceed to an interpretation. He rearranged the features of the landscape, a tree here, a cottage there, to please his sense of composition. He used the full range of Nature's mysteries and beauties to bring forth the richness of harmony and form, of color and light, as the true poet does—as Wordsworth did— to bring forth a picture fostered by true creative imagination. It was by his choice of details and by showing the bonds that unite them to each other that his art became poetry. Constable knew what he was about: "The whole object and difficulty of art (indeed of all the fine arts)," he said, "is to *unite imagination with nature.*"

Constable was a conscious innovator; in respect to painting he stands in somewhat the same position as Wordsworth in respect to poetry. He rebelled against a public that ran after art that was imitative or eclectic and that pleased by repeating what was familiar and soon estimated. He chose "to seek excellence at its primitive source NATURE" and, by close observation, to discover "qualities existing in her, which have never been portrayed before, and thus form a style which is original."[28] He set out to reproduce on canvas what he called "the evanescent effects of nature's chiaroscuro," that is, a landscape rendered in terms of light and shade "not only in its general effect on the 'whole,' and as a means of rendering a proper emphasis on the 'parts,' in Painting, but also to show its use and power as a medium of expression, so as to note the day, the hour, the sunshine, and the shade."[29] He wanted to arrest the luminosity of color in the most striking manner, "to give 'to one brief moment caught from fleeting time'[30] a lasting and a sober existence." He was out to slay the landscape of the picturesque formula, the painting with Sir George Beaumont's "brown tree" in it. "I was determined," he said to Leslie, "that my pictures should have chic if they had nothing else." As we have seen, after prolonged experimentation he discovered how even the most transitory appearances of Nature could be captured by new shorthand techniques and broken forms with spots and splashes of color to counterfeit the sun's glitter. His contemporaries, nurtured on tradition, were shocked and puzzled by his daring technique; the academicians scorned it and called it "concerted imbecility." Constable went his lonely way following the line of truth against the forces of falsehood and affectation. His unwavering objective was, as Sir Kenneth Clark puts it, "to paint the scenery he knew best and loved, to paint it under all conditions of weather, to render both transient effects of light and the eternal grandeur of nature; never to exaggerate, never to prettify, never to paint for effect and yet to make a picture, as Claude and Ruysdael had made pictures before him."[31] He once said: "My pictures will not be popular, for they have no *handling*. But I do not see *handling* in nature."[32] He knew that eventually he would be recognized because he rendered the universal truth of Nature and the human heart. In a letter to Fisher in 1824 he writes:

My Lock [*A Boat Passing a Lock*] is liked at the Academy, and indeed it forms a decided feature and its light cannot be put out,

THE HAY-WAIN

by John Constable (The National Gallery, London)

because it is the light of nature, the mother of all that is valuable in poetry, painting or anything else where an appeal to the soul is required. The language of the heart is the only one that is universal; and Sterne says he disregards all rules, but makes his way to the heart as he can. But my execution annoys most of them, and all the scholastic ones.[33]

C. R. Leslie acclaims him as "the most genuine painter of English pastoral landscape who has ever lived." There are some limitations to his art: his range of subject matter is not wide and his draughtmanship is not as expert as Turner's. Yet he deserves a very special crown of glory, for no painter has so consistently, so sincerely, and so truthfully captured and crystallized the fair beauty of pastoral England as it really was. As Lucas says: "He brought English people face to face with England: the delicious, fresh, rainy, blowy England that they could identify."[34]

Oddly enough, Constable's genius was first given its due not in England but in France when in 1824 three of his pictures, the *Hay-Wain*, a *Hampstead Heath*, and *A View on the Stour,* were exhibited at the Louvre. Their originality stunned and excited the French artists. The *Hay-Wain* is a masterly composition in which every object represented in the landscape from the grandest masses of the windswept cloudy skies to the smallest plant or spray seems instinct with, as it were, and breathing the very stillness of summer noon. The figures, too— the horses standing ankle deep in the cool stream, the boy fishing from the boat, and the farm dog—all seem naturally called forth by, and form part of, the landscape. There is depth and breadth, and the vividness of fresh-air fact in all its shimmering beauty. The French wondered where the brightness came from. One Frenchman said to another: "Look at these landscapes by an Englishman; the ground appears to be covered by dew." The effect of seeing what Constable had done was to send French landscape painters into new endeavors. It opened the eyes of a youth named Corot, and so astonished Delacroix, who panegyrized Constable as "la gloire de l'école anglaise," that he completely repainted his *Massacre of Scio* in four days, just before the opening of the exhibition. Constable's influence upon the Barbizon School was direct and specific. Rousseau was perhaps his closest follower, but Troyon, Daubigny, and Millet, in his landscapes, are all deeply indebted to him. Following the example set by Constable they went directly to Nature where they aimed to reproduce the ceaseless movement of sunlight and shadow in a new technique. They sought to portray "the moment of illumination" by the light they found in a particular place at a given time, and to portray that light in its natural color. Like Constable they said, "There is nothing beautiful but light and shade make it so." From the time of its dramatic impact upon the Barbizon School, Constable's doctrine of "chiaroscuro in Nature" became in sober fact the core of nineteenth-century painting. Thus the "poetic moment of illumination" directly links Wordsworth, Constable, and the Impressionists.

We have taken note above of the first meeting of Constable and Wordsworth in the Lake Country and have suggested the possible far-reaching effects of that meeting in a dramatic freeing of Constable's style. Beckett thinks a second meeting must have taken place in London early in 1807, when Wordsworth and his sister came to stay with the Beaumonts from about 23 April to 8 June. Constable was so much in and out of the house in Grosvenor Square that they could hardly have avoided being thrown together.[35] Sir George and Lady Beaumont were at that time in the full tide of enthusiasm for Wordsworth, and proudly proclaimed the excellence of his poetry to any who would listen, sometimes to the annoyance of the artist Farington. Another meeting probably took place in the spring of 1812 at the Beaumonts' town house. Henry Crabb Robinson in his diary for 26 August 1824 records that he met Constable at the home of J. J. Masquerier, who said: "Constable knew Wordsworth formerly, took an interest in his conversation, and preserved some memorials of his composition when they met at Sir George Beaumont's. He furnished me with the lines from the third "Inscription in the Grounds of Coleorton" beginning:

> Beneath yon eastern ridge, the craggy bound
> Rugged and high of Charnwood's forest ground.[36]

Wordsworth did not compose these verses until 1811. By 1824, however, they would have acquired an added charm because of Constable's recent visit, in late fall, 1823, to the scenes described at the Beaumonts' country home. During that visit, which lasted for nearly six weeks, Constable became even better acquainted with Wordsworth's poetry. Sir George often read his verses aloud in the evenings. Constable tells of one such occasion in a letter to his wife: "Last evening (Sunday) he read a good deal of W's Excursion. It is beautiful but has some sad melancholy stories, and as I think only serve to harrow you up without a purpose—it is bad taste—but some of his descriptions of landscape are beautiful. They strongly wish me to get it."[37] Evidence for another possible meeting is offered by a note in the margin of David Lucas' copy of Leslie's *Life of Constable*. In this note, opposite the description of the spring, Leslie quotes from one of Constable's letters to his wife: "Everything seems full of blossom of some kind, and at every step I take, and on whatever subject I turn my eyes, that sublime expression of the Scripture, 'I am the resurrection and the life' seems as if uttered near me."[38] Lucas, repeating what Constable had told him, has written in the margin: "This remark was originally made by Wordsworth to Constable whilst walking by the side of an hedge the branches of which were just putting forth their green boughs in the early spring."[39] Leslie gives May, 1819, as the date, but Wordsworth did not visit London in that year. There were spring visits in 1812 and 1815, so that it could have been during one of them that the walk took place.

A letter from Wordsworth to Constable's daughters has recently come to light which shows that the poet and the painter met "with mutual pleasure," several times it would appear, in the latter part of Constable's life, that is, from about 1820 to 1837.[40]

Mr. Wordsworth presents his compliments to the Misses Constable and thanks them for the acceptable present of the Memoirs of their Father's life which he has just received. He lost no time in perusing the Book with which, on many accounts he has been much interested. Mr. Wordsworth had the pleasure of making Mr. Constables acquaintance when he visited this Country long ago; and through their common Friend Sir George Beaumont used often to hear of him, though he had not the good fortune to fall in with him, till the latter part of his life when they met with mutual pleasure. The engravings with which the Memoirs are illustrated, are eminently characteristic of the Painters mind. Mr. W— was not unacquainted with these works, as Mr. Constable had gratified him with a Copy of his English Landscape, a work most honorable to his Genius. Pity that he did not prolong his stay in this beautiful country, i. e. that we might have had its features reflected by his pencil.

RYDAL MOUNT
June 6th 1844

Wordsworth seems to have forgotten the several meetings with Constable at the Beaumonts' London home in the earlier years, but he clearly recalls with pleasure their later encounters. Constable's feeling for Wordsworth became more friendly, and over the years his enthusiasm for his poetry increased steadily. He frequently quoted Wordsworth's verses when they struck a responsive chord in his thought. He was reading Wordsworth early in 1823 before his visit to Coleorton and quoted from "Ode: General Thanksgiving" to give utterance to his own fervent love of England:

O England! dearer far than life is dear
If I forget thy prowess, never more
Be thy ungrateful son allowed to hear
Thy green leaves rustle, or thy torrents roar!

[vv. 139–42]

Later he used the same passage to preface his volume of *English Landscape*, 1830. When in 1833 he sent Mrs. Leslie a proof of his striking picture of *Weymouth Bay*, he explicitly associated it with Wordsworth. In his letter to Mrs. Leslie he said: "I shall now, to give value to the fragment I send, apply to it a line from Wordsworth:

This sea in anger and that dismal shore.

I think of Wordsworth, for on that spot perished his brother in the wreck of the Abergavenny."[41] An instance of shared delight in the rainbow is evidenced by Constable's transcription of "My heart leaps up when I behold," found among the painter's private papers in the possession of Col. J. Constable (quoted by permission) and copied out by Constable in 1829, when he was elected a full Academician. When Constable in 1830 set forth his thoughts about painting techniques in his Prospectus to *English Landscape*, he revealed his closeness to Wordsworth and his admiration for him by selecting the verse "to one brief moment caught from fleeting time" as the one that most fittingly expressed the essence of his thought about chiaroscuro. In 1836, when Constable sent *The Cenotaph* (a picture which honored the memory of Sir George Beaumont with that of Sir Joshua Reynolds) to the Academy for exhibition, he inserted in the catalog the "beautiful lines by Wordsworth" inscribed on the monument at Coleorton as a memorial to Reynolds. Perhaps it was this collocation of ideas on that occasion that led Constable to send Wordsworth an invitation to attend the four lectures on landscape art which he was to give at the Royal Institution in the late spring.[42]

The deep admiration that Constable had developed by the end of his life for Wordsworth's poetry is revealed in an unexpected way. A sonnet written by Constable and addressed to Wordsworth was discovered recently pasted in an autograph book of Dora Wordsworth.[43]

> Thou second Milton! in whose fervent strain
> The prayer was poured, that England's greatest bard
> His 'faith and morals' to this isle again
> Might in new glory give—that prayer was heard.
> In thee his presence hath been reassumed:
> High notes again have sounded in the ear
> Of those who virtue love and conquer fear
> In freedom's cause, who joy to be illumed
> By truths as pure as were the flowers that bloomed
> In sinless Eden. O maintain our cause!
> Nor let us dread that this proud land is doomed
> To yield to violent men her Church and Laws,
> While lays like thine are framed to glad the strong
> And give the lowly surest hope from wrong.
>   J. C. (28th June 1835)

For the painter this expression of esteem culminated a life-long admiration of the poet and was grounded in attitudes towards Nature that the two men shared at many points. These affinities may now be properly brought together and considered in some detail.

Constable shared Wordsworth's deep love of Nature and his belief that the beautiful objects of Nature can reveal moral and spiritual essences of their own. Both the painter and the poet were captivated by the charms of pastoral England where they grew up; both of them in manhood drew practically the whole of their emotive power from the scenes of their boyhood. Constable believed with Wordsworth that the simple scenes and situations of country life provided a source of human passion that could be more accurately contemplated and more powerfully depicted than any other, because it is incorporated with the moving spirit of Nature. Each put his trust in the senses, and each went to great lengths in his art to achieve a faithful adherence of the truth of Nature. Early in their careers, both Constable and Wordsworth were aware of the infinite variety of beauty in Nature that hitherto had never been captured in artistic form, and each was determined in his own way to remedy the deficiency. Constable found the smaller beauties of Nature under every hedge: "Lights— dews—breezes—blooms and freshness, not one of which has been perfected by any painter in the world." Similarly, Words- worth told Isabella Fenwick that the moment of composing a couplet in *Evening Walk,* expressing an appearance of Nature directly observed as he was crossing the Pass of Dunmail Raise, "was important in my poetical history; for I date from it my consciousness of the infinite variety of natural appearances which had been unnoticed by the poets of any age or country, so far as I was acquainted with them: and I made a resolution to supply in some degree the deficiency." Constable had writ- ten: "The world is wide; no two days are alike, nor even two hours; neither were there ever two leaves of a tree alike since the creation of the world."[44] On a sketching trip to the Lake Country in 1806, Constable appears to have been much im- pressed with Wordsworth and as a result of their meeting to have put into practice a new daring in style to capture light in motion at the poetic moment of truth. Constable and Words- worth in seeking a fresh, original reading of Nature turned to the concrete away from the abstract. Instead of Reynolds' ab- stract ideal of a tree, for example, Constable gives us *Elm Trees in Old Hall Park* and Wordsworth "Yew-Trees" in Bor- rowdale. Both the painter and the poet were ready to follow the steps of the Man of Science in his search for truth, in his accurate observation of things as they are in themselves, and with fidelity to describe them. The scientist in Constable is revealed in his rigorous study of cloud formations and his truthful rendition of them on canvas. The scientist in Wordsworth is to be discovered in the undeviating accuracy of his images of Nature constructed from direct and loving observation. But both the painter and the poet move beyond the visual report embodying the scientific fact to a poetic rendition of the totality of human experience. Each deeply felt in moments of inspiration the rapture in created things "clothed with the heavens, crowned by the stars." By such rapture Constable opens our eyes to delight in the poetic truth in such simple scenes as *Willows by a Stream* or *The Cottage in a Cornfield*, and Wordsworth awakens our imagination to the visionary wonders of the commonplace, such as are to be discovered in the roaring of a mountain cataract or in the shout of the cuckoo. Both the artist and the poet were conscious innovators; both rebelled against what was imitative or stereotyped in art and sought by a close study of Nature to portray in a style that was original what never before had been portrayed. Constable set out to arrest on canvas, in new shorthand techniques and broken forms, "the one brief moment caught from fleeting time." Just so, Wordsworth, in a bold departure from convention and using the language of common life, created a body of original poetry built upon moments of insight, "spots of time." Both Constable and Wordsworth were ridiculed by their contemporaries and were slow to reach public acceptance. Constable was acclaimed by French artists in 1824 but never by the English during his lifetime. Membership to the Royal Academy was delayed until 1829, after the death of his wife, when it no longer could have meant very much to him. Wordsworth suffered the public abuse of Lord Jeffrey in the *Edinburgh Review* until after his fiftieth year. Their friends urged them to conform more closely to tradition to gain acceptance. Sir George Beaumont was always trying to persuade Constable to imitate the paintings of others, and Farington repeatedly advised him to give his pictures a smoother finish. Samuel Rogers once said to Wordsworth that if he would let him edit his poems, "and give him leave to omit some half-dozen and make a few trifling alterations," he guaranteed he would be "as popular a poet as any living."[45] But neither the artist nor the poet would yield his inner convictions to the expediency of popular favor. Wordsworth recalled Coleridge's observation that "Every great and original writer, in proportion as he is great or original, must create the taste by which he is to be relished: he must teach the art by which he is to be seen." And Constable acted upon the assumption that the principle applied to the original artist as well. Finally, it should be noted that both Constable and Wordsworth were passionate lovers of their native England, each his own portion of it, and that each wanted more than anything else to leave a record of his love that posterity would cherish. Each interpreted for the less gifted, in his own medium and in his own highly original way, the spirit of the place and age in which he lived.

As we have seen, Constable early in his career adopted Wordsworth's artistic principles with singular success in experiments to free his style, and as the years passed he steadily grew in esteem for the poet and his poetry. Wordsworth did not reciprocate the painter's admiration in the same measure that it was given, nor does it appear that Constable had any influence on Wordsworth either in suggesting poetic themes or in advancing his taste in landscape painting. Wordsworth's relationship with Constable was always cordial. He praised the engravings of his paintings done by Lucas, "a work most honourable to his genius," and he subscribed a guinea to the fund raised in 1837 as "a tribute of respect to so admirable a painter as Constable."[46] But nowhere is there any indication on the part of Wordsworth that he understood or appreciated Constable's originality. The poet's lack of appreciation was probably due, more than to any other single factor, to the myopic

vision of Sir George Beaumont, Wordsworth's mentor in pictorial art. Sir George never quite seems to have grasped what
Constable was up to. Beaumont, misunderstanding Sir Joshua
Reynolds, thought that Reynolds meant for painters to study
only the masters in attempting to achieve the artistic ideal and
to follow established rules and practices. Sir George evidently
believed that he had inherited the responsibility to foster and
maintain Reynolds' "rules of art." When Constable was visiting
the baronet in 1823, at a time when the artist had reached the
height of his creative originality, he complained to his wife
that Sir George wanted him to imitate pictures. Beaumont
tried to convince Constable that he should ape the golden
brown of the masters. Constable always remained on good
terms with Beaumont but continued in his original way to in-
terpret the poetry of the landscape in a heightened and expanded color range. Following Beaumont's lead, Wordsworth
seemed unable to understand the crucial advances, similar to
his own in poetry, that Constable was making in painting.
Wordsworth's insensitivity to Constable's originality was due
partly to his lack of interest in technique. Today we wonder at
the blindness of the poet who argued eloquently for freedom
of style in his own artistic medium but who did not sense its
presence or need in another medium. Wordsworth did not
seem to penetrate to the poetry of *The Hay-Wain* or *The Leaping Horse,* though the poetry was there and something of the
spirit of it was taken from Wordsworth himself.

Turner and Wordsworth

J. M. W. Turner (1775–1851), that other great experimenter
and pioneer in landscape painting of the romantic age, was
like Constable a keen observer of Nature. He saw and por-

trayed the sublimity of light and the grandeur of the forms of clouds. He had the great gift of rendering a very true impression of a particular scene. In his pictures of the sea (*The Slave Ship, The Burial at Sea*) he could awaken a sense of mystery and some of the old reverential fear; in many of his pictures he crossed over into the realm of the supernatural. Sometimes he painted purely decorative effects and too often gave himself up to fantastic extravagances of his imagination. But with Constable he helped to make the palette of our landscape painters brighter and gayer.

Turner shared with Wordsworth a delight in poetic interpretations of scenery. Each has done pictures of the Lake Country, the rivers of England, scenes from Yorkshire and Scotland, castles, and ruined abbeys, as well as scenes from France, Switzerland, and Italy. Each remembered the human interest in the scenes he portrayed. But in style and handling there is scant parallel between them. Turner overwhelms the scene with a dramatic blaze of color swirling with emotion. Wordsworth renders the scene with distinct pictorial imagery quietly offering the affectionate associations linked with the daily life and work of man. Neither did Wordsworth appreciate Turner. And again, as with Constable, his attitude was largely influenced by Sir George Beaumont. Sir George was relentless in his attack on Turner. He belittled him in public; said his vague foregrounds were an abomination and his colors in bad taste. William Hazlitt, whose judgment in art was about as discerning as anyone's at that time, supported Beaumont in his crusade against Turner. Hazlitt found Turner unintelligible, thought he lacked a feeling for harmony, and criticized his high range of colors. Wordsworth had copies of Rogers' works containing numerous engravings by Turner, and he had seen some of Turner's watercolors at exhibitions in London: *The Sun Rising through Vapour*, 1807; *Hannibal Crossing the Alps*,

1812; *Crossing the Brook*, 1815; *Dido Building Carthage*, 1815. As we should expect, Wordsworth did not care much for the exhibitions, one of which included *The Sun Rising through Vapour*, and he thought Ruskin overpraised Turner in *Modern Painters*, "to the disparagement of others."

Wordsworth as Art Critic

In the latter portion of his life Wordsworth took increasing pleasure in viewing works of art. In 1823 he visited the art museums of Holland, where he admired the magnificent pictures of Rubens. He saw a Ruysdael, of which he gives a description, showing the view from a cathedral tower, including woods and spires, and "the sea and sand—hills beyond the flats glowing under a dazzling western sky."[47] He admired Bewick's engravings on wood—"transcripts from nature, that I look at with ever-recurring pleasure, and wonder at the variety and texture the artist contrived to produce upon such difficult material."[48] He acquired by gift from Robinson in 1839 a Ruysdael and a Van der Weyden, and in 1843 he purchased a print by Leonardo da Vinci, a favorite artist with Wordsworth. He took pleasure in the sketching of Westall and had a knowledge of Peter de Wint's watercolors. Hazlitt pays tribute to Wordsworth's taste and judgment in the art of landscape painting:

[Wordsworth] greatly esteems Bewick's woodcuts, and Waterloo's sylvan etchings. But he sometimes takes a higher tone, and gives his mind fair play. We have known him enlarge with a noble intelligence and enthusiasm on Nicolas Poussin's fine landscape-compositions, pointing out the unity of design that pervades them, the superintending mind, the imaginative principle that brings all to bear on the same end; and declaring he would not give a rush for any landscape that did not express the time of day, the climate, the period of the world it was meant to illustrate, or had not this character of *wholeness* in it. His eye also does justice to Rembrandt's fine and masterly effects. In the way in which that artist works something out of nothing, and transforms the stump of a tree, a common figure into an *ideal* object, by the gorgeous light and shade thrown upon it, he perceives an analogy to his own mode of investing the minute details of nature with an atmosphere of sentiment.[49]

But as between the arts, Wordsworth gives the palm to poetry over painting. He tells how in North Wales (summer, 1824) at Haford, near the Devil's Bridge, while Dora was attempting to make a sketch of the chasm in the rain, he composed by her side a sonnet addressed to the torrent: "How art thou named?" He describes the features of the scene; but adds, as the painter cannot, allusions to other famous heights and waterfalls.[50] The point is that the painter is restricted primarily to the scene before him, while the poet may range the world as his imagination leads him. Robinson, after his and Wordsworth's trip to Italy in 1837, reported to Barron Field that Wordsworth found the picture galleries more attractive than the museums of sculpure. But he would not allow "the plastic artist of any kind to place himself beside the poet as his equal."[51] Wordsworth even went so far, on a visit to Paris in 1820, as to express a preference for the exhibitions of untamed Nature at the *Jardin des Plantes* over the works of art at the Louvre:

Nothing which I have seen in this city has interested me at all like the *Jardin des Plantes*, with the living animals, and the Museum of Natural History which it includes. Scarcely could I refrain from tears of admiration at the sight of this apparently boundless exhibition of the wonders of the creation. The statues and the pictures of the Louvre affect me feebly in comparison.[52]

When he visited the Louvre again in 1837, he had nothing favorable to say about the exhibit of modern French landscape painting, which had received a fresh impetus after 1824, when

Constable's *Hay-Wain* was acclaimed.[53] As a critic of art, Wordsworth had much to say that is fundamental and illuminating about landscape painting and about the principles that underlie all the varied manifestations of beauty. But, like most of his generation, he was on the side of tradition when it came to making judgments on particular pictures or artists. Regrettably, he failed to recognize the genius of Constable and of Turner, who share the honor with Wordsworth of being the most imaginative and influential artists of landscape of their time.

THREE

Wordsworth and Landscape Gardening

Wordsworth's Principles of the Art of Landscape Gardening

Wordsworth considered landscape gardening as an art worthy to be bracketed with painting and poetry. He once good-humoredly told Perceval Graves that he thought Nature had furnished him with qualifications for success in the three related callings of poet, landscape gardener, and critic of works of art.[1] Early in his life he began acquainting himself with works on gardening and picturesque travel. His library eventually contained many volumes on these subjects, including the well-known ones by Knight, Price, Hutcheson, and Gilpin. He was well-informed on the controversy between the Brownists and the champions of picturesque gardening that was going full-blast during his young manhood. He scribbled marginalia in a copy of Knight's *Principles of Taste*[2] and probably read his *Landscape* when Dorothy was reading it in 1800.[3] He was a close student of Uvedale Price and thought he was "of great service in correcting the false taste of layers out of Parks and Pleasure-grounds."[4] In due course of time he became personally acquainted with Price, but after a visit to Price's Foxley, he confessed to Sir George Beaumont that he found fault with the taste of the owner as applied to his own estate. He thought Price had become unnecessarily fastidious in his control over the scenery, "impoverishing and monotonizing Landscapes which, if not originally distinguished by the bounty of Nature, must be ill able to spare the inspiriting varieties which Art, and the occupations and wants of life in a country left more to itself never fail to produce. This relish of humanity Foxley wants."[5] Wordsworth realized that most people of his generation had wrong-headed, conventional notions about gardens and scenery that often not only hindered their pleasure in the sight of common beauty but would even turn it into disgust. He cites as an example how a respectable person, one of his neighbors, once wanted to do away with "all the black and dirty stuff from the wall" in his garden at Rydal Mount. "The wall was backed by a bank of earth, and was exquisitely decorated with ivy, flowers, moss, and ferns, such as grow of themselves in like places; but the mere notion of fitness associated with a trim garden-wall prevented, in this instance, all sense of the spontaneous bounty and delicate care of Nature."[6] One of Wordsworth's life-long ambitions was to correct aberrant taste, such as his neighbor's, and to develop among the public a proper delight in the naturalness and beauty of the landscape. He realized that good taste in gardening, as in poetry, was slow in developing and had to be implanted gradually. Nevertheless, he bent his efforts in that direction. His basic purpose in writing *A Guide to the Lakes* was to inculcate a better taste for landscape among newcomers to the Lake Country. He even urged his youngest son to go into landscape gardening seriously as a profession.[7] This shows how far ahead of his time Wordsworth was, for although modern gardening had been developing in England for more than a century, it was mainly a gentleman's hobby in that day. His own taste was impeccable, and his skill in developing gardens remarkably well advanced. "He combined, beyond any man with whom I ever met," said

John Taylor Coleridge (nephew of the poet), "the most un-
sophisticated poetic delight in the beauties of nature with a
somewhat artistic skill in developing the sources and conditions of them. In examining the parts of a landscape he would
be minute; and he dealt with shrubs, flower-beds, and lawns
with the readiness of a practised landscape-gardener."[8]

Wordsworth set forth his principles governing the art of
landscape gardening in a letter to Sir George Beaumont dated
17 October 1805[9] and in the third section of *A Guide to the
Lakes*, 1810. He reminds Beaumont, who at the time was engaged in building a mansion on the family estate at Coleorton,
that "with respect to the grounds, you have there the advantage of being in good hands, namely, those of Nature." He says
in the letter that if Beaumont will let his house belong to the
country and not the country to the house, he cannot be wrong.
There is no justification for a nobleman to thrust himself in
beween us and Nature. When a person is in the midst of a
large estate, he ought to feel that the owner of it is "not the
victim of his condition" or "the spoiled child of worldly grandeur." A nobleman ought to be possessed of lowly mind and
human feelings, and have a true relish of simplicity. He should
do his utmost to be surrounded with tenants living comfortably
in happy-looking houses set among flourishing fields. And in
that part of his estate devoted to park and pleasure-ground
"let him keep himself as much out of sight as possible; let Nature be all in all, taking care that everything done by man
shall be in the way of being adopted by her."

As he writes, Wordsworth remembers the offensive "tremen-
dously long ell-wide gravel walks of the Duke of Athol, among
the wild glens of Blair, Bruar Water, and Dunkeld, brushed
neatly, without a blade of grass or weed upon them, or anything that bore trace of a human footstep."[10] He also recalls
the mistaken project undertaken by Thomas Wilkinson, master
of the grounds at Lord Lowther's estate near Penrith. Wilkin-

son began the construction of a gravel walk through a forest ground where it would, if completed, "efface the most beautiful specimen of a forest pathway ever to be seen by human eyes, and which I have paced many an hour when I was a youth, with some of those I best love." Wordsworth's imagination kindles with the remembrance of that lovely spot, and his language becomes poetical:

This path winds on under the trees with the wantonness of a River or a living Creature; and even if I may say so with the subtlety of a Spirit, contracting or enlarging itself, visible or invisible as it likes. There is a continued opening between the trees, a narrow slip of green turf besprinkled with Flowers, chiefly Daisies; and here it is, if I may use the same kind of language, that this pretty path plays its pranks, wearing away the turf and flowers at its pleasure. When I took the walk I was speaking of, last summer, it was Sunday. I met several People of the Country posting to and from church, in different parts; and in a retired spot by the River-side were two musicians . . . playing upon the Hautboy and Clarionet. You may guess I was not a little delighted.

The indulgence of sentiment in recalling the idyllic charm of the pathway in Lowther Woods leads Wordsworth into a statement of basic principles:

All just and solid pleasure in natural objects rest upon two pillars, God and Man. Laying out grounds, as it is called, may be considered as a liberal art, in some sort like Poetry and Painting; and its object, like that of all the liberal arts, is, or ought to be, to move the affections under the controul of good sense; that is, of the best and wisest, but speaking with more precision, it is to assist Nature in moving the affections. . . . No liberal art aims merely at the gratification of an individual or a class, the Painter or Poet is degraded in proportion as he does so; the true servants of the Arts pay homage to human kind as impersonated in unwarped and enlightened minds. If this be so when we are merely putting together words or colours, how much more ought the feeling to prevail when we are in the midst of the realities of things; of the beauty and harmony, of the joy and happiness, of living creatures; of men and children, of birds and beasts, of hills and streams, and trees and flowers; with the changes of night and day, evening and morning, summer and winter; and with all their unwearied actions and energies, as benign in the spirit which animates them as they are beautiful and grand in that form and clothing which is given to them for the delight of our senses.

Wordsworth censures the removal of tenant cottages and villages from great mansions (as was the practice of the Brownists) and is glad that Lord Beaumont will not follow that customary course. As for his part, he says in conclusion:

. . . strip my Neighborhood of human beings, and I should think it one of the greatest privations I could undergo. You have all the poverty of solitude, nothing of its elevation. In a word, if I were disposed to write a sermon . . . upon the subject of taste in natural beauty, I should take for my text the little pathway in Lowther Woods, and all that I had to say would begin and end in the human heart, as under the direction of the divine Nature conferring value on the objects of the senses, and pointing out what is valuable in them.

Wordsworth's letter to Beaumont is at once practical and imbued with poetical feeling. His fundamental principle is simple: Art can never succeed until it has learned the lessons which Nature has to teach, in so far as Nature is the art of God; and art never will touch the heart until it is united to the needs of man.[11] Cunning art practiced with pride and for the purposes of ostentation and selfish pleasure is false and cannot endure. This proposition is the theme of Wordsworth's poem "Hart-Leap Well," in which a knight, proud of his conquest of a gallant stag that at the chase's end with three prodigious leaps fell breathless and stone-dead, vowed to build a pleasure house and garden to mark the spot. For a time "the dancer's and the minstrel's song/Made merriment within that pleasant bower." But that was long ago. Now the great Lodge is dust and the place overgrown.

> This Beast not unobserved by Nature fell;
> His death was mourned by sympathy divine.

So Nature, working with her co-partner Antiquity, leaves these objects to a slow decay and "puts on her beauty and her bloom," as a reminder to mankind never to blend pleasure or pride "With sorrow of the meanest thing that feels."

In the third section of *A Guide to the Lakes,* entitled "Changes, and Rules of Taste for Preventing their Bad Effects," Wordsworth points out numerous examples of the desecration of landscape beauty perpetrated by newcomers to the Lake District and proposes ways to enhance, not destroy, this beauty. Settlers, he observes, thoughtlessly fell venerable native woods and plant anew whole islands with Scotch firs, "left to spindle up by each other's side—a melancholy phalanx"; they erect tall square buildings, "with four sides exposed, like an astronomer's observatory," and around these novel structures station platoons of firs; they pare off the shores of islands and surround them with embankments, giving an artificial appearance to the whole and destroying the infinite variety of natural beauty; they plant imported larches over the rocky steeps in place of native hollies and ash trees. Wordsworth laments that one can no longer travel through the more frequented tracts of the district without being offended by an introduction of discordant objects disturbing the peaceful harmony and color that formerly existed. He conjectures that most transgressions from good taste originate in unpracticed minds from their delight in formality and harsh contrasts. He cites as example the disfigurement of the hill of Dunmallet, at the foot of Ullswater, which resulted from dividing it into different portions by avenues of fir trees with a green and almost perpendicular lane descending the steep hill through each avenue. He asks his reader to contrast this quaint appearance with the same hill overgrown with self-planted wood—each tree springing up in the situation best suited to it with its forms and colors endlessly melting and playing into each other.

He would applaud—not condemn—a man's desire to decorate his residence and possessions and would attempt to show how the best results might be attained. "The rule is simple: with respect to grounds—work, where you can, in the spirit of Nature, with an invisible hand of art" and with respect to buildings with "Antiquity, who may be styled the co-partner and sister of Nature." Houses or mansions should be "not obvious, not obtrusive, but retired." Their color ought, if possible, to have the cast or shade of the soil: the principle being that "the house must harmonize with the surrounding landscape." White houses are, generally speaking, a blemish and to be avoided; though "a small white building, embowered in trees may, in some situations, be a delightful and animating object." He finds especially objectionable the introduction of exotic features that disrupt the harmony of Nature. Wordsworth in this connection vehemently censures the extensive planting of imported larch and fir. The larch as a tree, he asserts, has no variety in its youth and little dignity even when it attains its full growth. In the spring, when the larch is green, its color finds nothing to harmonize with; in summer it is of a dingy, lifeless hue; in autumn it is "of a spiritless unvaried yellow"; and in winter it appears "lamentably and absolutely dead." At no season has sunshine or shadow power to adorn the surface of its form. In short, the larch is a poor thing—it won't do! Generally, if exotic plants are chosen for adorning grounds close to a dwelling, "a transition should be contrived, without abruptness, from these foreigners to the rest of the shrubs, which ought to be of the kinds scattered by Nature through the woods—holly, broom, wild rose, elder, dogberry, white and black thorn, etc.,—either these only or such as would harmonize with them in form and color."[12] Trees should be natives of the country—birch, Scotch fir, sycamore, etc.,—plantings that by Nature take their own shape without constraint. As for the proper management of tree plantings:

. . . let the images of Nature be your guide, and the whole secret lurks in a few words; thickets or underwoods—single trees—trees clustered or in groups—groves—unbroken woods, but with varied masses of foliage—glades—invisible or winding boundaries—in rocky districts, a seemly proportion of rock left wholly bare, and other parts half hidden—disagreeable objects concealed, and formal lines broken—trees climbing up to the horizon, and in some places, ascending from its sharp edge, in which they are rooted, with the whole body of the tree appearing to stand in the clear sky—in other parts, woods surmounted by rocks utterly bare and naked, which adds to the sense of height, as if vegetation could not thither be carried, and impress a feeling of duration, power of resistance, and security from change![13]

The comments made by Wordsworth and his sister upon estates that they have visited confirm the principles of taste and its abuse that Wordsworth sets forth in his letter to Beaumont and in A Guide to the Lakes. In her Alfoxden Journal Dorothy laments the sad intrusion of formal art and foreign plantings upon the squire's grounds at Crookham, though there is some cause for giving cheer:

Quaint waterfalls about, about which Nature was very successfully striving to make beautiful what art had deformed—ruins, hermitages, etc. etc. In spite of all these things, the dell romantic and beautiful though everywhere planted with unnaturalised trees. Happily we cannot shape the huge hills, or carve out the valleys according to our fancy.[14]

Dorothy comments in her Grasmere Journal upon the pitiful

appearance of the shrubberies on Mr. Curwen's island on Lake Windermere, where he has made with them no natural glades, but merely a lawn with "a few miserable young trees, standing as if they were half-starved, and no sheep, no cattle upon these lawns."

It is neither one thing or another—neither *natural,* nor wholly cultivated and artificial, which it was before. And that great house! Mercy upon us! if it *could* be concealed, it *would* be well for all who are not pained to see the pleasantest of earthly spots deformed by man. But it *cannot* be covered. Even the tallest of our oak trees would not reach to the top of it.[15]

Recalling their visit to the estate of the Duke of Argyle, Dorothy tells of their regret at seeing the landscape rounded and shorn of its native beauty after the manner of "Capability" Brown:

The hills near the lake are smooth, so smooth that they might have been shaven or swept; the shores, too, had somewhat the same effect, being bare, and having no roughness, no woody points. . . . Behind the Castle the hills are planted to a great height, and the pleasure grounds extend far up the valley of Arey. We continued our walk a short way along the river, and were sorry to see it stripped of its natural ornaments, after the fashion of Mr. Brown, and left to tell its tale (for it would not be silent like the river at Blenheim) to naked fields and the planted trees on the hills.[16]

On their visit to Bothwell Castle in 1831 William and Dorothy were displeased to see formally laid out flower borders taking the place of "the natural overgrowings of the ruin, the scattered stones, and wild plants." Yet they recognized that there was some excuse in adorning the venerable castle ruin because it was so close to the Douglas mansion and the pleasure grounds must of necessity have extended beyond it.[17]

In a letter to John Taylor Coleridge dealing at some length with the arrangement of flower gardens, Wordsworth states certain principles upon which his mind had been clearly made up for a long time:

> . . . whenever a house fronts a grand or sublime scene of mountains, I would not admit beds of flowers and shrubs, with lawns interspersed, those diversities of shape which are so pleasing when we meet with them in wild Nature. I would either have no flowers, or an architectural garden with terraces and formal beds, after the manner of the French or Italians. But a scheme of this kind requires something of an antique air in the house to correspond with it. In such a site, or with such a building, the garden would at once be referred to the house, and would obviously depend upon it, without having other pretensions. Nevertheless, we often see, in such situations, a disposition of flowers and shrubs and lawns, which is neither Art nor Nature, and accordingly it is to me displeasing to look upon. . . . When the Landscape has no grandeur, but is somewhat Arcadian, a little Cyclades of exotic shrubs and flowers may be introduced in front of a house with good effect.[18]

Wordsworth cherished the indigenous English flowers and in his later years feared that the increasing practice of importing plants and flowers "from every portion of the globe" would drive some of his old favorites out of fashion. After a visit to Addington Park he wrote to Mrs. Howley (Sir George Beaumont's granddaughter) that he missed the hollyhock in her grounds. He warmly praised the stately beauty of the hollyhock and mentioned several lofty ones in his own garden which were still in flower in mid-November; he could scarcely bear the thought that "the Dahlia, and other foreigners recently introduced should have done so much to drive this imperial flower out of notice."[19] The poet's and Dorothy's comments affirm his stated principle that Art can never succeed until it learns the lessons which Nature has to teach in the service of man. Happily, they sometimes found gardens tastefully managed, as were the Duke's gardens on the Isle of Man:

Then to [the] Duke's gardens, which are beautiful. I thought of Italian villas, and Italian bays, looking down on a long green lawn adorned with flower-beds, such as Eve's, at one end; a perfect level with gravel walks at the sides, woods rising from it up the steeps. . . . The gardens beautifully managed,—wild, yet neat enough for plentiful produce; shrubbery, forest trees, vegetables, flowers, and hot-houses, all connected, yet divided by the form of the ground. Nature and art hand in hand.[20]

The Orchard-Garden at Dove Cottage

Wordsworth's own first undertaking in the art of landscape gardening had nothing to do with great houses or landed estates but with a modest cottage garden created in fulfillment of a long-cherished personal dream. Since boyhood he had been possessed with the idea of a remote golden age, when man lived in tranquil surroundings free from cares and sorrows. Wordsworth's thought of a paradise on earth was no idle conceit or fiction but a deep and abiding current of thought which constantly brought before him images of a splendid past. The problem was to find the lost paradise, the loss of which was not so much to be lamented as its rediscovery was to be sought. During his childhood he had caught a glimpse of such a state in the freeborn shepherd presiding in his own domain as lord and master amidst tracts more exquisitely fair than "Gehol's matchless gardens." On his travels in young manhood Wordsworth had beheld "sweet coverts" of pastoral life in enticing Alpine valleys where, it appeared, shepherds found freedom, dignity, and contentment in the pursuit of their daily tasks. For himself a cottage with a garden shared by one he loved could in very truth, he thought, be transformed into a place as fair as Paradise itself. So the Solitary describes the cottage garden in the Quantocks where he brought his bride:

. . . all was life
To us, all Nature, breathing love, was filled
With fragrance universal. . . .
Wild flowers transplanted with a tender hand
They from their various birthplaces were brought
And throve assembled in our small domain!
Blest occupation, pastimes innocent. . . .
Thus love . . . not only wrought
In that Enclosure to redress and guard
And to maintain, but also could find space
To introduce new touches of his own,
Heightened the beauties of a finished spot
Finished and fair as Paradise itself
Where the first Adam dwelt with sinless Eve.

[*The Excursion,* Book III]

Once as a roving school boy Wordsworth caught sight of
Grasmere Vale and (though never dreaming it might be his
fortune) thought it would be paradise to live there. But it did
happen on a turbulent December day in 1799 that his wish
became a reality; at that time he and his sister Dorothy came
to Grasmere Vale to make their home at Dove Cottage.

. . . possession of the good
Which had been sighed for, ancient thought fulfilled
And dear Imaginations realized
Up to their highest measure, yea and more.

[*The Recluse,* vv. 106–9]

Wordsworth rapturously pours forth the swelling gladness in
his heart on that occasion in a salutation to Grasmere. Here is
the last, best spot on earth where they will find

. . . the sense
Of majesty, and beauty, and repose,
A blended holiness of earth and sky,
Something that makes this individual Spot,

This small Abiding-place of many Men,
A termination, and a last retreat,
A Centre, come from wheresoe'er you will,
A Whole without dependence or defect,
Made for itself; and happy in itself,
Perfect Contentment, Unity entire.

[*The Recluse*, vv. 142–51]

Wordsworth did not come to Grasmere expecting to find perfection among all men in the valley. He was born and bred in the region and "wanted not a scale to regulate" his hopes. He looked for "Man/ The common Creature of the brotherhood,/ Differing but little from the Man elsewhere,/ For selfishness, and envy, and revenge,/ . . . strife and wrong." But love could be a redeeming power, and beauty an exaltation. Dismissing, then, "all Arcadian dreams" and "golden fancies of a golden Age," yet finding within themselves "Enough to fill the present time with joy," William and Dorothy anticipated the future years in the beautiful and quiet home where the poet would compose his verses and the two of them would find a refuge and a place of peace in Nature's midst.

Dove Cottage lay at the foot of the hill where the old road from Ambleside descends from White Moss Common to the side of Grasmere Lake. When the Wordsworths first came to live there, a farm stood at the top of the hill and another on the opposite side of the road from the cottage. None of the buildings then existed that are now across the street and block the view of the water and of Silver How. The Wordsworths' home had formerly been an inn, The Dove and Olive Branch, and is now known simply as Dove Cottage; the family, however, for some years spoke of it as Town-end, which was the local name. The outside walls of the cottage were rough-cast with white lime and gleamed hospitably upon the sight of the traveler as he passed its door. Downstairs there were two rooms, a wainscoted room used as the kitchen and a room leading out of it, which Dorothy made into a bedroom. Upstairs there were two fair-sized rooms that looked towards the lake, the larger of which became the "living room"; the other, in which the chimney "smoked like a furnace," became William's bedroom. Two other small rooms on this floor completed the accommodation. The premises were indeed humble, but in them the poet and his sister turned their dream into reality.

In Wordsworth's Edenic vision the house and the garden went together. The garden encompassed and beautified the home and was a living extension of the home for the delight and comfort of those living within. At Dove Cottage the orchard garden-ground was the creation of the whole family and was regarded by all with pride and partiality. John Wordsworth helped to make it; he planted trees in it and sodded the wall. Coleridge discovered a rock seat in the orchard and cleared away the brambles. Tom Hutchinson helped in the planting of flowers. But the planning and labor were chiefly the work of William and Dorothy: "My trees they are, my sister's flowers." They began by enclosing a strip of ground between the road and the cottage and planting it with roses and honeysuckles. In a year's time the outside wall was "covered all over with green leaves and scarlet flowers," for they had trained scarlet beans upon threads, which, as Dorothy said, "are not only exceedingly beautiful but very useful, as their produce is immense."[21] Next they pulled down the fence at the rear of the cottage which formerly divided the garden from the orchard. The entire area was small, and behind the house the ground sloped steeply upwards. Here the poet and one of his cottage neighbors, John Fisher, laid out stepping stones. These led to steps cut in the living rock and on to a short terrace walk which curved beneath a few apple trees. Above was a grassy bank where Wordsworth and his sister built a moss-hut, or arbor, backed by a rude stone wall built up and planted by Wordsworth himself, every interstice of

DOVE COTTAGE

Photograph by the author

THE DOVE COTTAGE GARDEN

Photograph by Blake N. White

which he filled with fern. Beyond the wall a dark wood rose
to the fells and crags. Below the terrace was a little rocky well:

> If you listen, all is still
> Save a little neighbouring rill
> That from out the rocky ground
> Strikes a solitary sound.
>
> ["The Kitten and Fall-
> ing Leaves," vv. 81–84]

Near this tiny fountain-head and in among the stones they
planted primroses. To fill their garden home with the wild
growing things that they loved, William and Dorothy roamed
the lakeside and the fells and brought back thyme, columbine,
daisies, snowdrops, orchises, foxglove, and gowans; also ferns,
lichens, and mosses. From their village neighbors they transported loads of native garden plants—white and yellow lilies,
London Pride, periwinkles, Lochety Goldings (globeflowers),
Christmas roses, boxwood, and rosemary. Sometimes Dorothy
was so late in returning from her foragings for wild plants that
she had to set them out by moonlight. Wordsworth wrote with
delight of the snow-drops planted around a stone in the orchard:

> Who fancied what a pretty sight
> This Rock would be if edged around
> With living snow-drops? circlet bright!
> How glorious to this orchard-ground! . . .
>
> It is the Spirit of Paradise
> That prompts such work, a Spirit strong,
> That gives to all the self-same bent
> Where life is wise and innocent.
>
> [vv. 1–4, 15–18]

To this day many of the wild things set out by the poet and
his sister more than a century and a half ago still thrive there.

And in early spring, clustering in the rocks above the well, and throughout the orchard, are scores of wild daffodils and in May quantities of bluebells.

With their own hands they had made their orchard-garden into "the calmest, fairest spot on earth." The Moss Hut, because of its retirement and the excessive beauty of the prospect from it, was the choicest niche of all. Wordsworth described it to his brothers as "a charming little Temple" and wrote a dwarf inscription for it. From the hut they had clear and expansive views of the lake, the valley, and the mountains. Dorothy characteristically records her responses to what they beheld:

Grasmere very solemn in the last glimpse of twilight. It calls home the heart to quietness. . . . Grasmere was so beautiful that my heart was almost melted away. . . . What a beautiful spot this is—the greenest in all the earth, the softest green covers the mountains to the very top—Silverhow is before my eyes, and I forget that I have ever seen it so beautiful.[22]

Through the pleasant days of the growing season they happily mixed garden tending, idling, reading, and composing. It was not long before the whole place was haunted with memories. Dorothy describes a sweet May morning when they had put the finishing stroke to their bower and were sitting in the orchard upon a seat under the wall:

It is a nice, cool, shady spot. The small birds are singing, lambs bleating, cuckow calling, the thrush sings by fits, Thomas Ashburner's axe is going quietly (without passion) in the orchard, hens are cackling, insects humming, the women are talking together at their doors, plumb and pear trees are in blossom. . . . The stitchwort is coming out, there is one budding lychnis, the primroses are passing their prime, celandine, violets, and wood sorrel for ever more, little geraniums and pansies on the wall.[23]

A number of Wordsworth's choicest poems are closely associated with the garden. Walking up and down the terrace he first recited "The Cuckoo"; "The Butterfly" describes the garden; the first two poems on the Daisy were made as the poet looked on the flower where under his own apple trees it starred the dappled grass; the "Green Linnet" is a vibrant expression of the spirit of the place. In "The Kitten and Falling Leaves" Wordsworth speaks like a prince with pride and joy of his palace-garden. In its shade "The Leechgatherer" was partly composed.

In 1802 William and Dorothy left the cottage for some months to go to France and later to Yorkshire for William's marriage. This departure meant the end of the "sole companionship" of brother and sister in the garden-paradise they had created and loved together. Dorothy poignantly records her feelings: "O, beautiful place! . . . I must prepare to go. The swallows, I must leave them, the well, the garden, the rose, all. Dear creatures!! . . . Well, I must go. Farewell."[24] William expressed his deep affection for the garden of their joyous sharing in "A Farewell":

> O happy Garden! whose seclusion deep
> Hath been so friendly to industrious hours;
> And to soft slumbers, that did gently steep
> Our spirits, carrying with them dreams of flowers,
> And wild notes warbled among leafy bowers.

>   ✿   ✿   ✿

> Sweet garden-orchard, eminently fair,
> The loveliest spot that man hath ever found,
> Farewell!—we leave thee to Heaven's peaceful care.

>   [vv. 57–61, 5–7]

Of all Wordsworth's gardening activity none better exemplifies his ideal of Art working with the spirit of Nature in the service of Man than the orchard-garden he and Dorothy created at Dove Cottage. They had found a sheltered spot that they reconstructed in harmony with the hills and planted with the wild and native things that grew in Nature's midst. With love they wrought in response to the needs of their hearts for beauty and harmony and joy. The touches they added of their own were always in keeping with Nature's images and ways— touches to "heighten the beauties of the finished spot/ Finished and fair as Paradise itself." So the garden at Dove Cottage, like the poetry written there, fulfilled deep creative impulses rising freely and naturally and not prompted by precept and man-made rules.

In his poetry, Wordsworth identifies several Edenic spots in the Lake Country, secure and protected, such as would make ideal locations for a home, and he extols the natural beauty and charm of a number of mountain cottages. In "Septimi Gades" (1794), verses freely adapted from Horace and addressed to Mary Hutchinson, the poet hails Grasmere's quiet vale as "the sweet scene of peace" among sequestered hills, "delicious spot secure" where he will take his bride to live in idyllic happiness "for many a golden year." In *The Excursion*, Book I, he hails the vale at Blea Tarn as "a sweet Recess" where man would be tenderly protected and surrounded on all sides with images of the pristine earth. In Book VII he describes an Elizabethan knight whose imagination had been captured when he was a young man by fair images of Grasmere, whence in later years he was drawn from the world "To make that paradise his home." In Book VII the poet is pleased to see that the pastor living in a mountain cottage has planted trees that shelter it from wintry blasts and that in the summer the dark shadows of the leaves "Danced in the breeze, chequering its mossy roof." In Book VI he describes the Grasmere widower's cottage, seeming to be sprung self-raised or grown from the living rock and adorned by Nature only; but a closer look discovers that the place was made lovely by his daughters, who planted wild honeysuckle round the porch and roses that climb upon the roof, and in the garden herbs and wild flowers with which were intermingled bright stones gathered from the hills—"a studious work of many fancies." In all instances Wordsworth considers the charm of the Lakeland cottage as compounded of native, natural elements in a kind of sacred union of the cottager and the cottage, with "its own dear brook, its own small pasture, almost its own sky."[25]

The Winter Garden at Coleorton Hall

Wordsworth's next substantial undertaking in landscape gardening was at Coleorton Hall, the estate of Sir George and Lady Beaumont in Leicestershire. When, in 1805, extensive alterations on the manor house were begun and plans for landscaping the grounds were being considered, Wordsworth in response to his patron's request wrote a letter, quoted in part on pp. 93–5, setting out his principles on the fine art of gardening. He insisted, it will be recalled, that all must be done with an eye to naturalness; for all Art is grounded in Nature. On this basic faith in Nature Wordsworth and Beaumont were strongly united. Sir George painted it, Wordsworth poetized it; in the life of both it was a permanent resource to which they constantly deferred.

> One wooed the silent Art with studious pains:
> These groves have heard the Other's pensive strains;
> Devoted thus, their spirits did unite
> By interchange of knowledge and delight.
> ["The Embowering Rose," vv. 5–8]

Moreover, Wordsworth took note that "painters and poets have had the credit of being reckoned the fathers of English gardening." Thus he felt that he and Beaumont were honorably joined

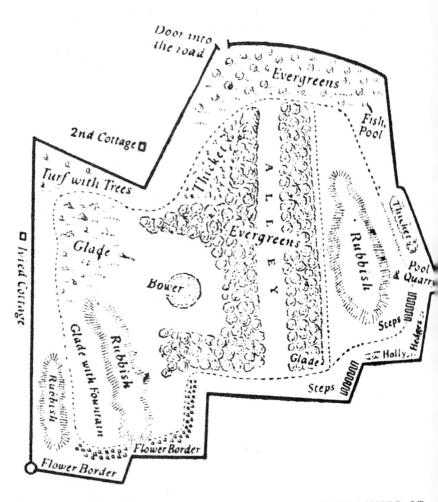

Door into the road

Evergreens

Fish Pool

2nd Cottage

Thicket

ALLEY

Thicket

Turf with Trees

Evergreens

Rubbish

Pool & Quarry

Ivied Cottage

Glade

Bower

Steps

Rubbish

Glade with fountain

Rubbish

Glade

Holly Hedges

Steps

Flower Border

Flower Border

THE WINTER GARDEN AS WORDSWORTH PLANNED IT

from *Letters of the Wordsworth Family*, ed. William Knight (London, 1907) I, 285 in the line of succession in this art. Unfortunately, Beaumont's addiction to the picturesque in painting tended to pull Wordsworth's taste in that direction in gardening as well as in painting. Under Beaumont's influence he seems to have become more consciously aware of intricate and studied effects in the landscape, especially in the working out of details; but his fine sense of propriety seems to have prevented him from per n.t-ting any disharmony in his gardens that would have marred the beauty of the whole landscape.

Dove Cottage had become too small for the Wordsworth family; consequently, in the autumn of 1806, when Sir George offered them the use of the spacious farmhouse on his estate, Wordsworth, his sister, his wife, and children took up their residence there. During that winter and in the spring and fall of 1807 the poet gave many weeks of careful and methodical thought to the replanning of the estate at Coleorton—the groves and lawns, the hedges and fences, the cottages and outbuildings —and in his letters to Beaumont made many excellent suggestions full of professional detail. His special project and the one in which he took the greatest pride was the design and construction of the Winter Garden. The idea of it seems to have originated with Addison, who, as Wordsworth pointed out, had a pleasing paper on this subject in *Spectator* 477. Addison had mentioned the laurel, the hollies, and the hornbeam as plants that he wanted his winter garden to be full of. Wordsworth, always partial to holly, picked up this suggestion approvingly and passed it on to the Beaumonts: "Let the holly be scattered here in profusion," he wrote. "It is of slow growth, but it does grow and somebody, we hope, will enjoy it."[26] Lady Beaumont chose the spot for the Winter Garden. The plot of ground, where stone had once been quarried, was hollow in shape, something over an acre in size, and about 250 yards from the manor house. The surface of the ground was marked by hillocks and slopes of rubbish overgrown with weeds and brambles—an unpromising prospect—but the site was protected at one end (toward the manor house) by a massive buttressed and recessed wall that offered shelter from the winter winds and provided a setting which invited enclosure. Wordsworth was pleased with the location and proceeded to lay before Lady Beaumont an elaborate plan for its development which, in fact, was carried out.[27] Mindful of the effects he wanted to create overall and also in the various compartments of the Winter Garden, he marshalled his horticultural materials accordingly.

To visualize the design, Wordsworth asked Lady Beaumont to imagine with him that they were standing upon the terrace above the newly built wall and looking down from it upon the garden. First he suggested that the entire space be enclosed with evergreen shrubs intermingled with cypress, and behind these he would put a row of fir trees, so as to give "the greatest appearance of depth, shelter, and seclusion possible." This he considered essential to the *feeling* of the place—"a spot which the winter cannot touch, ... when the face of Nature everywhere else is cold, decayed, and desolate." One opening in the boundary fence should be made to present the best view of the most interesting *distant* object. This break would provide the meditative mind with a contrast between the cares of a bleak worldly existence and the peace and protection of the garden recess. As for the treatment of the border within the enclosing fence of evergreens, Wordsworth thought that the wall should be covered with ivy and pyracanthus or any other winter plants that bear scarlet berries. The bank or *scar* before the ivied cottage should be planted along the top with ivy, periwinkle, or other brilliant evergreen plants, which should hang down and leave the earth visible in different places. The second cottage, which offered an "irregular and picturesque form, its tall chimney in particular," should be retained and planted with ivy. Above the little quarry, the scar should be adorned with trailing plants, and juniper, box, and yew. A stretch next

to this, where an old ugly wall had been built to prevent the
bank from falling in, should be covered with a bed of hollies,
but trimmed so as to create a green wall that would ascend to
the roots of the fir trees planted on top of the bank. Wordsworth also suggested formal beds of flowers edged with boxwood for the top of the wall and "at the risk of being tedious"
gave details of planting (omitted here). A path should wind
around the garden mostly near the boundary line, accompanied by wild flowers except where it led through the formal
closure. So much for the circumference.

As for the interior, this should be divided into several compartments, bowers, and alleys. The first compartment—the
one before the wall—should be "formal as characterized by
ornament of architecture as in the wall," and "by showiness
and splendor in flowers and shrubs." In this glade, if water
could be provided without undue expense, Wordsworth
wanted a stone fountain. In the next glade the ancient cottage
with wild flowers scattered everywhere would provide the
presiding image. The winding path around the garden would
lead through a dark thicket or grove past the second cottage
across the end of a long alley to a small glade encircled with
evergreens. In this glade there should be a basin of water inhabited by two goldfish or silverfish, the "genii" of the pool and
place. "The enclosure of evergreen, the sky above, the green
grass floor, and the two mute inhabitants, the only images it
should present, unless here and there a solitary wild-flower."
From this glade the path would lead to the little quarry, filled
with a pool of water to reflect the rocks "with their hanging
plants, the evergreens upon the top, and, shooting deeper than
all, the naked spire of the church." A flight of steps would be
made to lead out of the quarry to the clipt holly hedge, where
the stroller would come to a large open glade and a stream of
water flowing from the base of the wych-elm. Having passed
through this glade and before coming to the newly built wall,

POOL AND GROTTO in the Winter Garden

Photograph by Ross Lockridge

STEPS TO THE WYCH ELM in the Winter Garden

Photograph by Ross Lockridge

he would cross the other end of the alley and continue to the glade where the second cottage stands. This alley—to extend across the whole length of the garden—would be quite straight and perfectly level, and shaded with laurel. The ground, when the trees overshadowed the walk, would become mossy so that the whole would be "still unvaried, and cloistral, soothing and not stirring the mind, or tempting it out of itself." From the middle of this alley, on the left side, should be a small blind path leading to a bower with a mossy seat and a small stone table in the midst. These are the features of consequence. Intermediate plantings of evergreens would be used to fill in open spaces and "break up any unpleasing formality which alley and bower, or any other parts of the garden, might otherwise give to it, when looked at from above." Wordsworth concluded that if there should be added to the features he had described a seat in some sunny spot, or perhaps a small shed or alcove, there would be introduced "as much variety within the compass of an acre as my fancy is capable of suggesting."

Wordsworth realized that he had written "a very pretty romance" in his letter to Lady Beaumont and when he looked at the site in its actual state, he was afraid that she would call him "an enthusiast and a visionary." He was nevertheless convinced that if proper pains were taken in the selection and care of the plantings, "less than six years would transform it into something that might be looked at with pleasure; fifty would make it a paradise." Dorothy shared the enthusiasm of her brother. Coleridge was delighted with the plan, though he had doubts about the fountain. He also thought that an intermingling of birch trees somewhere should be added because of the richness of the color of the naked twigs in winter (an opinion in which Dorothy concurred).

To Wordsworth was assigned the overseeing of the construction of the Winter Garden, an employment that he greatly enjoyed. He generally visited the garden twice a day to guide the workmen in their progress. Mr. Craig, the Beaumonts' head gardener, though perhaps "inwardly rather petted" (as Dorothy thought), was coöperative in carrying out Wordsworth's ideas. Some days the two of them journeyed to a Nottingham nursery fourteen miles distant to procure plants. One day they returned with a load of American azaleas which were set in the first compartment to make it "splendid and adorned." While the work was moving forward, Wordsworth addressed a sonnet to Lady Beaumont letting his fancy shape the dream of transformation that time and Nature would work upon their efforts.

> Lady! the songs of Spring were in the grove
> While I was shaping beds for winter flowers;
> While I was planting green unfading bowers,
> And shrubs—to hang upon the warm alcove,
> And sheltering wall; and still, as Fancy wove
> The dream, to time and nature's blended powers
> I gave this paradise for winter hours,
> A labyrinth, Lady! which your feet shall rove.
> Yes! when the sun of life more feebly shines,
> Becoming thoughts, I trust, of solemn gloom
> Or of high gladness you shall hither bring;
> And these perennial bowers and murmuring pines
> Be gracious as the music and the bloom
> And all the mighty ravishment of spring.

After some weeks of Wordsworth's inspired direction and the sustained labor of the garden workmen, the ground surface was reshaped, the paths and walks were constructed, water was channeled to fill the quarry pool, hundreds of trees and shrubs were set in place, and the grass plots and flower beds were planted. When all was finished and Wordsworth and Mr. Craig proudly viewed from the high wall the newly-built paths and gleaming stone work amidst a multitude of freshly set trees and shrubs, the poet was no doubt keenly aware that

the man-made garden before them—contrived by art—fell far
short of his vision of green unfading bowers "as fancy wove the
dream." But in just a few years, with Nature's help, his dream
began to take the shape of reality. In the fall of 1811 Sir
George wrote to Wordsworth: "You cannot imagine how beautiful the winter garden grows. The trees are sufficiently grown
to give intimacy."[28] With the passing of time the garden was
transformed into an ideal winter retreat of evergreens and
red-berried vines, with glades and arbors fit for a poet's walk,
where variety was happily joined with unity and wildness with
the charm of cultivation. Wordsworth was especially pleased
to note, on a visit some years after, how subtly the boundary
plantings merged to lose their identity:

> We see not nor suspect a bound,
> No more than in some forest wild;
> The sight is free as air—or crost
> Only by art in nature lost.
> ["A Flower Garden," vv. 27–30]

In some verses sent to Lady Beaumont, "the happy Eve of this
fair spot," he wrote proudly of the protection provided:

> This delicate Enclosure shows
> Of modest kindness, that would hide
> The firm protection she bestows;
> Of manners, like its viewless fence,
> Ensuring peace to innocence.
> ["A Flower Garden," vv. 44–48]

Uvedale Price was pleased with the Winter Garden, though
he wished that the straight walk were not there as he thought
it interfered with the whole by dividing it.[29] Price's criticism,
though perhaps valid at the time he made it (one year after
construction had been completed), was less justified when the
trees and shrubs through years of growth had brought a unify-

ing naturalness to the whole garden. The straight walk, it should be noted, was a favorite garden feature with Wordsworth, one that expressed his need for a place of retirement in which to pace as he composed his poems aloud. Even the orchard-garden at Dove Cottage had its terrace below the moss-hut; and the garden at Rydal Mount was distinguished by a long, straight terrace walk constructed by the poet for his special use—but neither feature is necessarily divisive or disunifying.

Over the years the Beaumonts consulted Wordsworth about alterations and upkeep in the Winter Garden. He reminded Lady Beaumont that one may go too far in trying to avoid expense in maintenance, especially in mowing:

A wilderness of shrubs is a delightful thing as a part of a garden, but only as a part. You must have open space of lawn, or you lose all the beauty of outline in the different tufts or islands of shrubs, and even in many instances in their individual forms. This lawn cannot be had without mowing.[30]

Perennial plants and flowers should be the mainstay of the garden, but a few late-blooming annuals might with little trouble and great advantage be interspersed among them.[31] During the lifetimes of Sir George and Lady Beaumont the Winter Garden was watched over carefully and kept in harmony with Wordsworth's original design; but when Coleorton passed into the hands of their successors, foreign materials and lapses in maintenance marred the poet's creation. On a visit in the summer of 1841 Wordsworth was distressed to see an aviary, introduced by the younger Lady Beaumont,[32] "which took up room that could not be spared, shuts out of view the ornamental masonry of the high terrace wall, and is altogether out of character with the place."[33] He also thought the evergreens had been far too much thinned, leaving some parts cold and bare; and the little nook where the pool was, seemed too

SCOTT'S SEAT in the Winter Garden
Photograph by Ross Lockridge

much dressed with shells and pretty ornaments.[34] When William Knight visited Coleorton in 1886, the Winter Garden retained enough of the condition of its prime so that he could call it a monument of the poet's "insight into the principles of Art as applied to landscape gardening."[35] Today all that remains of the original plantings are a few gnarly old holly and yew trees in the border. The bowers and alleys are all gone. In their place is the private garden, mostly open lawn, of a Coal Board official who has a neat modern house on the south border. Under the high wall are beds of modern floribunda roses which would have amazed Wordsworth with their brilliance and long flowering season. It is still a beautiful place, and it still retains a number of the physical features of Wordsworth's original layout: the bordering path and stone steps, the moldering brick chimney and walls of the second cottage, the old quarry hole (once a pool) over which the church steeple can be sighted, the rock cavern with some of the shell decorations still in place, and the niche in the sandstone rock scooped out by Wordsworth, his wife, and his sister while the laborers were at work.[36] With these landmarks in the hollow and Wordsworth's detailed description to guide us it is possible to trace out with some certainty the features of the Winter Garden as shown on the old map reproduced in the volume of letters to the Beaumonts.

Also of interest at Coleorton are the inscriptions written by Wordsworth which were engraved in stone and set up as memorials on the estate grounds. The practice of erecting memorial inscriptions goes back to ancient times and was much favored in the picturesque gardens of eighteenth-century England. Shenstone especially helped to popularize the practice by composing a number of poems which were carved on stone tablets and placed about his estate, the Leasowes. Wordsworth had written several inscriptions for favored places in the Lake District including a miniature one for the moss-hut in the garden at Dove Cottage. In keeping with tradition Sir George proposed in a letter to Wordsworth (4 November 1811) that the sonnet he had addressed to Lady Beaumont (quoted above p. 119) should be engraved on stone and placed, with Wordsworth's approval, in a circular gothic structure which he was to assist in designing.[37] Encouraged by Sir George's lead, Wordsworth composed three additional inscriptions for the grounds at Coleorton and forwarded them to his patron (16 November), one to the memory of Sir John Beaumont (1583–1627) and his brother Francis ("The embowering rose, the acacia, and the pine"), a second to commemorate the seat cut out of sandstone in the Winter Garden ("Oft is the medal faithful to its trust"), and a third to memorialize Sir Joshua Reynolds ("Ye lime-trees, ranged before this hallowed Urn").[38] Further encouraged by Sir George's enthusiasm for these inscriptions, Wordsworth soon wrote and forwarded a fourth one honoring the family of Beaumont, which for generations had resided at Coleorton, and especially Sir Francis Beaumont, the friend of Shakespeare ("Beneath yon eastern ridge, the craggy bound"). He also sent along a sonnet to John Dyer ("Bard of the Fleece, whose skilfull genius made"), which Sir George thought "Might find an appropriate place in Powell's rough, at a distance from the hall."[39] Wordsworth had a clear conception of what he was trying to accomplish in these inscriptions, though he feared he had fallen short of his goal. He wished, he said, to create a dramatic, yet anonymous, effect—as if the reader of the verses were speaking them to himself—and thought that some of the inscriptions might suggest comparison with the poems of Theocritus and the Greek Anthology.

In the following year, 1812, three of Wordsworth's inscriptions were engraved on stone and erected in the groves at Coleorton, the two honoring the Beaumonts and the one in memory of Sir Joshua Reynolds. In 1823 John Constable, during his stay with Sir George, painted a picture of the urn

MONUMENT TO SIR JOSHUA REYNOLDS at Coleorton

Photograph by Ross Lockridge

honoring Reynolds. In composing the picture, Constable set the urn in the avenue of lime trees and enlivened the scene with a stag. Constable's painting now hangs in the National Gallery. And the lime trees "Planted by Beaumont's and by Wordsworth's hands" flourish to this day, providing a shaded avenue and circle before the "hallowed urn." In these inscriptions Wordsworth evokes the spirit of each honored spot. He calls upon his readers, as in the lines honoring Sir Francis Beaumont, to revive the inspired art of the heroic past:

> Here may some Painter sit in future days,
> Some future Poet meditate his lays;
> Not mindless of that distant age renowned
> When Inspiration hovered o'er this ground.
> ["The Embowering Rose," vv. 13–16]

In later years Wordsworth wrote several inscriptions for the grounds at Rydal Mount, which have been engraved on tablet and native stone. But the most impressive inscriptions to behold, as well as the most inspiring, are the ones carved in stone at Coleorton. By means of poetical inscriptions both at his Lake Country homes and at Coleorton, Wordsworth added to his landscape gardening an attractive feature intimately his own.

Rydal Mount

In the spring of 1813, to provide more commodious quarters for his family, Wordsworth moved from the Rectory in Grasmere two miles southeast to Rydal Mount, a residence that was part of the estate of Sir Michael Le Fleming. The house was large and comfortable, beautifully situated on the hillside under Nab Scar. Here the poet lived for the remaining years of his life, and here he indulged his avocation of landscape gardening to the full. Before he was done, he had turned the grounds at Rydal Mount into a garden paradise.

When he first moved into his new home, there was a heavy growth of shrubs and trees on the place, several open spaces of lawn, a few flower beds, and an extensive kitchen garden. But there was nothing very special in the layout, only the gravelled semicircular area in front of the house and stone steps descending to an ancient mound at a distance beyond it. The location commanded fine views, and the grounds offered great possibilities. What Wordsworth did over the years was to capitalize upon these possibilities by creating in the landscape a variety of features each of which had its own distinct appeal but blended harmoniously into its rustic setting. He raised the mound, giving it two ascents; he reduced the kitchen garden, transforming part of it to lawn; he constructed three terraces, each having its special use and attractiveness; he built a summer house, strategically located; he cleared and walled a well, and built a pool for goldfish and silverfish; he laid out pathways and stone steps; he planned gates and gravelled walks; he wrote inscriptions which were engraved in the rocks; and he set out innumerable native shrubs, trees, and flowers on the slopes.

Rydal Mount is today not much changed from what it was at the time of Wordsworth's death as Christopher Wordsworth describes the estate in his *Memoirs*. So we can see exactly what Wordsworth created and how the separate parts fit together to make a unified whole. In front of the house is the semicircular area of grey gravel, bordered with flower beds and shrubs. From this area there is a descent by a flight of stone steps to an open piece of lawn and then an ascent to a grassy mound. Some sort of a mound was built here centuries ago by Norsemen to serve as a lookout post commanding the valleys. Wordsworth liked the spot and raised the height of the mound by a second ascent so as to improve the views of Wansfell, Windermere, and the fells of Loughrigg. The kitchen garden originally occupied a large glade overhung with rhododendrons sloping gently to the west. Wordsworth made a lawn out of the section towards the house, laid out parterres within it, and planted flowering shrubs along its borders. He was much pleased with the new-made lawn. "Hundreds of times," he said, "have I watched the dancing of shadows amid a press of sunshine, and other beautiful appearances of light and shade, flowers and shrubs. What a contrast between this and Cabbages and Onions and Carrots that used to grow there on a piece of ugly-shaped unsightly ground!"[40] He recorded his meditations on this new garden feature in the poem "This Lawn, A Carpet All Alive."

Among Wordsworth's most distinguishing constructions at Rydal Mount are the three terrace walks to the west of the house. The first of these is the *sloping terrace,* as it was called, a straight walk of about 250 feet running along the stone wall at the north boundary. It is reached by fourteen steps of stones about nine feet long in the interstices of which in Wordsworth's day grew yellow flowering poppy and wild geraniums. In its entire length it is shaded by laburnums, laurels, mountain ash, and fine walnuts and cherries. This terrace walk was close to Wordsworth's heart, and once in 1826, when he thought he was going to have to leave Rydal Mount, he tendered the terrace walk a fond farewell in verse:

> Yet on the mountain's side
> A Poet's hand first shaped it; and the steps
> Of that same Bard—repeated to and fro
> At morn, at noon, and under moonlight skies
> Through the vicissitudes of many a year—
> Forbade the weeds to creep o'er its grey line.
> No longer, scattering to the heedless winds
> The vocal raptures of fresh poesy,
> Shall he frequent these precincts; locked no more
> In earnest converse with beloved Friends,
> Here will he gather stores of ready bliss,

THE SLOPING TERRACE at Rydal Mount

Photograph by the author

As from the beds and borders of a garden
Choice flowers are gathered!

      ["The Massy Ways Carried across
         These Heights," vv. 5–17]

The *sloping terrace* is flanked on the south by a stone wall, coped with rude slates and covered with lichens, mosses, and wildflowers. The fern still waves on the wall, as Christopher Wordsworth said it did in the poet's time, and at its base grow the wild strawberry and foxglove. Beneath the wall is the *level terrace* constructed by Wordsworth for Isabella Fenwick and used by the poet in old age. Both terraces command fine views of winding Rothay River and of Lake Windermere. The *ascending terrace* leads to a small summerhouse from which, passing onwards and after opening a latched door, one sees a breath-taking view of Rydal Lake, of the long wooded hill of Loughrigg above and beyond it, and of Langdale Pikes in the far distance. To the west of the summerhouse is a spacious field sloping down to the road by the lakeside and filled with beautiful trees. In this field, which the poet bought for Dora, there is a terrace path following a serpentine line along the hillside for about 150 feet, where the path ends at a little gate. Beyond the gate is a beautiful well of clean water—"The Nab Well." (See Wordsworth's descriptive lines in "To the Nab Well.") He entered into the construction of what came to be called the *far terrace* with great enthusiasm and busied himself in the spring of 1830 day after day out-of-doors among the workmen. "Today we have Hayes digging among the gooseberries," he wrote to Dora, "and Tom Jackson and his boy preparing the Gate of Entrance to the new Terrace. This walk charms everyone that has seen it."[41] From the summerhouse a narrow flight of stone steps descends to the kitchen garden, and a path through it southward leads to a gate which opens upon "Dora's Field." To the right of the gate, in Wordsworth's day, was a pollard oak

STEPS TO THE TERRACE at Rydal Mount

Photograph by Ross Lockridge

where a wren built its nest. (See the poem "A Wren's Nest.")
In a hazel nook nearby is a stone upon which are inscribed
these verses written by the poet:

> In these fair Vales, hath many a tree
> At Wordsworth's suit been spared,
> And from the builder's hand this Stone,
> For some rude beauty of its own,
> Was rescued by the Bard;
> Long may it rest in peace! and here
> Perchance the tender-hearted
> Will heave a gentle sigh for him
> As One of the Departed.

On the left of the gate was another oak, and beneath it a pool,
to which goldfish and silverfish, once swimming in a bowl in
the library of the house, were transported for the enjoyment of
greater liberty. (See "Gold and Silver Fishes in a Vase" and
"Liberty.") Beyond the pool, stone steps lead down the slope
past a large rock upon which is engraven an inscription allu-
sive to the steepness of the descent. This rock marks the far
boundary of the garden.

Wordsworth loved this garden home on the mountain side
that he had created with Nature as his guide and help. He
loved its terraces and summerhouse, its garden and lawn, and
its thriving trees and shrubs. He took particular delight in the
abundant growth of native laurel:

> Rydalian Laurels! that have grown
> And spread as if ye knew that days might come
> When ye would shelter in a happy home
> On this fair Mount, a Poet of your own,
> One who ne'er ventured for a Delphic crown
> To sue the God; but, haunting your green shade
> All seasons through, is humbly pleased to braid
> Ground-flowers, beneath your guardianship, self-sown.
>
> ["Adieu, Rydalian Laurels," vv. 1–8]

He spent many hours with his gardener, James Dixon, consulting about the maintenance of the grounds and the superintending of its culture. Ellis Yarnall on a visit in August, 1849, reported, "It was evident that the greatest attention had been paid to the grounds, for the flower-beds were tastefully arranged, and the gravel walks were in complete order."[42] In the earlier years of his residence at Rydal Mount the poet strode the *sloping terrace* and composed reams of verses along its path. After the *far terrace* was built, he spent no small part of the long bright summer days under the shade of the oaks there. When friends came to visit, and even friendly strangers, he took them about and showed his favorite views, and with special delight the dramatic view of Rydall Water from the summerhouse. Ellis Yarnall reports a typical reaction to the scene.

[Wordsworth] led the way . . . to a small summer-house. The moment we opened the door, the water-fall was before us; the summer-house being so placed as to occupy the exact spot from which it was to be seen; the rocks and shrubbery around closing it in on every side. The effect was magical. The view from the rustic house, the rocky basin into which the water fell, and the deep shade in which the whole was enveloped, made it a lovely scene.[43]

Many visitors to Rydal Mount have paid affectionate tribute to the enchanting garden created by Wordsworth. Nathaniel Hawthorne, who visited there in 1855, wrote:

Wordsworth's residence . . . so delightfully situated, so secluded, so hedged about with shrubbery and adorned with flowers, so ivy-grown on one side, so beautiful with the personal care of him who lived in it and loved it, that it seemed the very place for a poet's residence; and as if, while he lived so long in it, his poetry had manifested itself in flowers, shrubbery, and ivy.[44]

A German visitor was charmed by the noble groves of Rydal Mount and the luxuriant growth of massive ivy that entirely covered the front of the house, "all alive with bees, like a flow-

SHADOWS ON THE LAWN at Rydal Mount

Photograph by the author

ery hillside." He thought the summerhouse the only building of its kind he had ever seen wholly consistent with the character of its location. The entire place in shadow and sunshine, breeze and calm, seemed a "quiet garden of Eden."[45] The Rev. R. P. Graves believed that Wordsworth had proved his qualifications as landscape gardener "by the surprising variety of natural beauties he managed to display to their best advantage, from the very circumscribed limit of the garden at Rydal Mount, 'an invisible hand of art everywhere working' (to use his own exquisite expression) 'in the very spirit of Nature.' "[46].

Wordsworth often wondered what would become of Rydal Mount after his day. "Will the old walls and steps remain in front of the house and about the grounds," he asked, "or will they be swept away with all the beautiful mosses and ferns and wild geraniums and other flowers which their rude construction suffered and encouraged to grow among them?"[47] He need not have worried, for residents who have since lived in the poet's old home have been proud to maintain the lovely garden much as he left it. It is now in private hands, but each year, when the rhododendrons are in full bloom the house and garden are opened to the public. The flowers of the modern hybrid plants are more resplendent than those that bloomed for Wordsworth, but the beautiful mosses, lichens, and ferns and other wild growths so dear to his heart are permitted to flourish and help to keep it a place of "Nature's own."

Wordsworth as Garden Consultant and Public Benefactor

Wordsworth's activity in landscape gardening at Rydal Mount was not limited to his own grounds but reached out into the neighboring slopes and to the homes and gardens of his neighbors. When Dr. Thomas Arnold decided in 1833 to make his summer home in the Lake District, Wordsworth found for

him the small property of Fox How. It is beautifully situated
on the winding Rothay River with an expansive view of "noble"
Fairfield Mountain all before and the fields in back rising to
the top of Loughrigg. The poet helped to fix the spot for the
house and while it was being built, in the absence of Dr. Arnold, was frequently on the place watching the proceedings of
the contractors. Wordsworth was zealously attentive to the design and construction of the chimneys. In the words of one of
the local masons:

Wudsworth was a girt un for chimleys, had summut to saay in the
makkin' of a deal of 'em hereaboot. There was 'maist all the chimleys Rydal was built efter his mind. I can mind he and the Doctor
[Arnold] had girt argiments aboot the chimleys time he was building Foxhow, and Wudsworth sed he liked a bit o'colour in 'em. And
that the chimley coigns be natural headed and natural bedded, a
lile bit red and a lile bit yallar. For there is a bit of colour i' t'
quarry stean up Easedale way. And heid a girt fancy an' aw for
chimleys square up hauf way, and round t'other. And so we built
'em that road."[48]

The chimney stacks at Fox How and throughout the valley are
so many monuments to Wordsworth. Wherever he went, he
noted with an eye of love

> The smoke forth issuing whence and how it may,
> Like wreaths of vapour without stain or blot.

After the house was completed, Wordsworth and Dr. Arnold
spent hour after hour arranging the planting. The location of
each tree and shrub was studiously chosen. Not only were the
plants viewed individually and in combination with one another, but their relation with the surrounding landscape was
considered. One greatly amused rustic eye-witness recalled the
bobbing up of a head behind one bush and then another as
Wordsworth glided from spot to spot noting appearances and
visualizing mature growth.[49] One of the birches that Words-

worth planted at Fox How became a great and admired tree. This was destroyed by a gale of cyclonic force in 1893, when nearly a hundred trees around the house went down; but a magnificent Canadian beech that was planted by the poet and Dr. Arnold on the south edge of the lawn is still standing. Much of the sylvan beauty of Fox How and of the adjacent valley along the Rothay was shaped by Wordsworth's hand.[50]

Another neighbor who was greatly helped by Wordsworth in setting up her home and in landscaping it was Mrs. Eliza Fletcher, widow of an Edinburgh lawyer. When in 1839 Mrs. Fletcher consulted Wordsworth about the small farm of Lancrigg under Helm Craig that was then for sale, he waxed enthusiastic over its tangled copse and natural terrace, which had for many years been a favorite summer haunt of the poet and his sister when they lived at Dove Cottage. He said of the little "Rocky Well" by the terrace walk, "I know it by heart."[51] He was a great admirer of the view from a great rock by the back boundary wall, which commands the wild mountain view into Far Easedale on one side, and the more cultivated glimpse into the Vale of Grasmere on the other. In Lancrigg wood the poet largely composed *The Prelude* as he paced the green terrace walk. When Mrs. Fletcher decided to purchase Lancrigg, Wordsworth acted as her agent; and he assisted her in every detail of the remodeling of the house and the beautifying of the grounds. Lady Richardson, daughter of Mrs. Fletcher, reports how Wordsworth in his seventy-third year planted holly berries on her place "for posterity":

Wordsworth was in a very happy, kindly mood. We took a walk on the terrace, and he went as usual to his favourite points. On our return he was struck by the berries on the holly tree, and said, "Why should not you and I go and pull some berries . . . and then we can go and plant them in the rocky ground behind the house." We pulled the berries, and set forth with our tool. I made the holes, and the poet put in the berries. He was as earnest and eager

about it as if it had been a matter of importance; and as he put
the seeds in, he every now and then muttered, in his low solemn
tone, that beautiful verse from Burns's *Vision*—

> And wear thou this, she solemn said,
> And bound the holly round my head.
> The polished leaves and berries red
>   Did rustling play;
> And like a passing thought she fled
>   In light away.

He clambered to the highest rocks . . . and put in the berries in
such situations as Nature sometimes does with such true and beautiful effect. He said "I like to do this for posterity."[52]

On my visit to Lancrigg in the spring of 1963 the hillside in
back of the house was dotted with magnificent specimens of
holly, which I have no doubt were started from the berries
Wordsworth planted.

As we should expect, Wordsworth was an expert on trees,
and his advice about them was often sought. When his family
moved to Allan Bank, their landlord, Mr. Crump, asked
Wordsworth's opinion about the laying out of the grounds.
The great trees in the park-land below Allan Bank still survive
as witness to his taste. Dorothy considered the appointment of
her brother as planter of the trees as quite a public benefit.[53]
One of the natives had this to say:

> Wordsworth was distant, ye man saäy, verra distant . . . . but
> efter a time fwoaks began to tak his advice, ye kna aboot trees,
> and plantin, and cuttin' and buildin' chimleys, and that mak o'
> things. . . .
> He was yan as keppit his heäd doon and eyes upo' t'ground, and
> mumbling to hissel; but why, why, he 'ud never pass folk draining,
> or ditching, or walling a cottage, but what he stop and say, "Eh
> dear, but it's a pity to move that stean, and doant ya think ya might
> leave that tree."[54]

Another dalesman tells how the natives sought Wordsworth's opinion on tree trimming:

> I've seen him many a time lig o' his back for long eneuf to see whedder a branch or a tree sud gang or not. I mind weel I was building Kelberrer for Miss S—, and she telt me I mud get to kna Wudworth's 'pinion.[55]

An old retainer at Rydal Mount praised his knowledge and respect for trees:

> He was a man as noticed a deal o' steans and trees, verra particular aboot t' trees, or a rock wi' ony character to it. When they cut down coppy woods in these parts they maistly left a bit of t'coppy just behint wall to hide it for him, he was a girt judge in sic things, and noticed a deal.[56]

Besides the trees and shrubs that he planted on his own grounds and those of his neighbors must be mentioned the stately yews he set out in Grasmere Churchyard. The money for purchasing them was provided by Sir George Beaumont, and the trees—eight of them—were transplanted from Loughrigg in 1819. Wordsworth watched over them with devoted care, watering them and providing enclosures for them at his own expense. Today they are all thriving, one of them only a few paces from the poet's grave. When Harriet Martineau moved to Ambleside, Wordsworth gave her good advice about the landscaping of her grounds and on her invitation planted two stone pines under her terrace wall. The poet took the planting very seriously, performed his task admirably, and when it was done "washed his hands in the watering pot, took my hand in both of his, and wished me many happy years in my new abode."[57]

The preservation, as well as the planting, of native trees was, of course, a matter of great interest and concern to Wordsworth. It pained him to see the lordly trees in his neighbor-

YEW TREE in Grasmere Churchyard

Photograph by Ross Lockridge

hood felled and sold for lumber. One day, as he was crossing Rothay Bridge, he saw to his great sorrow several trees that grew near it by the waterside levelled to the ground. They were a great ornament and a few were still standing. Mr. Cookson, the proprietor, was there and Wordsworth entreated with him earnestly to spare them—but in vain.[58] The poet looked upon the lumbermen of the region as destroyers. The lumberman, he wrote, takes

> One after one, their proudest ornaments.
> Full oft his doings leave me to deplore
> Tall ash-tree, sown by winds, by vapours nursed,
> In the dry crannies of the pendent rocks;
> Light birch, aloft upon the horizon's edge.
> A veil of glory for the ascending moon;
> And oak whose roots by noontide dew were damped,
> And on whose forehead inaccessible
> The raven lodged in safety.

> [*Excursion*, VII, 594–602]

The household fir that fences off the fierce winds, the sycamore that spreads its protecting shade, the "joyful elm" around whose trunk the maidens dance in May, and the "lord's oak"— "would plead their several rights/In vain, if [the lumberman] were master of their fate." When the Kendal and Windermere Railway was projected, one of Wordsworth's chief objections to it was that its construction would call for the levelling of a multitude of magnificent trees; indeed, many of their yeomen owners would rather have fallen on their knees in worship of the trees than sell them for profit. When Wordsworth was touring Scotland in 1803, he was so moved by the report of the despite of Lord Douglas in ordering a great forest to be cut down that he wrote a sonnet condemning his action:

> Degenerate Douglas! oh, the unworthy Lord!
> Whom mere despite of heart could so far please,

And love of havoc, (for with such disease
Fame taxes him,) that he could send forth word
To level with the dust a noble horde,
A brotherhood of venerable Trees,
Leaving an ancient dome, and towers like these,
Beggared and outraged!—Many hearts deplored
The fate of those old Trees; and oft with pain
The traveller, at this day, will stop and gaze
On wrongs, which Nature scarcely seems to heed:
For sheltered places, bosoms, nooks, and bays,
And the pure mountains, and the gentle Tweed,
And the green silent pastures, yet remain.

Wordsworth sent the poem to Scott, who often quoted it to support his plea for keeping the old estates undespoiled. In his own Lakeland, Wordsworth saved many a tree from the axe. As one dalesman put it: "He couldn't bide to see t' faäce o' things altered, ya kna. It was all along of him that Grasmere folks have their Common open."[59] And Moss Common today still stands a beautiful, unspoiled woodland because of Wordsworth's love and protection of it.

FOUR

Wordsworth and the Art
of Scenic Travel

Wordsworth's Response to the
Beauty of the Landscape

The enjoyment of natural beauty was with Wordsworth an absorbing passion and roaming the world in search of it a lifelong habit. He began as a child to drink in the spectacle of beauty surrounding him. From the terrace of his father's house at Cockermouth he could see great Skiddaw a few miles off rising to a lofty height and over the lower hills a road stretching towards the mountain. This road became for him a symbol of the unexplored world, a cherished "invitation into space." In his childhood when passing along the shore of Bassenthwaite on the way to Penrith he came to know the bronzed flanks of Skiddaw. From Penrith he perhaps ranged as far as Ullswater and from Cockermouth as far as Crummock Water. But when as a nine-year-old boy he went to Hawkshead, swiftly the whole Lake District became his inheritance. Joyously he wandered through the hollows and over the cliffs, embarked by boat upon the surface of the lakes, and followed the rivers to their sources on the lonesome mountain peaks. He reached the far limits of the district when he and his companions on hired ponies rode as far afield as Furness Abbey and at Cartmel raced their mounts "in wantonness of heart" on the level sea sands. All scenes, "beauteous and majestic," habitually became

> . . . dear, and all
> Their hues and forms were by invisible links
> Allied to the affections.

As a college youth, during his second summer holiday (1789),
he went scene-hunting in the Peak country ("making a quest
for works of art,/Or scenes renowned for beauty," *Prelude*, VI,
190) and with his sister explored "hidden tracts" of his own
native region in the neighborhood of Penrith. He tells in *The
Prelude* of a memorable moment when he and Dorothy viewed
the wide landscape from the ruins of Brougham Castle:

> . . . when, having clomb
> The darksome windings of a broken stair,
> And crept along a ridge of fractured wall,
> Not without trembling, we in safety looked
> Forth, through some Gothic window's open space,
> And gathered with one mind a rich reward
> From the far-stretching landscape, by the light
> Of morning beautified, or purple eve.
>
> [VI, 212–19]

During his third summer holiday (1790), he deliberately
slighted his college studies in order to make a tour of the Alps
with his fellow student, Robert Jones. He was at the time, as
he wrote to Dorothy, "a perfect enthusiast in his admiration of
Nature in all her forms" and would not be satisfied until he had
experienced first hand the beauty and sublimity of the famed
Swiss and Italian Alps. This adventure he records twice in
poetry: in *Descriptive Sketches* and in *The Prelude*, Book VI.
In the summer of 1791 he accompanied Jones on a three weeks'
tour of the Welsh mountains. He seems not to have been as
impressed with their beauties as he was by the Alps and his
own Lake District. Yet there is one magnificent memorial of
that tour, in the description of the midnight ascent up Mt.
Snowdon to see the sunrise (*The Prelude*, Book XIV). In later

years Wordsworth took many tours, including some memorable ones which were productive of worthy poetry, such as his tour of Scotland with Dorothy in 1803. All his life he was a keen student of the literature of travel and touring. He knew intimately the travel books of Gilpin, Gray, Clarke, West, and others.[1] He encouraged his friends in their travel plans and often prepared tour notes for them. He talked of doing an analysis of the region of North Wales around Snowdon, and after his return from a tour in Ireland wanted to do "a judicious topographical work on [the district of Kerry] that would be really useful, both for the lovers of nature and the observers of manners."[2] He wrote his *Guide to the Lakes* to instruct tourists on how to enjoy the landscape of the Lake District and how to find the spots where the best prospects were. Throughout his life Wordsworth counted the pleasures of wayfaring as indispensable to his existence and the rewards they offered to him as a poet as paramount.

Wordsworth tells us that in his childhood it was collaterally through sports and adventures that Nature first peopled his mind "with beauteous forms and grand." When he was aroused with feelings of delight or awe—climbing, trapping, boating, skating—the scenes in which these events took place filled his mind with their own images. The boy blew mimic hootings to the owl, and while he hung in deep silence listening,

> a gentle shock of mild surprise
> Has carried far into his heart the voice
> Of mountain torrents; or the visible scene
> Would enter unawares into his mind,
> With all its solemn imagery, its rocks,
> Its woods, and that uncertain heaven, received
> Into the bosom of the steady lake.
>
> [*The Prelude*, V, 382–88]

There were times, also, when a power worked upon him directly through the "hallowed and pure motions of sense." Images were "drunk in" as a bee sucks honey from a flower.

> I held unconscious intercourse with beauty
> Old as creation, drinking in a pure
> Organic pleasure from the silver wreaths
> Of curling mist, or from the level plain
> Of waters coloured by impending clouds.
>
> [*The Prelude*, I, 562–66]

The boy in *The Excursion* is described (in Wordsworthian terms) as having

> . . . attained
> An active power to fasten images
> Upon his brain, and on their pictured lines
> Intensely brooded, even till they acquired
> The liveliness of dreams. Nor did he fail,
> While yet a child, with a child's eagerness
> Incessantly to turn his ear and eye
> On all things which the moving seasons brought
> To feed such appetite—
>
> [I, 144–52]

Thus in the midst of adventure or quietly through the senses the beauty of the physcial world was absorbed with delight: gradually all he saw was fastened with joy upon his memory. When he beheld the sun rise up and bathe the world in light

> . . . his spirit drank
> The spectacle: sensation, soul, and form,
> All melted into him; they swallowed up
> His animal being; in them did he live,
> And by them did he live; they were his life.
> In such access of mind, in such high hour
> Of visitation from the living God,
> Thought was not; in enjoyment it expired.
>
> [*Excursion* I, 206–13]

Through the years his mind became "peopled" with "pleasant images"; it became "a mansion for all lovely forms," as vivid as the external world itself. Eventually the orginal, vivid physical vision became the foundation of a fuller vision that transcended sense. But for several years during his young manhood the tyranny of the physical eye held him in thraldom. Wordsworth's visual powers were of a very special intensity. "The bodily eye," he says, "in every stage of life is the most despotic of our senses." Apparently this period began as early as his Cambridge days, that is from the age of seventeen,[3] and continued intermittently until after his first tour of the Wye when he was twenty-three. These years also cover the time when he was drawn to the popular loco-descriptive poetry of the eighteenth century and the prose writings of "picturesque" travel.

Wordsworth first consciously saluted the awakening of his creative powers at a moment when the beauty of the landscape was heightened by contrasting light and shadow. It happened during an evening picnic with his companions in the summer of his fourteenth year. He was resting in a boat under a magnificent row of sycamore trees on the western shore of Coniston Lake. From under the wide-spreading branches, which made a heavy shade, he beheld the tops of the hills opposite flushed with sunset light, though the sun was "himself unseen" and the lake and vale were lying in deep shadow. Suddenly Wordsworth spoke:

> And there I said,
> That beauteous sight before me, there I said . . .
> That in whatever region I should close
> My mortal life I would remember you,
> Fair scenes! that dying I would think on you,
> My soul would send a longing look to you:
> Even as that setting sun while all the vale
> Could nowhere catch one faint memorial gleam
> Yet with the last remains of his last light

> Still linger'd and a farewell lustre threw
> On the clear mountain tops where first he rose.[4]

So he wrote of the event fifteen years later in *The Prelude,* but while still a schoolboy he had put his vow into poetic form in "The Vale of Esthwaite," a lengthy topographical poem in octosyllabic couplets concerning his own adventures and the scenery of the region in which he was brought up. "The Vale of Esthwaite" vividly records many directly felt sensual impressions of the landscape. Out of the early morning mists the shepherd's dog emerges and disappears:

> And on yon summit brown and bare,
> That seems an island in the air,
> The shepherd's restless dog I mark,
> Who, bounding round with frequent bark,
> Now leaps around the uncovered plain,
> Now dives into the mist again.
>
> [vv. 13–18]

The ploughboy moves along the lane striking the ash leaves with his whip:

> The ploughbow by his gingling wain
> Whistles along the ringing lane,
> And, as he strikes with sportive lash
> The leaves of thick o'erhanging ash,
> Wavering they fall; while at the sound
> The blinking bats flit round and round.
>
> [vv. 193–98]

The sun drops behind a massive oak tree and sets off its boughs and leaves in stronger lines:

> While in the west the robe of day
> Fades, slowly fades, from gold to gray,
> The oak its boughs and foliage twines
> Mark'd to the view in stronger lines,

Appears with foliage marked to view,
In lines of stronger browner hue,
While, every darkening leaf between,
The sky distinct and clear is seen.

[vv. 95–102]

The pictures of the shepherd's dog and of the oak tree, as well as some others, Wordsworth retained in *An Evening Walk,* his first published poem (1793). *An Evening Walk,* like "The Vale of Esthwaite," was constructed directly upon his visual experiences of the Lake District. Wordsworth in his seventy-third year told Miss Fenwick that he recollected when and where most of them had occurred. He mentioned as an example the instance of the shepherd dog barking and bounding among the rocks to intercept the sheep, of which Wordsworth was an eye-witness for the first time while crossing the Pass of Dunmail Raise. He also said that he recalled distinctly the very spot where he first noticed the darkening boughs and leaves of the oak tree "fronting the bright west": "It was in the way between Hawkshead and Ambleside and gave me extreme pleasure." He said further:

The moment was important in my poetical history; for I date from it my consciousness of the infinite variety of natural appearances which had been unnoticed by the poets of any age or country, so far as I was acquainted with them; and I made a resolution to supply, in some degree, the deficiency. I could not have been at that time above 14 years of age. . . .[5]

Two Early Travel Poems: An Evening Walk *and* Descriptive Sketches

An Evening Walk is a topographical poem offered to the reading public as an album of beautiful landscape scenes of the Lake District. It is a poem that fulfilled Wordsworth's resolution to supply in poetical form an abundant variety of directly observed natural appearances. But the poet was hindered in his attempt at originality because he had not yet found his own medium of expression. In this early work he often used the language of "poetic diction" and personification and described scenery in accordance with the principles of the "picturesque" school of topographical poets like Darwin and Rogers, and the famous delineator of "picturesque" scenes, William Gilpin. He also followed certain conventionalities of the then popular region-poems. As in these poems, the young poet pictures himself as far from his friend, makes use of early memories, is sadly pensive, and indulges in moralizing on the vanity of human life. He presents scenes, views, and prospects after the best manner of the English landscape school. *An Evening Walk* is, then, a conventional region-poem describing the country of several Wordsworthian rambles chiefly around Lake Windermere, but Wordsworth reminds his readers that "the plan of it has not been confined to a particular walk or place," for he was "unwilling to submit the poetic spirit to the chains of fact and real circumstances." What Wordsworth was attempting was what Reynolds saw Claude doing in his landscapes—masterfully combining separate scenes of Nature into one idealized whole. Also like Claude, Wordsworth was concerned with the way light can reveal the qualities of objects and give meaning to scenes. The poem is largely structured on the picturesque variations of landscape as revealed in the gradations of evening light: sunset, twilight, and moonlight.

As the sun declines, the "bright obscurity" produced by the dazzling sunset melts the landscape into an harmonious whole, while the rich, golden light picks up some features and sets them in heightened relief: the silvered kite wheels in the slanting sunlight; "the lonely mountain horse" brightly beams as he feeds amid the purple heath; the quarry's moving trains are dwarfed by the distance and dimmed by the shadows between the cliffs; a long blue bar of cloud, dividing the setting sun, flings its purple shadow on the cliffs; the cliffs "with tow'rs and woods" become a " 'prospect all on fire' "; the slips of lawn between the broken rocks shine in light "with more than earthly green"; and the babbling brooks high upon the mountains by the sun's light are turned to "liquid gold." With the coming of twilight the sunset is tempered by "the solemn colouring of night." In the growing darkness the foreground scene appears as a "mass of shade"; the "thickened darkness" makes the mountains seem like "a black wall"; and the eastern hills and valleys are clothed in shadow. At the same time, the dark foreground contrasts with the radiant background, where the western hills are brightened by the setting sun, and the poet is enabled to depict both the mass of shadowy objects and the detail of illuminated ones. (This was a convention often employed by English picturesque artists, such as Gilpin.) Moonlight then shines upon the same scene with a clear, silver light which emphasizes the peace and harmony of the region. The wreaths of charcoal smoke from the cottager's chimney enliven but do not disturb the universal serenity of the valley.

A picturesque feature commonly found in paintings and used by Wordsworth was the addition of figures which harmonized with the general character of the landscape. In *An Evening Walk* the human and animal inhabitants, the shepherds and dogs, the muleteers and their trains, the peasant and his horse, all enhance the pastoral calm. The swans, in particular, reflect the idyllic character of their natural surroundings. Their curving, twisting motions resolve into a feeling of harmony, which corresponds to the movement of the "evening shadows" as they "sail on slowly-waving pinions, down the vale." The swan's bower, moreover, "Where leafy shades fence off the blustering gale," is described in terms paralleling an idyllic shepherd's cottage. Contrasted to the idyllic life of the swan and her brood is the beggar woman and her starving children at the mercy of cruel storms and freezing weather. (She serves as a humanitarian figure with romantic appeal as well as a contrasting pictorial figure in the foreground.) Another literary feature (in imitation of the inclusion in travel books of regional ghost stories) is the description of local "apparitions" of the Lake Country. In a note to the poem Wordsworth refers to Clarke's *Survey of the Lakes* as an example of picturesque writing that includes an apparition in the landscape.

These scenes and others like them are rendered through visual images and their composition is pictorial. As the shadows deepen and the stars come out, the poet offers images full of aural observations:

> Sweet are the sounds that mingle from afar,
> Heard by calm lakes, as peeps the folding star.

Included among these sweet evening sounds are: the dabbling duck amid the rustling sedge; the feeding pike; the swan stirring the reeds; the heron shooting upward, "darting his long neck before"; the char fish leaping for the may fly; the droning insect that strikes the wanderer and drops to his feet; the whistling farmboy that "plods his ringing way" by the slow wagon; the "sugh" of swallows moving through the air; the solemn curfew; the "talking boat" (a very Wordsworthian touch); the boys bathing afar off; the restless sandpiper on the lakeshore; and the remote bleating of the sheep as they are folded. To conclude his poem, with what is its finest passage, Wordsworth draws predominantly upon auditory images:

> The song of mountain-streams, unheard by day,
> Now hardly heard, beguiles my homeward way.
> Air listens, like the sleeping water, still,
> To catch the spiritual music of the hill,
> Broke only by the slow clock tolling deep,
> Or shout that wakes the ferry-man from sleep,
> The echoed hoof nearing the distant shore,

The boat's first motion—made with dashing oar;
Sound of closed gate, across the water borne,
Hurrying the timid hare through rustling corn;
The sportive outcry of the mocking owl;
And at long intervals the mill-dog's howl;
The distant forge's swinging thump profound;
Or yell, in the deep woods, of lonely hound.

[vv. 365–78]

An Evening Walk is the work of a young poet and has its faults: the imagery is overloaded and is often obscured by the language of convention. But the poem makes its impact; it is intense and for all its allegiance to tradition it is daringly new. It is a well-composed piece of landscape painting filled with a wonderful collection of precise and delicately perceived eye-observations and ear-observations that catalog Nature's charms. The poet can make us feel the nocturnal mountain calm, its "cold blue nights," and the "song of mountain streams unheard by day." At times his landscape-artist's eye achieves a visual effect beyond painting. Just after the description of Rydale Falls he tells of a naked waste of scattered stone, where "the thistle can scarce grow its beard or the foxglove peep." The use of sound images in this poem goes beyond anything Wordsworth ever did again except in that deliberate bravura "The Power of Sound." In time he learned to curb his use of sound images (there are but three of them in "Tintern Abbey"), and eventually he learned to free his visual images from the constrictions of poetic diction. But before Wordsworth was ready to create landscape poetry of the highest order he would have to break from the bondage of the outward-seeking physical eye.

The walking tour of the Alps with Robert Jones in 1790 brought Wordsworth into direct contact with mountain sublimity so stupendous that the attempt to render it in poetic form confronted him with problems he was unable to solve until years afterwards. The drama of that crucial time can be recovered from *Descriptive Sketches*, written in 1791–92, and published jointly with *An Evening Walk* in 1793. Wordsworth's chief reason for going on this tour was to feed his mind with the "mighty forms" of Nature (*Prelude*, VI). A long letter written to Dorothy near the end of his tour recorded the rapturous delight which the scenic wonders of the Alps had upon him.[6] Then on the point of quitting the most sublime and beautiful parts, he wrote, he was "filled with melancholy regret at the idea." He was "a perfect enthusiast" in his admiration of Nature in all her various forms. He had so long looked upon, conversed with, and enjoyed the objects which that country presented to his view that the idea of parting from them oppressed him with a sadness similar to what he had always felt in quitting a beloved friend. He regretted most of all the inability of his memory to retain "a more strong impression of the beautiful forms" before him and again and again returned to a fortunate station "with the most eager avidity" in the hope of bearing away a more lively picture. He was cheered by the reflection that his future days would derive some happiness from the landscape images then floating before his mind. This last was no idle thought, for the Alpine tour provided a great store of images that he drew upon for the rest of his life. The impressions of a three hours' walk down Simplon Pass he correctly prophesied would never be effaced.

The journey was carried forward with military speed: "Earth did change her images and forms/Before us, fast as clouds are changed in Heaven" (*Prelude*, VI, 492). Wordsworth's spirits were in a perpetual hurry of delight, and his eye was busy seeking out forms and colors that would satisfy his thirst for the "picturesque." He says in *The Prelude* that when he traveled through the Alps, he was not addicted to scene-hunting and that his attitude towards Nature was the same as it was before he left his native hills to go to Cambridge:

I felt, observed, and pondered; did not judge,
Yea, never thought of judging; with the gift
Of all this glory filled and satisfied.

[XII, 188–90]

But the record of his travels as given in his letter to Dorothy
and in *Descriptive Sketches* does not altogether support his
testimony in *The Prelude*, especially those sections that describe the scenery of the Italian lakes. In his letter to Dorothy,
Wordsworth described with pertinent detail the "succession of
scenes" that opened to his sight at every turn of the charming
path along the shore of Lake Como. He noted that the surface
was not less interesting than its shores, "part of it glowing
with the richest green and gold, . . . and part with a soft blue
tint." Finally, he added the detail that would bring a climax
of delight to any scene-hunter, that of the sails moving slowly
on the water: "The picture was still further diversified by the
number of sails which stole lazily by us as we paused in the
woods above them." In *Descriptive Sketches* he exults in the
blessed eye that greets the open beauties or the lone retreats
of Lake Como and its shores. As the sun sets he is intrigued by
the "picturesque" contrasts of light and shade:

Here half a village shines, in gold array'd,
Bright as the moon, half hides itself in shade.
From the dark sylvan roofs the restless spire,
Inconstant glancing, mounts like springing fire,
There, all unshaded, blazing forests throw
Rich golden verdure on the waves below.
Slow glides the sail along th'illumined shore,
And steals into the shade the lazy oar.

[vv. 106–13]

In the scenes describing the lake there is a well-conducted,
harmonious time sequence in the passage from sunset to twilight to starlight and the next morning in the progress of the

rising sun. The management of light and the spirit of repose in these "lovely scenes" (Wordsworth's own words) remind one of the landscape paintings of Claude Lorrain. By way of contrast, to heighten the romantic effect of "savage" scenes in the mountains, he seems to evoke the spirit of Salvator Rosa by placing human types as foreground figures in the landscape. Upon the dull-red steeps "in solemn gloom" he has the gypsy pitch her tent:

> The Grison gypsey here her tent has plac'd,
> Sole human tenant of the piny waste;
> Her tawny skin, dark eyes, and glossy locks,
> Bend o'er the smoke that curls beneath the rocks.
> [vv. 188–91]

And to heighten the terror of a mountain storm he embellishes the scene with Gothic trappings worthy of Salvator's paintings, even to the banditti:

> —Bursts from the troubl'd Larch's giant boughs
> The pie, and chattering breaks the night's repose.
> Low barks the fox: by Havoc rouz'd the bear,
> Quits, growling, the white bones that strew his lair;
> The dry leaves stir as with the serpent's walk,
> And, far beneath, Banditti voices talk.
> [vv. 229–34]

Wordsworth disclaims the "picturesque" formula as applying to his sketches of the mountains. In his footnote to the stormy sunset passage he writes:

I had once given to these sketches the title of Picturesque; but the Alps are insulted in applying to them that term. Whoever, in attempting to describe their sublime features, should confine himself to the cold rules of painting would give his reader but a very imperfect idea of those emotions which they have the irresistible power of communicating to the most impassive imaginations. The fact is, that controuling influence, which distinguishes the Alps from all other scenery, is derived from images which disdain the pencil.

It should be noted, however, that there are two types of land-scape featured in *Descriptive Sketches*: one a mild beauty represented by the "delicious scenes" of the Italian lakes and the other the more fearful beauty of the Alps. The former, though heightened in form and color above anything Wordsworth had seen before, fulfilled his expectations of the pictorial components and reposeful sensations of Arcadian landscapes. "At the lake of Como," he wrote to Dorothy, "my mind ran through a thousand dreams of happiness, which might be enjoyed on its banks, if heightened by conversation and the exercise of the social affections." When confronted with the more awesome beauty of the higher Alps, however, he had no man-made guides to accompany him: "Among the more awful scenes of the Alps, I had not a thought of man, or a single created being; my whole soul was turned to him who produced the terrible majesty before me."

In the high Alps Wordsworth saw Nature on a scale mightier and more awe-inspiring than hitherto he had ever dreamed of and evocative of sensations that approximated sublimity. Many scenes vexed his sight and many overwhelmed him. There were swift variations of dark and light, vacillations of mighty opposites. Often his eye was led by bewildering contrasts from scene to scene without finding a surface where its power might rest. His imagination sought helplessly for an inner vision to rest upon. When in 1791–92 Wordsworth recorded his experiences in *Descriptive Sketches,* he was still seeking for an Idea of Nature adequate to express the essential truth of Nature in the lofty Alps. *Descriptive Sketches* is for the most part the record of his failure in that quest.[7]

As Beatty has pointed out, when Wordsworth first wrote out

his impressions of the Alps he leaned heavily upon the writings of two earlier travelers to Switzerland, William Coxe and Ramond de Carbonnières. Ramond especially is a colorful writer who describes mountains from the point of view of their effect upon him while at the same time he keeps "his eye on the object." Wordsworth uses Ramond for scenic details and for vocabulary, but overall the Frenchman was not much more than a crutch for him to lean on. The impression of the Alps upon Wordsworth was so awe-inspiring and so dazzling that in the recording of it in *Descriptive Sketches* he widened the contrasts and multiplied the locus of life. Through personification and animism he made a separate (visual) entity of nearly everything his glance encountered.[8] In *Descriptive Sketches* few single "prospects" satisfied him; he spread the swift interchanges of seasons, times, and landscapes over Nature as a whole. It was not until ten years later in *The Prelude* that moments of "grateful vicissitude" were brought by the poet's imagination into a magnificent instance of *visionary* contrasts. A harmonizing vision expressed at last the idea of Nature that was haunting his mind—of a form-bound but not time-bound image of the Absolute Mind:

> The immeasurable height
> Of woods decaying, never to be decayed,
> The stationary blasts of waterfalls,
> And in the narrow rent at every turn
> Winds thwarting winds, bewildered and forlorn,
> The torrents shooting from the clear blue sky,
> The rocks that muttered close upon our ears,
> Black drizzling crags that spake by the way-side
> As if a voice were in them, the sick sight
> And giddy prospect of the raving stream,
> The unfettered clouds and region of the Heavens,
> Tumult and peace, the darkness and the light—
> Were all like workings of one mind, the features

Of the same face, blossoms upon one tree;
Characters of the great Apocalypse,
The types and symbols of Eternity,
Of first, and last, and midst, and without end.

[VI, 624–40]

As Hartman observes, the distance between *The Prelude,* written in Wordsworth's maturity, and *Descriptive Sketches* is enormous. *Descriptive Sketches* shows him still blind to his own power by an inner blindness of too much sight. The eyes defeat themselves by looking everywhere, "Still craving combinations of new forms,/New pleasure, wider empire for the sight."[9] Furthermore, the heroic couplet, which was the traditional form for loco-descriptive poems, and the one which Wordsworth chose for *Descriptive Sketches,* inclined him to divide, particularize, and balance his landscape rather than to develop a blended or transcendent meaning of it. As Aubin points out, Wordsworth tends in *Descriptive Sketches* to jump nimbly from one spot to another indulging his bent for *picturesque genre scenes.*[10] In his period of maturity he is constantly concerned with the thought that the physical eye's activity should be reduced until it becomes "an eye made quiet by the power/Of harmony, and the deep power of joy." Then it will perceive the blended vision of the landscape as in "Tintern Abbey," where the visual and the ideal are joined.

In the sunset storm passage of *Descriptive Sketches,* however, there is a striking instance wherein Wordsworth breaks from the hold of the "outer eye" and reaches inner vision; not through a blending of images of sight but through a supercharged excess of them.[11] After the storm in the mountains, the sun breaks through the clouds, flashes light upon the eagle, makes glitter the "wood-crown'd cliffs," turns the Alpine streams to flaming pillars, and sets the mountains aglow like coals of fire. At the moment of climax, the light of sense is ex-

tinguished and "Characters of the great Apocalypse" blaze in
the mind:

> 'Tis storm; and hid in mist from hour to hour
> All day the floods a deeper murmur pour,
> And mournful sounds, as of a Spirit lost,
> Pipe wild along the hollow-blustering coast,
> 'Till the Sun walking on his western field
> Shakes from behind the clouds his flashing shield.
> Triumphant on the bosom of the storm,
> Glances the fire-clad eagle's wheeling form;
> Eastward, in long perspective glittering, shine
> The wood-crown'd cliffs that o'er the lake recline;
> Wide o'er the Alps a hundred streams unfold,
> At once to pillars turn'd that flame with gold;
> Behind his sail the peasant strives to shun
> The west that burns like one dilated sun,
> Where in a mighty crucible expire
> The mountains, glowing hot, like coals of fire.
>
> [vv. 332–47]

The thrust of imaginative power in the sunset storm passage
is an almost isolated example in *Descriptive Sketches* of what
in Wordsworth's period of maturity was to become an often
repeated response to the landscape. The poem remains, then,
in a crowded sequence of sketches, a record, on the one hand,
of aesthetic pleasures felt and satisfactions derived from viewing the pastoral landscape of the Swiss and Italians and in
meditating upon their customs and history. It is a record, on
the other hand, of a restless, shifting pursuit with his eye,
amidst the massive lights and shadows of the awe-inspiring
cliffs and thunderous gorges of the Alps, of some inner vision
of meaning—a pursuit which, except in one blinding moment
of light, failed.

Wordsworth's Thraldom
to the Picturesque

Wordsworth tells us in *The Prelude* that soon after his return from France (December, 1792) his faculties fell under the dominance of the analytic intellect, abetted by his allegiance to a radical social philosophy,[12] and that they remained so enthralled until his deliverance by his sister Dorothy subsequent to their settling at Racedown in 1795. His response to Nature was contaminated; his mind

> . . . so far
> Perverted, even the visible Universe
> Fell under the dominion of a taste
> Less spiritual.
>
> [*The Prelude*, XII, 88–91]

Though, as he says, he was never one who took much stock in "picturesque" analysis of the landscape—he rather scornfully defines "picturesque" in his *Guide to the Lakes* as "a fad for relishing the select parts of natural scenery"[13]—he fell under its spell at that time. He was then obsessed by the habit of comparing scene with scene and of observing the "meagre novelties of colour and proportion":

> . . . even in pleasure pleased
> Unworthily, disliking here, and there
> Liking; by rules of mimic art transferred
> To things above all art; but more,—for this,
> Although a strong infection of the age,
> Was never much my habit—giving way
> To a comparison of scene with scene,
> Bent overmuch on superficial things,
> Pampering myself with meagre novelties
> Of colour and proportion; to the moods

> Of time and season, to the moral power,
> The affections and the spirit of the place,
> Insensible.
>
> [*The Prelude*, XII, 109–21]

He also says that this period of intellectual thraldom coincided
with the tyranny of the bodily eye which drove him insatiably
to seek "new forms,/New pleasure, wider empire for the
sight":

> Nor only did the love
> Of sitting thus in judgment interrupt
> My deeper feelings, but another cause,
> More subtle and less easily explained,
> That almost seems inherent in the creature,
> A twofold frame of body and of mind.
> I speak in recollection of a time
> When the bodily eye, in every stage of life
> The most despotic of our senses, gained
> Such strength in *me* as often held my mind
> In absolute dominion . . . . My delights
> (Such as they were) were sought insatiably.
> Vivid the transport, vivid though not profound;
> I roamed from hill to hill, from rock to rock,
> Still craving combinations of new forms,
> New pleasure, wider empire for the sight,
> Proud of her own endowments, and rejoiced
> To lay the inner faculties asleep.
> Amid the turns and counterturns, the strife
> And various trials of our complex being,
> As we grow up, such thraldom of that sense
> Seems hard to shun.
>
> [*The Prelude*, XII, 121–31, 140–51]

His attitude towards Nature in these lines is identical to that
which he experienced on his first visit to Tintern Abbey in
1793, when

> Like a roe
> I bounded o'er the mountains, by the sides
> Of the deep rivers, and the lonely streams,
> Wherever nature led: more like a man
> Flying from something that he dreads than one
> Who sought the thing he loved. For nature then
> (The coarser pleasures of my boyish days,
> And their glad animal movements all gone by)
> To me was all in all.—I cannot paint
> What then I was. The sounding cataract
> Haunted me like a passion: the tall rock,
> The mountain, and the deep and gloomy wood,
> Their colours and their forms, were then to me
> An appetite; a feeling and a love,
> That had no need of a remoter charm,
> By thought supplied, nor any interest
> Unborrowed from the eye.
>
> [vv. 67–83]

On his walking tour of the Wye Valley, Wordsworth's passion for the colors and forms of Nature was rapacious, and the hold of physical Nature upon his eye was absolute. But as the foregoing comments have shown, the period of the eye's dominance (and the concomitant appeal of the pictorial and the picturesque in the landscape) was by no means limited to that time. Wordsworth indicates in the above-quoted passage from *The Prelude* that the bodily eye is "in every stage of life/The most despotic of our senses." He calls it almost inherent in the creature, and such depictions as "The Ruined Cottage," vv. 85–108 (*Poems,* V, 381–82), suggest, as Hartman points out, that this dominance is always latently present.[14] It achieved varying degrees of *accidental* dominance throughout the poet's period of apprenticeship. As we grow up, he reminds us, "thraldom of the sense is hard to shun." It even strove for mastery as late as 1799, when he was struggling to get under way with his philosophical poem. His days then were frustrated and his powers locked up by morbid introspection; he falsely trusted "an anxious eye/That with intrusive restlessness beats off/Simplicity and self-presented truth" (*The Prelude*, I, 247f).

It was through Dorothy's ministrations that Wordsworth escaped from the bondage under which he had fallen. She did not seek Nature in terms of the intellectual subtleties of the picturesque.

> Her eye was not mistress of her heart;
> Far less did rules prescribed by passive taste,
> Or barren intermeddling subtleties,
> Perplex her mind.
>
> [*The Prelude*, XII, 153–56]

In the midst of all, by openness of heart and benignity of spirit, Dorothy led her brother back to his true self. He had felt too forcibly in early life the visitations of imaginative power for the imprisonment of his sight to last. In the course of time he was restored to a condition where the eye's eager delight was subdued by a mighty passion and he stood again in Nature's presence "a sensitive, and a creative soul."

Wordsworth's Enthusiasm for the Scenic Shared by Dorothy and Coleridge; the Tour of Scotland, 1803

Wordsworth broke free from the tyranny of the "picturesque" and the hold of the bodily "eye" just at the time when, in the closing years of the century, the fad for the "picturesque" was beginning to wear thin with the general public. Having himself advanced beyond false taste, he was in a position to direct his countrymen to a new awareness of beauty in the landscape. In order to do this, he reduced his own rendering of scenes to their barest essentials unadorned by false associations and shorn of any excess load of sensuous detail. In his

Guide to the Lakes he laid down basic principles to be followed by the seeker after natural beauty. Sometimes he leaned upon the vision and vocabulary of the "picturesque" school. But his passion for Nature was so intense and so exalted that he was able to lift the pursuit of the scenic to a new vitality. Wordsworth's enthusiasm was shared by members of his family and his friends but by none more keenly than his sister Dorothy. She never wearied of watching the myriad goings-on in the natural world and of recording what she saw. Her journals are filled with the records of her responses to Nature and its scenic beauty. And she was as passionately fond of touring the countryside to view the landscape as was her brother. In April, 1794, the two of them made a trip to Windy Brow (near Keswick) from Halifax, the first of innumerable journeyings which they were to make together in the next forty years. They went by coach to Kendal, and then, says Dorothy, "I walked with my brother at my side, from Kendal to Grasmere, 18 miles, and afterwards from Grasmere to Keswick, fifteen miles, through the most delightful country that ever was seen." They were always to remember "that happy ramble, that most happy day and hour." It was a foretaste of many more such days that the two "glad Foot-travellers" were to share in the future. They explored together the countryside about Racedown in Dorsetshire, rambled over the Quantock hills and valleys in Somersetshire, and were together when Wordsworth returned to the Wye valley, a worshipper unwearied in the service of Nature, to scenes both dear to him for themselves and for his sister's sake. They toured Scotland and western Europe together; but no region could ever quite equal the delight they took in the Lake District, the place of their birth and their home throughout most of their lives. In December, 1799, their three days' journeying from Yorkshire to Grasmere to take up their abode together at Dove Cottage was a kind of triumphal march towards the possession of an earthly paradise. They moved forward in exhilaration of spirits, drinking in the scenic beauty of the winter landscape. At Askrigg they turned aside to see the waterfall, and then visited another at Hardraw a few miles farther on. This detained them some time, for it was a scene of true magnificence made more wonderful by the ice and icicles of all shapes that festooned the walls of the hollow limestone behind the falls. They were enchanted by the effect produced by "this Arabian scene of colour." Wordsworth describes in detail in a lengthy letter to Coleridge all the pictorial charms of these natural wonders. But the climax of their journey, long anticipated, came when they entered Grasmere Vale. It was

> A blended holiness of earth and sky,
> Something that makes this individual Spot,
> This small Abiding place of many Men,
> A termination, and a last retreat,
> A Centre, come from wheresoe'er you will,
> A Whole without dependence or defect,
> Made for itself, and happy in itself,
> Perfect Contentment, Unity entire.
>
> [*The Recluse,* I, 142–49]

Within this vale and the regions lying near it the poet and his sister could indulge their love of scenic beauty without going on extended tours to far-off places. The hills and lakes at hand offered an infinite variety of prospects, and the changing seasons multipled them. Dorothy's *Grasmere Journal* is filled with entries of "beautiful prospects" and identifications of stations for viewing them:

Walked to Ambleside in the evening round the Lake, the prospect exceedingly beautiful from Loughrigg Fell. [18 May 1800]

In the morning walked up to the rocks above Jenny Dockeray's, sate a long time upon the grass, the prospect divinely beautiful. [28 May 1800]

A succession of delicious views from Skelleth to Brathay. [16 June 1800]

The view exquisitely beautiful, through a gate, and under a sycamore tree beside the first house going into Loughrigg. [23 June 1800]

After William had composed a little, I persuaded him to go into the orchard. We walked backwards and forwards. The prospect most divinely beautiful from the seat; all colours, all melting into each other. [15 October 1800]

The tops of G[ras]mere mountains cut off. Rydale was very, very beautiful. The surface of the water quite still, like a dim mirror. The colours of the large island exquisitely beautiful, and the trees still fresh and green were magnified by the mists. The prospects on the west side of the Lake were very beautiful. We sate at the "two points" looking up to Park's. [19 October 1800]

. . . [from] the western side of Rydale. The lights were very grand upon the woody Rydale hills. Those behind dark and topp'd with clouds. The two lakes were divinely beautiful. Grasmere excessively solemn and the whole lake was calm and dappled with soft grey ripples. [20 October 1800]

And so the record continues: "glorious, glorious sights" from Helvellyn; "the whole prospect very soft" from Heifer Crags; "a pretty field with 3 pretty prospects" from Parson's field in Easdale; "The view above Ambleside very beautiful"; the prospects of Wensley Dale "most beautiful each way"; Rydale Lake perfectly still with "all the beautiful colours" melted into one another.[15] Dorothy could very well be summing up her impressions of all Lake Country scenery in her letter to Jane Marshall describing the views from Allan Bank. "The views," she writes, "wherever you turn are enchanting."[16]

In her *Grasmere Journal* Dorothy does not ignore, neither does she exploit, "picturesque" features of the landscape. She notes how effectively a tree over a gate frames a picture of the landscape.[17] She sensitively describes the patternings of light and darkness on a moonlit night (but how unlike the uninspired analyses of tour guidebooks!):

As I climbed Moss [White Moss Common], the moon came out from behind a mountain mass of black clouds. O, the unutterable darkness of the sky, and the earth below the moon! and the glorious brightness of the moon itself! There was a vivid sparkling streak of light at this end of Rydale Water, but the rest was very dark, and Loughrigg Fell and Silver How white and bright, as if they were covered with hoar frost. The moon retired again, and appeared and disappeared several times before I reached home. Once there was no moonlight to be seen but upon the island-house and the promontory of the island where it stands. "That needs must be a holy place," etc. etc. I had many very exquisite feelings, and when I saw this lowly Building in the waters, among the dark and lofty hills, with that bright, soft light upon it, it made me more than half a poet.[18]

She has a gift for selecting the features of the landscape which when added together make up an uncontrived yet joyous beauty. She tells of one April day when she and her brother came to the foot of Brothers' Water:

I left William sitting on the bridge, and went along . . . the side of the Lake through the wood. I was delighted with what I saw. The water under the boughs of the bare old trees, the simplicity of the mountains, and the exquisite beauty of the path. There was one grey cottage. I repeated *The Glow-worm* as I walked along. I hung over the gate, and thought I could have stayed forever.[19]

Dorothy's never-failing power in Nature's presence is her happiness of soul, which formed new delight in all she looked upon.

> She welcomed what was given, and craved no more.
> Whate'er the scene presented to her view,
> That was the best.
> [*The Prelude*, XII, 158–60]

In the *Grasmere Journal* Dorothy wrote out in more detail than was her custom her responses to scenic beauty during excursions taken with William up Scawfell and along the banks of Ullswater. In the ascent to the top of Scawfell she describes the majesty of mountain prospects, the stillness "not of this world" felt in the lofty solitude of the Pike, the splendor of gloom and sunshine, and the spectacle "of the grandeur of heaven and earth commingled" during a mountain storm. In their ramble beside Ullswater she notes the effects and appearances produced by the changeableness of the atmosphere, especially the surprise occasioned by the transforming powers of vapors; the exquisite mixture of sober and splendid colors of autumn trees; the *felt* presence of mountains on a moonlit night; the picturesque details in different settings of "two storm-stiffened black yew-trees"; "four or five goats" bounding among the rocks; and a group of three fishermen dragging a net beneath the high crags. In these prose pieces Dorothy shows a high degree of artistic competence in reporting an intimate sharing with her brother the sublimity, the beauty, and the mystery of the landscape. Wordsworth esteemed them sufficiently to rework them and publish them as part of his *Guide to the Lakes.*

Coleridge shared the enthusiasm of Dorothy and her brother for the scenic beauty of the landscape. Even before their days of close comradeship in Somersetshire, he had become interested in scene-hunting and had gone on a "picturesque" tour of Wales in 1794. Coleridge's typical response to viewing a prospect in Wales is recorded in a letter that he wrote to Henry Martin:

Three miles from Denbigh . . . is a fine Bridge with *one Arch*— of great grandeur—stand at a little distance, and *through* it you see the woods waving on the *Hill-bank* of the River in a most lovely point of view. A *beautiful* prospect is always more picturesque, when seen at some little distance thro' an Arch. I have frequently thought of Mich. Taylor's way of viewing a Landscape by putting his head between his thighs.[20]

In October-November, 1799, Coleridge joined Wordsworth in a tour of the Lake Country. He carried with him a small clasp notebook in which he took notes of the scenes before him. He identifies "stations" and describes scenes in the best tour-guide fashion. He becomes increasingly enthusiastic over a succession of prospects as they open to view:

'Tis a sweet country which we see before us. . . . We have curved round the hill, and at my back and before me, O God, what a scene! The foreground a wood sloping down to the river and meadow; the serpent river; beyond the river and wood terminated by Melbreak, . . . and where the wall ends a peep of Crummock Water.[21]

He exclaims over the view that opens from the shore of Ulls-water beyond the first great promontory: "What a scene! Where I stand on the shore is a triangular bay, taking in the whole of the water view." He is intrigued by the "deep wall of mist" and the miraculously shifting lights and shadows that strangely move in the wondrous scene before him:

On the opposite shore is a straight deep wall of mist, and behind it one third of the bare mountain stands out, the top of the wall only in the sun—the rest black. And now it is all one deep wall of white vapour, save that black streaks shaped like strange creatures seem to move in and down it, . . . And over . . . the cliff behind, in shape so like a cloud, the sun sent cutting it his thousand silky hairs of amber and green light. . . . Now as we return the fog begins to clear off from the lake . . . and clings viciously to the hill. All the objects on the opposite coast are hidden, and yet all are reflected in the lake; trees, the Castle, Lyulph's Tower and the high cliff which dwarfs it—divine![22]

In August, 1802, Coleridge made a tour of the mountains of the Lake District by himself. He was thrilled by "heart-raising scenes," "noble views," and "beautiful sea views." He climbed to the very summit of Scawfell, found a nook where he could lie protected from the winds but from whence just under his feet dropped "huge perpendicular precipices" frightening to behold. In his descent he all but fatally trapped himself on a narrow ledge from which he apparently could neither descend nor ascend. From this station of danger he was overawed by the sight of the crags above him on each side, and the impetuous clouds just over them, moving luridly and rapidly northwards. In a letter to Southey he wrote: "Of all earthly things which I have beheld, the view of Scafell and from Scafell (both views from its own summit) is the most heart-exciting."[23]

In pursuit of new vistas of landscape beauty Coleridge set out in August, 1803, with William and Dorothy Wordsworth on a tour of Scotland, but because of ill-health he separated from his companions at Loch Lomond. The Wordsworths continued on by themselves, and their six-weeks' journeying is recorded in Dorothy's *Recollections of a Tour Made in Scotland*, written after their return, from copious notes taken day by day. It covers a wide range of subjects, including gardening, agriculture, architecture, social conditions, customs, dress, peculiarities of speech, and so on, in which she shows a lively and good-natured sympathy. But most of all she was interested, and it is evident that her brother was equally interested, in landscape. They were unashamedly scene-hunting and reacted with great enthusiasm to pictures framed by trees, prospects yielding patterns of sun and shadow, and mountains shaped in picturesque forms. At Loch Lomond: "We had some beautiful distant views, one in particular, down the high road, through a vista of over-arching trees."[24] Along the shoreline of the lake: "A deep shade hung over the road. . . ; and when we came nearer, saw 3 or 4 thatched huts under the trees, and at the same moment felt that it was paradise."[25] Looking towards the foot of Loch Lomond:

We had not climbed far before we were stopped by a sudden burst of prospect, so singular and beautiful that it was like a flash of images from another world. . . . The sun shone, and the distant hills were visible, some through sunny mists, others in gloom with patches of sunshine; the lake was lost under the low and distant hills, and the islands lost in the lake, which was all in motion with travelling fields of light, or dark shadows under rainy clouds . . . so that the land seemed endless as the water.[26]

They took pleasure in the Highland ferryman who chose scenic beauties "with greater skill than our prospect-hunters and 'picturesque travellers.' "[27] Yet sometimes when they looked upon mountains, hills, and valleys they themselves fell back upon the analytical comparisons used by tourists. The top of Ben Lomond, as seen from Glenfalloch "being of a pyramidal form," is "much grander than with the broken outline, and stage above stage, as seen from the neighbourhood of Luss."[28] The lines of the hills of the Tweed valley "are flowing and beautiful, the reaches of the vale long; in some places appear the remains of a forest, in others you will see as lovely a combination of forms as any traveller who goes in search of the picturesque need desire."[29]

Throughout their tour it was most of all an emotional involvement with the landscape that the two travelers sought; yet they never allowed their senses to be sullied by the intrusion of false sentiment. At Loch Katrine they experienced a heightened sense of solitude:

It was an entire solitude; and all that we beheld was the perfection of loveliness and beauty; we had been through many solitary places since we came into Scotland, but this place differed as much from any we had seen before, as if there had been nothing in common between them; no thought of dreariness or desolation found entrance here; yet nothing was to be seen but water, wood, rock, and heather, and bare mountains above.[30]

Near Inverary a single white cottage enclosed by trees became an "image of romance" to be compared to scenes in Spenser:

We came to one spot which I cannot forget, a single green field at the junction of another brook with the Arey, a peninsula surrounded with a close row of trees, which overhung the streams, and under their branches we could just see a neat white house that stood in the middle of the field enclosed by the trees. Before us was nothing but bare hills, and the road through the bare glen. . . . This house . . . even in the fertile parts of Somersetshire it would have been a delicious spot; here, " 'Mid mountain wild set like a little nest", it was a resting-place for the fancy, and to this day I often think of it, the cottage and its green covert, as an image of romance, a place f which I have the same sort of knowledge as of some of the retirements, the little vallies described so livelily by Spenser in his *Fairy Queen*.[31]

A high point of imaginative involvement in the scene before them occurred when they came suddenly at dusk upon a lonely Highland boy:

While we were walking forward, the road leading us over the top of a brow, we stopped suddenly at the sound of a half-articulate Gaelic hooting from the field close to us; it came from a little boy, whom we could see on the hill between us and the lake, wrapped up in a grey plaid; he was probably calling the cattle home for the night. His appearance was in the highest degree moving to the imagination: mists were on the hillsides, darkness shutting in upon the huge avenue of mountains, torrents roaring, no house in sight to which the child might belong; his dress, cry, and appearance all different from what we had been accustomed to. It was a text, as Wm. has since observed to me, containing in itself the whole history of the Highlander's life—his melancholy, his simplicity, his poverty, his superstition, and above all, that visionariness which results from a communion with the unworldliness of nature.[32]

To Wordsworth the supreme gift of the tour came from just

such moments of visionariness that fed his imagination and that became transformed in the due course of time into poetry. A full examination of Wordsworth's poetic vision of the landscape, including interpretations of selected poems from the Scottish tour, will be given in the next chapter. In the remainder of the present one I shall take a closer look at Wordsworth's artistic principles—for the traveler viewing a landscape—as they are set down and illustrated in his classic *A Guide to the Lakes,* 1810.[33]

A Guide to the Lakes *and* the Duddon Sonnets

Wordsworth was well acquainted with the popular tourbooks on the Lakes,[34] and in his own work, especially where he gave advice on the several approaches to the district, he followed their method and their vocabulary. He was impatient, however, with their usual practice of investing the scenery with more emotional significance than it could bear. Accordingly, he undertook to teach the Touring World, which had become very numerous, "to look through the clear eye of understanding as well as through the hazy one of vague Sensibility."[35] In the opening sentence of his *Guide* he states that it is his principal wish "to furnish a Guide or Companion for the *Minds* of Persons of taste, and feeling for Landscape, who might be inclined to explore the District of the Lakes with that degree of attention to which its beauty may fairly lay claim." His guide, then, is not merely a book for a traveler seeking directions on the road, but a manual of sound philosophical principles, teaching how Nature is to be contemplated, and how her beauties are to be preserved, cherished, and improved.

Wordsworth conceives of the natural landscape as shaped into beauty by a universal spirit indwelling in the edges of the lake and of the wood and in the farthest reaches of the mountain crags. We should never contemplate these boundaries without some awareness, more or less distinct, of the powers of Nature by which they are imposed and an awareness that if they are defaced by man, the scars will gradually disappear before a healing spirit. Wordsworth sees man as deeply involved in Nature, his work seeming to be Nature's and Nature's that of man. The thoughtful man, then, does not look upon Nature as a superficially pretty picture, but as endowed with spiritual power ceaselessly speaking to him and working upon him. He must learn to admire the grandeur and harmony of Nature's order, to receive her with a "feeling intellect," and to carry her power into the distracted fields of human existence. Nature's book lies open, but we have to be taught to read it. This is what Wordsworth was doing in his *Guide to the Lakes* for the tourists who swarmed into the district.

Wordsworth reminds his traveler that his benefits, whether of pleasure or profit, must principally depend upon what he brings along within himself. Nature is not merely to be observed with the eye but assimilated by the whole being. He cautions against the invidious comparisons of countries. "Nothing," he says, "is more injurious to genuine feeling than the practice of hastily and ungraciously depreciating the face of one country by comparing it with that of another."[36] The best guide to which we can entrust ourselves in matters of taste is "a disposition to be pleased." The viewer must learn to love the landscape before it will seem worthy of his love.

> Vain is the glory of the sky,
> The beauty vain of field and grove,
> Unless, while with admiring eye
> We gaze, we also learn to love.
> ["Glad Sight Wherever
> New with Old," vv. 5–8]

The vital life with which Nature is endowed is capable of
transmitting through sight and sound a deep responsive joy.
Wordsworth himself expresses joy in reading the living face of
Nature. Over and over again his poetry records his spirit as
lifted by an "enchanting scene." The *Guide* is quickened by a
contagious spirit of joy in Nature which he wishes to impart to
his readers. He recognizes that the beauty of living Nature

> . . . cannot be portrayed
> By words, nor by the pencil's silent skill;
> But is the property of him alone
> Who hath beheld it, noted it with care,
> And in his mind recorded it with love!

> [*Excursion*, IX, 513–17]

It is not in the poem on the printed page or in the sketch on the
painter's canvas that the total record of Nature's impact is to
be recovered. It is upon the individual traveler that she works:

> Ye only can supply
> The life, the truth, the beauty: she confides
> In that enjoyment which with You abides,
> Trusts to your love and vivid memory.

> [Dedication of *Memorials of a
> Tour on the Continent*, 1820]

The reader familiar with Wordsworth's poetry will recall how
frequently the memory of "beauteous scenes" consoled him and
brought a power

> . . . as sweet
> And gracious, almost might I dare to say,
> As virtue is, or goodness; sweet as love,
> Or the remembrance of a generous deed,
> Or mildest visitations of pure thought,
> When God, the giver of all joy, is thanked

Religiously, in silent blessedness;
Sweet as this last herself, for such it is.

[*The Prelude*, VI, 680–87]

Wordsworth knew from first-hand acquaintance that fine scenery is widely spread in European countries, and he has words of praise particularly for the mountain scenery of Swit- · erland, Scotland, and North Wales. But the varied loveliness of his own Lake District he felt was not to be matched anywhere in Europe. And he wanted to keep its beauty unspoiled. As visitors flocked to the Lakes from all parts of England the fancies of some became so smitten that they decided to become settlers. Then it was, Wordsworth complains, that the despoiling of Nature's paradise began: These newcomers built monstrous houses on the summits of the hills, planted platoons of Scotch firs, shaved the shorelines of the lakes, and in general introduced a jumble of discordant objects throughout the district that disturbed the peaceful harmony of form and color, which had long been happily preserved. Dorothy's correspondence echoes the refrain of this complaint. Items from her letter to Lady Beaumont will serve as a good sampling of the thoughts the Wordsworths shared on the desecrations of the improvers:

Poor Grasmere is a devoted place! You may remember that I spoke of the whitewashing of the Church, and six years ago a trim Box was erected on a hill-side; it is surrounded with fir and larch plantations, that look like a blotch or scar on the fair surface of the mountain. Luckily these deformities are not visible in the grand view of the Vale. But alas! poor Grasmere! The first object which now presents itself after you have clomb the hill from Rydale is Mr. Crump's newly-erected large mansion, staring over the Church Steeple, its foundation under the crags being much above the top of the Steeple. Then a farmhouse opposite to ours, on the other side of the Lake, has been taken by a dashing man from Man-

chester, who no doubt will make a *fine place* of it, and, as he has
taken the Island too, will probably erect a pavilion upon it, or it
may be an Obelisk. This is not all. A very beautiful little Estate has
been purchased in the more retired part of the Vale, and the first
thing the Gentleman has done preparatory to building his house,
has been to make a *Sunk Fence,* which you overlook on every side
from the rocks, thickets, and green sloping hills! Add to all that
Sir Michael Fleming has been getting his woods appraised, and
after Christmas the Ax is to be lifted against them, and not one
tree left, so the whole Eastern side of the Lake will be entirely
naked, even to the very edge of the water! but what could we expect better from Sir Michael who has been building a long high wall
under the grand woods behind his house which cuts the hill in two
by a straight line; and to make his doings visible to all men, he
has white-washed it, as white as snow.[37]

The *Guide* is full of similar passages of scorn directed
against those who would despoil or make artificial the wild
and fanciful play of Nature. Wordsworth was grateful for a
beautiful region of seclusion and repose, and he hoped to protect it from disfigurement by human hands. His protests were
made not so much for himself as in the name of Nature and
on behalf of future generations. His indignation was little and
his love much. The subtle essence of love rises again and again
in his book as the beauties of the countryside are quietly revealed. His affection even for minute features of the landscape
can be felt in his descriptions of such features as "the curved
rim of fine blue gravel thrown up in course of time by the
waves" along the shore of the lake, or the "plots of water-
lilies lifting up their large target-shaped leaves to the breeze,
while the white flower is heaving upon the wave." Wordsworth
interpreted every sight and sound of the mountains and the
lakes with the affection of one who reads the familiar features
of a good friend. His descriptions glow with a recollected love

and with the indignation which accompanies that love, when that which is dearly loved is injured or made less beautiful.

It is this deeply grounded affection that sharply distinguishes Wordsworth's response to the landscape from even such a gifted scene-hunter as Thomas Gray. Gray's response was aesthetic rather than natural. Like most "picturesque" travelers he was picture-conscious and sought the scene with eye appeal that would compose well. He carried about a Claude glass, and whenever he saw any scene he thought pretty, he sat down to contemplate it in this glass. Wordsworth agrees that Nature should be seen with an artist's eye, but not primarily with the purpose of making a picture of it. He notes that the Lakeland scenes are better suited to painting than those of the Alps, but adds that he "should be sorry to contemplate either country in reference to that art, further than as its fitness or unfitness for the pencil renders it more or less pleasing to the eye of the spectator, who has learned to observe and feel, chiefly from Nature herself."[38] In his own descriptions of the landscape he moves from objective description to a freer, introspective, and poetic rendering.

Wordsworth makes the commonsense observation that the pleasure derived from viewing mountains, lakes, and waterfalls often depends absolutely upon the weather and upon accidents: "The atmosphere is frequently unfavourable to landscape, especially when keen winds succeed the rain which are apt to produce coldness, spottiness, and an unmeaning or repulsive detail in the distance."[39] How all travelers recalling sad disappointments in scene-hunting, whether in the Lake District or elsewhere, will grant accord on this point! But Wordsworth gives abundant advice out of his own intimate knowledge of the country of the Lakes on how the traveler may minimize these disappointments and enhance his enjoyments. He suggests the advantages to be gained by visiting

the Lake District during the different seasons. The six weeks
following the first of September are among the most favorable:
"There is then an admirable compass and proportion of natural
harmony in colour, through the whole scale of objects." Mid-
May to mid-June affords "the best combination of long days,
fine weather, and variety of impressions." There is diversity of
foliage; spring flowers still linger on the mountain-sides; while
the open and sunny spaces are stocked with the flowers of approaching summer. The songs of birds are heard in the copses,
woods, and hedge-rows, and multitudes of lambs with their
snow-white color and their wild and light motions enliven the
pastures and meadows. During July and August the visitor is
likely to be caused some discomfiture by storms, but he may be
treated to "bold bursts of sunshine, descending vapours, wandering lights and shadows, and invigorated torrents and waterfalls, with which broken weather in a mountain region is
accompanied." As to the order in which objects are best seen,
a lake "will appear to most advantage when approached from
its outlet, . . . for by this way of approach, the traveller faces
the grander features of the scene, and is gradually conducted
to its most sublime recesses. . . . From amenity and beauty the
transition to sublimity is easy and favourable, but the reverse
is not so; for, after the faculties have been elevated, they are
indisposed to humbler excitement."[40] It is not likely, Wordsworth reminds us, that a mountain will be ascended without
disappointment if one is hoping for a "wide range of prospect."
If this be the object, one had better plan to reach the summit
before sunrise or remain until sunset or after. Mountain vales
should be traversed in the early morning on the eastern side,
otherwise the traveler "will lose the morning light, first touching the tops and thence creeping down the sides of the opposite hills. . . . In the evening, for like reasons, the contrary
course should be taken."[41] Wordsworth says that he does not
know of any tract of country "in which, within so narrow a

compass, may be found an equal variety in the influences of light and shadow upon the sublime or beautiful features of landscape."[42]

The mountains in the Lake District are endlessly diversified in forms and colors because of their varied mineral composition and also because of seasonal changes. In winter their forms are more strikingly displayed, and also in this season there is an almost inexhaustible variety of coloring. The lakes being of comparatively small size produce a greatly variegated landscape; their boundary-line also "is for the most part gracefully or boldly indented." Birds enliven the waters; but at times when the waters are still and crystalline clear, the reflections of the surrounding hills are frequently the perfect inverted "copy of the real scene." The newcomer to the region must not overlook the smaller waterfalls or cascades in which the principal charm "consists in certain proportions of form and affinities of colour, among the component parts of the scene."[43] Lesser lakes, or tarns, are found in some of the vales but are more numerous in the mountains. The mountain tarns "are difficult of access and naked; yet some of them are very grand." By the side of one of these mountain pools the feelings of melancholy and solitude are often solemnly experienced. In the mountain and lake country the streams tend to be large brooks rather than rivers; yet so various are the beauties of the rivers Derwent and Duddon, they may be compared with "any two rivers of equal length in any country." The woods in earlier times covered the whole country to a great height up the mountains. Beautiful traces of the sylvan appearance the country formerly had still survive in the beauty and intricacy with which the fields and coppice-woods are often intermingled. Many field flowers and shrubs diversify and give color to the landscape.

The beauty of the natural scene is often enhanced by man's handiwork as seen in the buildings, roads and bridges, and places of worship, when built in harmony with their surroundings. This is especially so with the mountain cottages, which have such a naturalness about them that they seem "to have risen, by an instinct of their own, out of the native rock—so little is there in them of formality, such is their wildness and beauty." In numerous recesses and projections in the walls and in the different stages of their roofs are seen "bold and harmonious effects of contrasted sunshine and shadow." The chimneys are of singular beauty, particularly those of quadrangular shape surmounted by a tall cylinder. Wordsworth affectionately notes the "pleasing harmony between a tall chimney of this circular form, and the living column of smoke, ascending from it through the still air." The rough and uneven surfaces of "both the coverings and sides of the houses have furnished places of rest for the seeds of lichens, mosses, ferns, and flowers. Hence buildings, which in their very form call to mind the processes of Nature do thus, clothed in part with a vegetable garb, appear to be received into the bosom of the living principle of things, as it acts and exists among the woods and fields; and by their colour and their shape, affectingly direct the thoughts to that tranquil course of Nature and simplicity, along which the humble-minded inhabitants have, through so many generations, been led."[44] Add its shed for beehives, its small bed of potherbs, its borders of flowers, an orchard, a cheese press, a cluster of sycamores for summer shade, a tall fir "through which the winds sing when other trees are leafless," and the little household rill or spout murmuring at all seasons—combine these incidents and images together, and you have "the representative idea of a mountain cottage in this country so beautifully formed in itself and so richly adorned by the hand of Nature."

Though the country is, Wordsworth admits, subject to much bad weather, the "skiey influences" that result, as they affect the appearance of the landscape may, upon the whole, be con-

MOUNTAIN COTTAGE at Loughrigg

Photograph by the author

sidered as fortunate. Wordsworth himself was keenly responsive to these influences, and in his description of passing showers, vapors, and fleecy clouds he becomes "more than half a poet":

Days of unsettled weather, with partial showers, are very frequent; but the showers, darkening, or brightening, as they fly from hill to hill, are not less grateful to the eye than finely interwoven passages of gay and sad music are touching to the ear. Vapours exhaling from the lakes and meadows after sunrise, in a hot season, or, in moist weather, brooding upon the heights, or descending towards the valleys with inaudible motion, give a visionary character to everything around them; and are in themselves so beautiful, as to dispose us to enter into the feelings of those simple nations (such as the Laplanders of this day) by whom they are taken for guardian deities of the mountains; or to sympathise with others who have fancied these delicate apparitions to be the spirits of their departed ancestors. Akin to these are fleecy clouds resting upon the hill-tops; they are not easily managed in picture, with their accompaniments of blue sky; but how glorious are they in Nature! how pregnant with imagination for the poet! and the height of the Cumbrian mountains is sufficient to exhibit daily and hourly instances of those mysterious attachments. Such clouds, cleaving to their stations, or lifting up suddenly their glittering heads from behind rocky barriers, or hurrying out of sight with speed of the sharpest edge—will often tempt an inhabitant to congratulate himself on belonging to a country of mists and clouds and storms.[45]

Wordsworth moves to a full poetical mode in the midst of prose when he contemplates the occasional perfect day that is offered in the Lake District to the lover of Nature, "worth whole months, even years." One of these favored days sometimes occurs in the springtime when "soft air is breathing over the blossoms and new-born verdure"; but it is in autumn that Nature is capable of putting on an aspect satisfying "the most intense cravings for the tranquil, the lovely, and the perfect" to which man is subject:

COTTAGE CHIMNEYS above Grasmere

Photograph by the author

The atmosphere seems refined, and the sky rendered more crystal-line, as the vivifying heat of the year abates; the lights and shadows are more delicate; the colouring is richer and more finely har-monized; and, in this season of stillness, the ear being unoccupied, or only gently excited, the sense of vision becomes more susceptible of its appropriate enjoyments. A resident in a country like this which we are treating of, will agree with me, that the presence of a lake is indispensable to exhibit in perfection the beauty of one of these days; and he must have experienced, while looking on the un-ruffled waters, that the imagination, by their aid, is carried into re-cesses of feeling otherwise impenetrable. The reason of this is, that the heavens are not only brought down into the bosom of the earth, but that the earth is mainly looked at, and thought of, through the medium of a purer element. The happiest time is when the equi-noxial gales are departed; but their fury may probably be called to mind by the sight of a few shattered boughs, whose leaves do not differ in colour from the faded foliage of the stately oaks from which these relics of the storm depend: all else speaks of tranquillity;— not a breath of air, no restlessness of insects, and not a moving object perceptible—except the clouds gliding in the depths of the lake, or the traveller passing along, an inverted image, whose mo-tion seems governed by the quiet of a time, to which its archetype, the living person, is, perhaps, insensible:—or it may happen, that the figure of one of the larger birds, a raven or a heron, is crossing silently among the reflected clouds, while the voice of the real bird, from the element aloft, gently awakens in the spectator the recollec-tion of appetites and instincts, pursuits and occupations, that de-form and agitate the world,—yet have no power to prevent Nature from putting on an aspect capable of satisfying the most intense cravings for the tranquil, the lovely, and the perfect, to which man, the noblest of her creatures, is subject.[46]

When Wordsworth's *Guide to the Lakes* was published in 1820 under his own name, the reviews gave it almost unani-mous praise. It was "by far the best specimen of his prose style ever given to the world"; "as topographically useful as it is poetically picturesque." *Blackwood's Edinburgh Magazine* said of the 1822 edition: "It is . . . full of fine feeling and fine philosophy. He analyses the country and shews all the sources of the pleasure which it is peculiarly fitted to yield to an enlightened and thoughtful mind." Judging from the widespread acceptance of the *Guide* (it went into a fifth edition in 1835), we may conclude that Wordsworth was well on the way towards fulfilling his hope of teaching the touring world who visited the Lake District "to look through the clear eye of understanding" at what they saw and to bind with affection to their hearts what was worthy.

The sonnet sequence on the River Duddon was also first published in 1820, in the same volume with *A Guide to the Lakes*. Like the *Guide* it describes the sights and sounds to be enjoyed in an open-air ramble. But unlike the prose work it is much less concerned with giving pleasure through pictorial images (though these are not lacking) than stirring thoughts that may elevate the mind. *The River Duddon* belongs in the main stream of topographical poetry and employs, as Aubin has pointed out, the typical devices of traditional river-poems—"apostrophe, local pride, historical reflection, catalog, moralizing, genre scenes, episode, early memories, prospect, ruin-piece, and Muse-driving ('On, loitering muse—the swift stream chides us—on!')."[47] The country through which the Duddon flows is somewhat bleak and austere, yet the poet garners many pleasures following the stream from its rise at the top of Wrynose Pass as it ripples, winds, and widens on its way to the sea. He delights in the shade cast by the green alders and the birch trees in silver colonnade along its banks. He awakens to the power of the stream "to heal and to restore, to soothe and cleanse." He has fanciful thoughts about stepping stones and a faery chasm. He hails a fair prospect which with one glance takes in

>   . . . one small hamlet, under a green hill
> Clustering, with barn and byre, and spouting mill.

He beholds with pleasure a gloomy niche where rocks appear shaped into sculpture as if man-made. He observes a country chapel and extols it. He muses upon the legend of a lovelorn maid who drowned herself. He delights in the cheer and bustle of sheep-washing in the river. He describes a mid-noon resting place, where "no zephyr breathes, no cloud its shadow throws." He reminisces over boyhood associations with the stream. He notes a castle in ruins and the burial grounds of peace-loving Quakers. He parts with the river when it passes swiftly through a rough copse, but affectionately joins it again in an open meadow. Finally, he watches it expand and glide in silence over the smooth, flat sands to meet the sea. In the closing sonnet, "After-Thought," he sums up the symbolic meaning of the poetical journey from mountain to ocean. The river has been the traveler's companion through the various stages of life. It is the eternal life-force "of man's spirit as it emerges from the unknown, runs its earthly course, and merges again with the eternal."[48] It represents the spiritual oneness of Man and Nature, "what was, and is, and will abide."

Poems of the Continental Tour, 1820; The Scottish Tour, 1831; The Isle of Man, 1833; Italy, 1837

During his middle and later years Wordsworth's love of travel did not abate, and he often used the objects and experiences of his tours as the subject matter for new poems. He also describes scenic discoveries in letters to his friends and family, though he usually leaves any extended prose account of his travel adventures to others. Mary and Dorothy made rather extensive notes in the field on the Continental Tour in 1820 and expanded them into full journal accounts after their return home. Dorothy also kept a day-by-day record of her tour in Scotland in 1822 and of her tour in the Isle of Man in 1828; Mary kept minutes of her tour with William in Holland in 1823 and afterwards wrote them up into a journal; and his daughter Dora kept a journal of her trip through Scotland in 1831. For the record it will be useful at this point to list the more important tours made by Wordsworth beginning with 1814 and the poems written to memorialize them: Tour of Scotland, 1814, taken with Mary and Sara Hutchinson (four poems, including "Yarrow Visited"); Tour in North Wales, 1824; Tour up the Rhine, 1828, with his daughter, Dora, and Coleridge; Tour through Ireland, 1829, with J. Marshall, M.P. for Leeds; Tour in Scotland with Dora, 1831 (twenty-seven poems published under the title "Poems: Yarrow Revisited and Other Poems"); Tour in the Isle of Man and in Scotland, 1833, with his son John and Henry Crabb Robinson (Forty-seven poems published under the title "Poems Composed or Suggested during a Tour in the Summer of 1833"); Tour through France and Italy, 1837, with Henry Crabb Robinson (twenty-six poems published under the title "Memorials of a Tour in Italy, 1837"); Tour through the Duddon Valley with the Quillinans and Lady Richardson, 1844.

In the tour poems of the later years Wordsworth gives less attention to the landscape than he does to the works of man— his buildings, his cities, his battle-fields, his paintings and sculptures, and his shrines. In memorializing the tour of the continent in 1820, for example, he offers poems on Cologne Cathedral, the Church of San Salvador, the city of Bruges, the town of Schwytz, the battle-field of Waterloo, the prostrate column of granite left abandoned when Napoleon fell, the ruins of Fort Fuentes, the painted tower commemorating William Tell, the mural of *The Last Supper* by Leonardo da Vinci,

and the lovely shrine high in the mountains of Our Lady of
Snow. Of a total of thirty-eight poems on the continental tour
only seven are primarily concerned with the landscape. In one
of the more interesting of these—the sonnet describing the
Meuse River between Namur and Liège—he turns from think-
ing about the battles fought along its shores to contemplating
its peaceful activities and to viewing the sweet prospect of the
river glade—

> With its grey rocks clustering in pensive shade—
> That, shaped like old monastic turrets, rise
> From the smooth meadow-ground, serene and still.
>
> [vv. 12–14]

He wrote a long letter to Sir Uvedale Price in which he compared the landscapes on the Meuse with those on the Rhine
and stated his wish that somebody would combine into one
work the scenes, circumstances, and objects of that region as
they were touched upon by his wife and his sister in their
journals. In the other poems that treat of Nature he muses
upon the source of the Danube River; he describes the sky-
born waterfall of Staubbach and the waterfall of the Aar-
Handegg; he takes delight in the cloud-shapes that hover like
celestial bands around Engelberg (Angel Mountain) and the
sky prospect of clouds over the plains of France that strangely
changed their shapes; and he spiritedly recounts the dramatic
changes wrought upon the Italian landscape during an eclipse
of the sun.

The twenty-six poems composed to memorialize his tour in
Scotland in the autumn of 1831 are almost wholly concerned
with tradition and antiquities (as he put it, in this sequence
the Muse serves "that sacred Power/The Spirit of humanity").
Only one poem addresses itself directly to Nature. This is "The
Trosachs" in which Wordsworth calls upon his reader to turn
from scenes of art and with watchful eyes feed his thought

... 'mid Nature's old felicities
Rocks, rivers, and smooth lakes more clear than glass
Untouched, unbreathed upon.

[vv. 7–9]

In the forty-eight poems composed or suggested during a tour of the Isle of Man, of Western Scotland, and parts of Cumberland in the summer of 1833, landscape scenes that casually meet the eye are practically ignored. In this series of travel poems Wordsworth addresses rivers, bays, seashores, islands, friths, castles, caves, monuments, and the legends that are sometimes associated with them; but he does not describe or memorialize the scenery. His sweeter pleasure, which he expresses in the concluding sonnet, is not in the "fair region" that "round the traveller lies" but rather in "some soft ideal scene,/ The work of Fancy, or some happy tone/ Of meditation, slipping in between/ The beauty coming and the beauty gone."[49]

In the poems of his last major tour Wordsworth more nearly balances his interest in the landscape with his interest in the works of man. When he entered Italy (near Aquapendente) with Crabb Robinson in the spring of 1837, he fed "his mind with watchful eyes" among the Apennines delighting in the exhilarating scene before him and anticipating the pleasures of touring which lay ahead. He expressed a wish that on his wanderings he might chiefly "cull with care/ Those images of genial beauty, oft/ Too lovely to be pensive in themselves/ But by reflexion made so." (This is a characteristic Wordsworthian response: nearly all the poems memorializing this tour were written several years after the poet had returned home, mostly during 1840–41.) At Savona he singled out for description a high cliff whose steep sides were covered with "a thousand herbs and shrubs"and from whose sides extended, far and near, "Garden and field all decked with orange bloom,/ And peach

and citron, in Spring's mildest breeze/ Expanding." From this
height, in a meditative mood, he anticipated seeking out in
magnificent Rome those spots associated with Virgil and other
honored Romans and the memorials hallowed by the presence
of early Christian leaders and martyrs. While in Rome he contemplated her glories and pleaded with historians to give a
true account of her past. He lamented her fallen state and
wished for a future of renewed greatness. At Laverna he addressed with delight the cuckoo whose voice greeted him, and
he raised his song in praise of St. Francis whose church he saw
high on the rock's edge above him. At Vallombrosa he was
pleased to take his ease under the shade of trees where Milton
had formerly reclined. At Florence he gazed pensively upon
the works of Raphael and Michael Angelo. He returned home
with his memory filled with "rich stores of Nature's imagery/
And divine Art."

Wordsworth as Interpreter
of Scenic Landscape

In the major series of tour poems after 1814 Wordsworth
does not ignore the landscape, but neither does he pursue it
single-mindedly as he did on his first visit with Robert Jones
to the Alps in 1790, or on his visits to the Wye Valley in 1793
and 1798, or on his tour of Scotland with Dorothy in 1803, or
at other times on rambles through the Lake District. Moreover,
in the later years, though he was always against judging a
scene primarily on its suitability for drawing or painting, he
tended more than in the earlier years to seek out pictorial aspects and features which were recognizably "picturesque." The
poet's increasing interest in landscape painting and his friend-
ships with painters, especially with Sir George Beaumont,
doubtless encouraged this trend. It is noticeable that both
Wordsworth and his sister Dorothy in their letters to the Beau-

monts took pleasure in identifying scenes that "compose" well as in a painting or that have picturesque features. Dorothy tells of how she became aware of the beauty of city streets when she first looked with the eyes of a painter upon what had formerly appeared to her as ugly. She writes of her discovery to Lady Beaumont, 14 August 1810:

I have several times, in the course of my travels, passed through Stamford, and used to think it a very ugly place; but, to my great surprise, whichever way I looked on Friday afternoon, I saw something to admire—an old house, a group of houses, the irregular line of a street, a church, or a spire; and it was a great satisfaction to me to be in this manner delighted with what I had passed over in my youth with indifference, perhaps even disgust.[50]

In her journal of the continental tour (1820), Dorothy repeatedly records her pleasure in pictorial and picturesque objects. She confides that she has learned since her youth to enjoy "the sight of ancient buildings" and writes that at Ghent "the buildings, streets, squares all are picturesque; the houses, green, blue, pink, yellow with richest ornaments still varying." And she muses, as a painter might, that it is strange "that so many and such strongly-contrasted colours should compose an undiscordant whole."[51]

Soon after his return from his second tour of the Alps (1820) Wordsworth writes to Sir George Beaumont that he is proud to think that his friend is busy painting English landscapes; for English scenery, he thinks, "loses little by comparison with the Alps."[52] "The English lakes and streams are not only more pure and crystalline," he reminds him, "but the crumbly surfaces of the rocks and crags and the courses of the streams present a far more attractive variety"—that is, they are more "picturesque." In this same letter Wordsworth describes the scenery along the course of the Eden River as it would be envisaged by a landscape-sketcher. Wordsworth even identifies the point where Beaumont might set up his canvas and fills in for him the pictorial composition:

It is a charming region, particularly at the spot where the Eden and the Emont join. The rivers appeared exquisitely brilliant, gliding under rocks and through green meadows, with woods and sloping cultivated grounds, and pensive russet moors interspersed, and along the circuit of the horizon, lofty hills and mountains clothed, rather than concealed, in fleecy clouds and resplendent vapours.[53]

During his visit to Wales in 1824 Wordsworth reports to Beaumont the "fine views" they had, departing for Llanberris, as they looked back at Conway Castle, the sea, and Anglesey:

A little before sunset [we] came in sight of Llanberris Lake, Snowdon, and all the craggy hills and mountains surrounding it; the foreground a beautiful contrast to this grandeur and desolation—a green sloping hollow, furnishing a shelter for one of the most beautiful collections of lowly Welsh cottages, with thatched roofs, overgrown with plants, anywhere to be met with.[54]

Wordsworth described to Dorothy some of the "sublime views" he saw on his tour of Ireland. The following passage from a letter dated 24 September 1829 describes an enchanting scene in the county of Kerry:

This morning I walked out before six at Manor Hamilton—it is seated among hills and Rocks of Limestone—The Sun though not above the horizon had filled the East with purple and gold—One mountain opposite of Majestic size and varied outline was steeped in deep purple, so were the battlements and towers of a Ruined castle at one end of the small town—the Ruin is one of the finest we have seen in Ireland—the stream was visible in the valley, blue smoke ascending from the thatched cottages, and in different parts of the valley forming itself into horizontal lines resembling vapour, and on the sides of the hills also, all was quiet and beautiful, glowing light and deep shadow.[55]

With his artist friend Benjamin Robert Haydon, Wordsworth shared glimpses of landscape beauty such as artists are keenly aware of. He writes to Haydon of one such sight of the snow-clad mountain that he saw while enjoying skating:

The splendor of the snow-clad mountains, by moonlight in particular is most charming; and the softness of the shadows surpasses anything you can conceive; this when the moon is at a particular point of elevation. I never saw anything so exquisite; though I believe Titian has; *and* so, therefore, perhaps may you.[56]

When the artist Inman visited Wordsworth he told of how the poet accompanied him twice on his sketching excursions, and pointed out various points of view which seemed favorable as subjects for the pencil.

In walking over his own grounds, he would pause occasionally to invite my attention to some fine old tree. . . . He would point to its gnarled and torturous trunk with the same gusto with which the statuary might scan a fragment from the chisel of Phidias. . . . The moss-covered rock, the shining cascade, the placid lake, or splintered mountain-pinnacle seemed each to constitute for him a prideful possession.[57]

Although Wordsworth always had a keen sense of the pictorial, he scorned the picturesque cult made up of empty-headed travelers who wander about the countryside in search of spots identified by the writers of guide books as distinguished for the sublimity or beauty of the landscape there to be seen. He equally disdained the want of taste in such writers as Scott who in a laborious manner place everything before the eyes of the reader for the production of a picturesque effect. Wordsworth says that in a good narration "the reader feels the pictures rise up before his sight, and pass away from it unostentatiously, succeeding each other. But when they are fixed upon the easel for the express purpose of being admired, the judicious are apt to take offence and even to turn sulky at the exhibitor's officiousness."[58] In his own writing Wordsworth strove constantly to move beyond a surface rendering of the landscape. In the travel poems he less often reached the deeper levels of meaning that he reached elsewhere, though he did so in "Tintern Abbey," in some of the poems of the Scottish tour of 1803, and in the passages on the Alps and Mt. Snowdon in *The Prelude*.

Wordsworth saw more than most men see in the world around them, and in what he saw he experienced greater joy. Even as a small boy he found delight in prospects and tells how he took so much pleasure from the beautiful view to be seen from the site on the rocks above Esthwaite Lake (some years before the first pleasure-house was built there) that he "led thither from Hawkshead a youngster about my own age, an Irish boy, who was a servant to an itinerant conjurer. My motive was to witness the pleasure I expected the boy would receive from the propect of the islands below and the intermingling water. I was not disappointed."[59] The joys he experienced as a boy in seeking out the beauty in the landscape and in sharing that joy with others were deep wellsprings of delight that endured throughout his lifetime. These were the rewards of his wanderings. The travel poems, *A Guide to the Lakes*, and the letters and journals of which we have given some account in this chapter are the record of these discoveries which he took pleasure in sharing with others. Wordsworth realized that it required time for a taste in natural scenery to be implanted. He thought that Burns, though he was sensitive to "the general powers of Nature exhibited in storm and stillness, in light or darkness, and in the various aspects of the seasons," showed little preference for one scene over another and "had not much taste for the picturesque."[60] We have seen that Wordsworth's own progress in reporting the beauty and sublimity of the landscape was gradual and beset with problems. Although in his early travel poems—in *Evening Walk* and

Descriptive Sketches—he gives us a multitude of directly-observed, fresh images, he was hampered in reporting them by the restrictions of eighteenth-century poetic form and by the tyranny of the physical eye. However, when he writes the first draft (1810) of *A Guide to the Lakes,* he not only knows what beauties to admire, but he can tell others what the particular beauties of each scene are or to what incidents they owe their especial charm.[61] In his letters and in Dorothy's letters and journals describing their travels there are many exquisite passages descriptive of landscape beauties. And although there was some falling off in the proportionate number of poems given over to landscape description in the travel poems after 1810, and a falling off in the imaginative power in these poems (as there was in nearly all of his poems in the later years), there seems to have been no lack of enthusiasm for or delight in scenery—either that which was newly discovered on his many tours, or that which was often rediscovered in his own beloved Vale of Grasmere or among the neighboring lakes and mountains of Cumberland and Westmoreland.

FIVE

The Art of Landscape
in Wordsworth's Poetry

"How Exquisitely the Individual Mind
to the External World Is Fitted"

Wordsworth in his period of apprenticeship (*An Evening Walk, Descriptive Sketches*) was a visualizer and knew the enslavement that could come from viewing the landscape pictorially. But he learned that landscape poetry to be successful must go beyond mere picture-making. This is the point he is upholding in his comments as reported by Aubrey de Vere:

I was once on a visit to Wordsworth . . . and we had a conversation about the different modern poets who had in late years described Nature. He expressed a low opinion as to their success in description. He took down several volumes, and he said, "Here is a descriptive passage by ——. It is exceedingly able writing, but it is not Nature. It is undoubtedly clever, but it is the writing of a person who vainly endeavours to blend together as much as he sees, whether congruous or incongruous, into a single picture. This is the way in which he did his work. He used to go out with a pencil and a tablet, and note what struck him, thus: 'an old tower,' 'a dashing stream,' 'a green slope,' and make a picture out of it." Then, turning to me, the old Poet added, with a flashing eye, "But Nature does not allow an inventory to be made of her charms! He should have left his pencil behind, and gone forth in a meditative spirit; and, on a later day, he should have embodied in verse not all that he had noted but what he best remembered of the scene; and he would have then presented us with *its soul,* and not with the mere visual aspects of it."[1]

Wordsworth was not a note-taker when the objects of Nature were before him. He scorned the analytic sight of the naturalist ("one who would peep and botanize upon his mother's grave"), because in his opinion this kind of reporting did not pierce through the substance to the life. Even Dorothy as she records her impressions of the landscape in her journals usually reports merely the literal detail. And Coleridge could do much the same thing in poetry, as in "This Lime-Tree Bower":

> . . . in this bower,
> This little lime-tree bower, have I not mark'd
> Much that hath sooth'd me. Pale beneath the blaze
> Hung the transparent foliage; and I watch'd
> Some broad and sunny leaf, and I lov'd to see
> The shadow of the leaf and stem above
> Dappling its sunshine! And that walnut-tree
> Was richly ting'd, and a deep radiance lay
> Full on the ancient ivy, which usurps
> Those fronting elms, and now, with blackest mass
> Makes their dark branches gleam a lighter hue
> Through the late twilight: and though now the bat
> Wheels silent by, and not a swallow twitters,
> Yet the solitary humble-bee
> Sings in the bean-flower!
>
> [vv. 45–59]

Wordsworth was not, however, opposed to the description of natural scenery. Writing of this kind is to be found throughout the whole body of his poetry; indeed he defends his own practice of it in a letter to Richard Sharp:

Gray, in one of his letters . . . , affirms that description, (he means of natural scenery and the Operations of Nature) though an admirable ornament, ought *never* to be the subject of poetry. How many exclusive dogmas have been laid down, which genius from age to age has triumphantly refuted! and grossly should I be deceived if . . . these local poems[2] do not contain many proofs that Gray was . . . wrong in this interdict. . . .[3]

What Wordsworth did object to was the descriptive inventory of scenery indulged in for its own sake and unenlivened by any quickening spirit or meaning.

Wordsworth himself responded to Nature with a physical, spontaneous gladness and in his poetry describes the common sights of earth and sky with a feeling heart and a clear eye. He developed a lifelong habit of close, accurate observation of the external world and insisted that poetic creation be based upon the facts and realities of that world:

> To the solid ground
> Of Nature trusts the Mind that builds for aye;
> Convinced that there, there only, can she lay
> Secure foundations.
> ["A Volant Tribe of Bards," vv. 5–8]

He incessantly fed his eye and ear upon all outward things and attained even from early childhood an active power to impress upon his memory the "colours and forms" of Nature. Thus the beauteous forms of landscape were translated into his inward life:

> . . . with an eye so rich
> As mine was, through the chance, on me not wasted,
> Of having been brought up in such a grand
> And lovely region, I had forms distinct
> To steady me; these thoughts did oft revolve
> About some centre palpable, which at once
> Incited them to motion, and control'd,
> And whatsoever shape the fit might take,
> And whencesoever it might come, I still

At all times had a real solid world
Of images about me . . . .

[The Prelude (1805), VIII, 594–604]

The "forms and images" that filled his mind were visible pictures, but they were charged with emotion and had substance.
They became for the poet configurations both in the mind and
in the external world. This simultaneous identity allowed him
to shift easily from inward vision to outward scene and back
again; to apply in the linguistic context the words "sense" and
"form" with equal accuracy to mind *and* Nature; and to set up
paradoxes of meaning that add a rich complexity to his descriptions. He can be at once mysterious and matter-of-fact, or
naturalistic.[4] Moreover, the forms of earth conceived both inwardly and outwardly are a manifest creation of pure Spirit, a
transparent veil for the mysteries they emblemize. They are "a
scene from the palette of the Eternal Artist," existing meta-
phorically yet also massively in three dimensions just as we
would expect a large-scale landscape to exist.[5]

Wordsworth's imaginative response to Nature is greatly different from those who followed the pattern marked out by
tradition. With the traditionalists, landscape description was
likely to be external, pictorial, and variegated; with Wordsworth, to be inward, metaphorical, and unified in tone and
feeling. Cowper's well-known description of the Ouse Valley
(*The Task*, Bk. I, 154–78) is one of the better examples in eighteenth-century poetry of the scene looked upon conventionally,
simply as a picture:

How oft upon yon eminence our pace
Has slacken'd to a pause, and we have born
The ruffling wind, scarce conscious that it blew,
While admiration, feeding at the eye,
And still unsated, dwelt upon the scene.
Thence with what pleasure have we just discern'd

The distant plough slow moving, and beside
His lab'ring team, that swerv'd not from the track,
The sturdy swain diminish'd to a boy!
Here Ouse, slow winding through a level plain
Of spacious meads with cattle sprinkled o'er,
Conducts the eye along its sinuous course
Delighted. There, fast rooted in their bank,
Stand, never overlook'd, our fav'rite elms,
That screen the herdsman's solitary hut;
While far beyond, and overthwart the stream
That, as with molten glass, inlays the vale,
The sloping land recedes into the clouds;
Displaying on its varied side the grace
Of hedge-row beauties numberless, square tow'r,
Tall spire, from which the sound of cheerful bells
Just undulates upon the list'ning ear,
Groves, heaths, and smoking villages, remote.
Scenes must be beautiful, which, daily view'd,
Please daily.

Like a landscape painter Cowper feeds his eye and sets forth
the objects before him in an orderly and rhythmical line. He
leaves out the painter's foreground, but gives details of the
middle distance (the ploughman and his laboring team, spacious meadows with cattle, the elms screening the herdsman's
hut) and of the far distance across the river (with hedge-rows,
square tower, tall spire, groves, heaths, and smoking villages
whence the sloping land recedes into the clouds). He tells us
several times over that the scene is beautiful and that he has
repeatedly viewed it with pleasure. Still he stands outside the
landscape. There is no identification of the living mind of the
poet with the objects of his picture. Wordsworth, on the other
hand, is often intimately involved in the landscape in a way
that neither Cowper nor any other eighteenth-century poet is.
This is evident in a passage describing birch woods resplendent in the early morning sunlight:

—How vast the compass of this theatre,
Yet nothing to be seen but lovely pomp
And silent majesty; the birch-tree woods
Are hung with thousand thousand diamond drops
Of melted hoar-frost, every tiny knot
In the bare twigs, each little budding-place
Cased with its several bead, what myriads there
Upon one tree, while all the distant grove
That rises to the summit of the steep
Shows like a mountain built of silver light.
See yonder the same pageant, and again
Behold the universal imagery
Inverted, all its sun-bright features touched
As with the varnish, and the gloss of dreams;
Dreamlike the blending also of the whole
Harmonious landscape; all along the shore
The boundary lost, the line invisible
That parts the image from reality;
And the clear hills, as high as they ascend
Heavenward, so piercing deep the lake below.

[The Recluse, I, 560–79]

As with Cowper, Wordsworth's eye ranges over the scene before him; but unlike Cowper, Wordsworth prepares no catalog
or inventory of what he sees. He selects those objects which
predominate and give emotional substance to the scene. These
he reports with a marvelous precision and accuracy. The parts
of the composition are clearly distinguished: the foreground
("birch-tree woods"); the middle distance ("grove that rises to
the summit of the steep"); and the far distance ("the clear
hills" ascending heavenwards). The world he describes is an
external, solid world of birch woods, groves upon the steeps,
and deep lake. Though no detailed description of landscape is
given, we are made aware of a landscape with depth and
space, harmoniously framed and centered. It is at the same
time a landscape that is intimately felt, that exists within the

mind. Wordsworth's paradoxical use of imagery serves him, as it often does, in good stead here. The "universal imagery" reflected in the lake is Nature's image-work; it belongs to the *real* world of the woods, hills, and so on. But by being inverted or mirrored in the lake it also becomes an *unreal* image. Dream-like it can cross the boundary in the mind, "the line invisible that parts the image from reality." By the double use of imagery Wordsworth establishes an interdependence, and an intellectual and emotional identity, of the outer and inner worlds. He is no mere painter of scenes but one who by a deep sympathy enters into the life of Nature and brings that life home in his poetry by the inspired selection of details, surcharged with metaphorical meanings that see into the life of things. The landscape does not simply remain "over there" against the eye. We are made to "feel" its presence as if it were a bodily experience.

Again and again in Wordsworth there is sympathetic involvement of Man and the physical world of Nature, as in *The Prelude* with the boy's (or man's) love of the sun:

> . . . a boy I loved the sun,
> Not as I since have loved him, as a pledge
> And surety of our earthly life, a light
> Which we behold and feel we are alive;
> Nor for his bounty to so many worlds—
> But for this cause, that I had seen him lay
> His beauty on the morning hills, had seen
> The western mountain touch his setting orb,
> In many a thoughtless hour, when, from excess
> Of happiness, my blood appeared to flow
> For its own pleasure, and I breathed with joy.
>
> [*The Prelude* (1805), II, 178–88]

The Prelude is filled with passages that further confirm the inextricable conjoining of man and Nature, and there are many other poems and passages throughout his works that do so. Indeed, the high argument for Wordsworth's *magnum opus* is no other than to affirm "How exquisitely the individual Mind/ . . . to the external World/ Is fitted:—and how exquisitely, too/ . . . The external World is fitted to the Mind." (*The Recluse*)

It must not be supposed, however, that all of Wordsworth's landscape descriptions deeply involve the participation of man or that they incorporate imaginative sympathy in equal measure. Just as he himself differentiated poems of "fancy" and poems of "imagination," so may we in classifying his poetry of natural scenery distinguish several levels. For a meaningful examination it will be helpful to select representative examples of his landscape poetry and arrange them roughly in an ascending order. Let us consider first representative examples of pictorial composition.

Scenes which Impress Themselves upon the Eye and Are Shaped into Some Sort of Pictorial Composition

"Ode" (1814) opens with a landscape "prospect" created by Fancy in a dream. It is a kind of idealized world of "intermingled pomp of vale and hill" more wonderful than even a Claude could paint. The parts of the scene described are well ordered and the whole brought into the focus of a mood of deep repose.

> When the soft hand of sleep had closed the latch
> On the tired household of corporeal sense,
> And Fancy, keeping unreluctant watch,
> Was free her choicest favours to dispense;
> I saw, in wondrous perspective displayed,
> A landscape more august than happiest skill
> Of pencil ever clothed with light and shade;
> An intermingled pomp of vale and hill,

City, and naval stream, suburban grove,
And stately forest where the wild deer rove;
Nor wanted lurking hamlet, dusky towns,
And scattered rural farms of aspect bright;
And, here and there, between the pastoral downs,
The azure sea upswelled upon the sight.
Fair prospect, such as Britain only shows!
But not a living creature could be seen
Through its wide circuit, that, in deep repose,
And, even to sadness, lonely and serene,
Lay hushed.

[vv. 1–19]

"Epistle to Sir George Beaumont" (1811) is a description of
Loughrigg Tarn such as a painter might execute, with a
"fancy" picture added in the reflections of the cottage that
Beaumont dreamed of building on its shore. Characteristically
the water image carries the poet in easy transfer from the real
world to the inner world of dreams.

Ah, Beaumont! when an opening in the road
Stopped me at once by charm of what it showed,
The encircling region vividly exprest
Within the mirror's depth, a world at rest—
Sky streaked with purple, grove and craggy *bield*,
And the smooth green of many a pendent field,
And, quieted and soothed, a torrent small,
A little daring would-be waterfall.
One chimney smoking and its azure wreath,
Associate all in the calm Pool beneath,
With here and there a faint imperfect gleam
Of water-lilies veiled in misty steam—
What wonder at this hour of stillness deep,
A shadowy link 'tween wakefulness and sleep,
When Nature's self, amid such blending, seems
To render visible her own soft dreams,
If, mixed with what appeared of rock, lawn, wood,

Fondly embosomed in the tranquil flood,
A glimpse I caught of that Abode, by Thee
Designed to rise in humble privacy,
A lowly Dwelling, here to be outspread,
Like a small Hamlet, with its bashful head
Half hid in native trees.

[vv. 171–93]

A scene described in *The Prelude,* Book X, is one that Wordsworth longed for skill to paint. It is composed as an artist would compose a picture with "foreground," an eye-picture of a picturesque ruin; "middle ground," a variegated crowd of travelers; and "background," the great sea at a distance. The mood is established as gentle and peaceful; the various features are skillfully selected and amplified with descriptive phrases.

As I advanced, all that I saw or felt
Was gentleness and peace. Upon a small
And rocky island near, a fragment stood
(Itself like a sea rock) the low remains
(With shells encrusted, dark with briny weeds)
Of a dilapidated structure, once
A Romish chapel, where the vested priest
Said matins at the hour that suited those
Who crossed the sands with ebb of morning tide.
Not far from that still ruin all the plain
Lay spotted with a variegated crowd
Of vehicles and travellers, horse and foot,
Wading beneath the conduct of their guide
In loose procession through the shallow stream
Of inland waters; the great sea meanwhile
Heaved at safe distance, far retired. I paused,
Longing for skill to paint a scene so bright
And cheerful.

[vv. 553–70]

Wordsworth admired light, changing or steady, and its complementary shadow in all their innumerable combinations. No English poet has dwelt so richly on the diverse effects of light and shadow upon the landscape. He has an instinct for strong contrasts; also an exquisite sense of subtle modulations. His recordings range from the beauty of the star-shaped shadow of the daisy upon the surface of a stone to the glorious pomp of massive light and shade ruled by the sovereign sun. To him the uprising sun was almost always associated with joy ("The sunshine is a glorious birth," *Ode on Immortality*). He dedicated himself to poetry when the eastern sky was kindling:

> Magnificent
> The morning rose, in memorable pomp,
> Glorious as e'er I had beheld—in front,
> The sea lay laughing at a distance; near,
> The solid mountains shone, bright as the clouds,
> Grain-tinctured, drenched in empyrean light;
> And in the meadows and the lower grounds
> Was all the sweetness of a common dawn.
>
> [*The Prelude*, Bk. IV, 323–30]

Momentous as was the dawn, Wordsworth loved the sunset and evening even better. The broadening of the setting sun, the shifting light accompanying it, and the sun's brightness on rocks never failed to interest him. Hazlitt reports in "My First Acquaintance with Poets" how Wordsworth, looking eastward at the close of the day, remarked, "How beautifully the sun sets on that yellow bank!" and thought within himself, "With what eyes these poets see nature!" Wordsworth also watched with delight the forms and hues of clouds as they changed before the setting sun. Stepping westward towards the radiant sky after sunset with the ground about him all gloomy seemed to him "A Kind of heavenly destiny" ("Stepping Westward").

He also admired the sun-bright landscape seen in softened perspective from a shady room (*Excursion,* VIII). In the scene which opens *The Excursion* (Bk. I) he offers a pictorial rendering of the shadow-dappled landscape set off in fine perspective by the cave's enclosure. An independent life animates natural objects and impregnates them with emotional tones. The clouds are *brooding,* the sunshine is *bright* and *pleasant,* the covert is *impending.* The repetition of "pleasant" as applied to sunshine and in the following line "pleasant" as applied to the observer himself reclining on the "soft cool moss" facilitates the transfer from outward to inward vision and the creation of images in the mind. His placement of himself within the cave and as in a half-conscious, dreaming mood further aids in the poetic construction of the scene. The huge cave that "casts a twilight of its own" adds a semi-ominous note to set off by contrast the cloud-spotted, pleasant landscape prospect.

> 'Twas summer, and the sun had mounted high:
> Southward the landscape indistinctly glared
> Through a pale steam; but all the northern downs,
> In clearest air ascending, showed far off
> A surface dappled o'er with shadows flung
> From brooding clouds; shadows that lay in spots
> Determined and unmoved, with steady beams
> Of bright and pleasant sunshine interposed;
> To him most pleasant who on soft cool moss
> Extends his careless limbs along the front
> Of some huge cave, whose rocky ceiling casts
> A twilight of its own, an ample shade,
> Where the wren warbles, while the dreaming man,
> Half conscious of the soothing melody,
> With side-long eye looks out upon the scene,
> By power of that impending covert thrown
> To finer distance.
>
> [vv. 1–17]

*Scenes in which Pictorial Features are Blended
or Translated to Establish the Poetic Mood*

Five examples of many that might be offered will show how
Wordsworth can create the poetic spirit of a place or scene and
set it off. The first of these is "Airey-Force Valley." The mood
is soothing solitude in the peaceful glen animated by the "soft
eye-music" of the pendent ash tree. As he often does, Wordsworth chooses language that describes human conditions and
emotions and impregnates natural and inanimate objects with
them. He speaks of the *bosom* of the leaf glen, the trees *stead-
fast* as the rocks, "a little breeze, perchance/ Escaped from
boisterous winds that *rage without*," the light ash *sensitive* to
the wind's *gentle touch*. The dominant mood of silent peaceful-
ness is enhanced by contrasting the undulating ash with the
sturdy oaks and the *raging* winds. A "soft eye-music" also sets
up an inner mental response of unheard melodies more sweet
than any external sound.

> —Not a breath of air
> Ruffles the bosom of this leafy glen.
> From the brook's margin, wide around, the trees
> Are steadfast as the rocks; the brook itself,
> Old as the hills that feed it from afar,
> Doth rather deepen than disturb the calm
> Where all things else are still and motionless.
> And yet, even now, a little breeze, perchance
> Escaped from boisterous winds that rage without,
> Has entered, by the sturdy oaks unfelt,
> But to its gentle touch how sensitive
> Is the light ash! that, pendent from the brow
> Of yon dim cave, in seeming silence makes
> A soft eye-music of slow-waving boughs,
> Powerful almost as vocal harmony
> To stay the wanderer's steps and soothe his thoughts.

Another of these sketches is from "Fidelity," in which Wordsworth concentrates the melancholy feelings aroused in the presence of a mountain tarn. He states in *A Guide to the Lakes* that a tarn is an object in Nature that forms in the mind of the observer "a centre or conspicuous point to which objects, otherwise disconnected or insubordinated, may be referred." He observes also a kind of perplexity that is induced by the tarn's physical appearance and its location and the solemn sense of solitude, "desolate and forbidding," that is impressed upon one there. "The imagination," he says, "is tempted to attribute a voluntary power to every change which takes place in such a spot." So the scene is animated in the poetic description, and all things are brought into the circle of the dominant tone of boding melancholy.

> It was a cove, a huge recess,
> That keeps, till June, December's snow;
> A lofty precipice in front,
> A silent tarn below!
> Far in the bosom of Helvellyn,
> Remote from public road or dwelling,
> Pathway, or cultivated land;
> From trace of human foot or hand.
> There sometimes doth a leaping fish
> Send through the tarn a lonely cheer;
> The crags repeat the raven's croak,
> In symphony austere;
> Thither the rainbow comes—the cloud—
> And mists that spread the flying shroud;
> And sunbeams; and the sounding blast,
> That, if it could, would hurry past;
> But that enormous barrier holds it fast.
>
> [vv. 17–33]

Reflections in the crystal-clear waters of the northern lakes were a constant delight to Wordsworth, and accounts of them frequently appear in his poetry. A sonnet "Composed by the Side of Grasmere Lake" (1807) takes us to the moment of twilight when the planets and stars are first beauteously revealed in mirror-smooth Grasmere Lake. Jupiter, Venus, and ruddy Mars, personified and individualized, shimmer in the abyss of the dark waters. Their reflections, being insubstantial, easily identify themselves with the imagery of the mind and with thoughts tranquil and spiritual. The living presence of the natural scene stirs in the voice of Great Pan himself "low-whispering" words of comfort and peace to mortals.

> Clouds, lingering yet, extend in solid bars
> Through the grey west; and lo! these waters, steeled
> By breezeless air to smoothest polish, yield
> A vivid repetition of the stars;
> Jove, Venus, and the ruddy crest of Mars
> Amid his fellows beauteously revealed
> At happy distance from earth's groaning field,
> Where ruthless mortals wage incessant wars.
> Is it a mirror?—or the nether Sphere
> Opening to view the abyss in which she feeds
> Her own calm fires?—But list! a voice is near;
> Great Pan himself low-whispering through the reeds,
> "Be thankful, thou; for, if unholy deeds
> Ravage the world, tranquility is here!"

Wordsworth heard and felt the stirrings of Nature's voices in the Langdale Pikes (*The Excursion*, Book II). Chiefly they speak when the storm rides high and the wind draws forth the wild concert from rocks, woods, caverns, and heaths; theirs, too, is the song of roaring cataract and echoing thunder. But more subtly they also have power

> . . . to yield
> Music of a finer tone; a harmony,
> So do I call it, though it be the hand
> Of silence, though there be no voice.

Animated by clouds, mists, shadows, motions of moonlight, setting suns, and stars in the blue vault, the Langdale Pikes have
a life of their own which even in silence stirs mute voices that
vibrate silently in the heart of man. The silent harmonics of
sight are transposed by the imagination to the inner, unheard
melodies of sound. A similar transposition is performed in
"Airey-Force Valley" ("The soft eye-music of slow-waving
boughs"), but the one on Langdale Pikes is more impressive
and on a more extended scale. Not only are pictorial features
of the mountains blended and harmonized to establish the poetic mood, but the busy stirrings of Nature are apprehended
through a multifold working of the imagination to the end that
all together they "shape a language not unwelcome to sick
hearts and idle spirits."

> Many are the notes
> Which, in his tuneful course, the wind draws forth
> From rocks, woods, caverns, heaths, and dashing shores;
> And well those lofty brethren bear their part
> In the wild concert—chiefly when the storm
> Rides high; then all the upper air they fill
> With roaring sound, that ceases not to flow,
> Like smoke, along the level of the blast,
> In mighty current; theirs, too, is the song
> Of stream and headlong flood that seldoms fails;
> And, in the grim and breathless hour of noon,
> Methinks that I have heard them echo back
> The thunder's greeting. Nor have nature's laws
> Left them ungifted with a power to yield
> Music of finer tone; a harmony,
> So do I call it, though it be the hand
> Of silence, though there be no voice;—the clouds,
> The mist, the shadows, light of golden suns,
> Motions of moonlight, all come thither—touch,
> And have an answer—thither come, and shape
> A language not unwelcome to sick hearts

And idle spirits:—there the sun himself,
At the calm close of summer's longest day,
Rests his substantial orb;—between those heights
And on the top of either pinnacle,
More keenly than elsewhere in night's blue vault,
Sparkle the stars, as of their station proud.
Thoughts are not busier in the mind of man
Than the mute agents stirring there:—alone
Here do I sit and watch.

[vv. 696–725]

The preëminence of interest held by painters at the turn of
the century in architectural remains and historical buildings of
various sorts was shared by Wordsworth and used by him to
good purpose. He was instinctively attracted to the beauty of
line and contour in the "lovely majesty of ruined halls" and has
left us fine poetical accounts of the ruins at Cockermouth,
Brougham, Carnarvon, Roslin, Furness, Kilchurn, and many
others. With respect to these ancient buildings he sees Antiquity working as sister and copartner with the Spirit of Nature.
Upon the ruins of a castle in North Wales, Time and Nature
work hand in hand to offer it "a soothing recompense":

Relic of Kings! Wreck of forgotten wars,
To winds abandoned and the prying stars,
Time *loves* Thee! at his call the Seasons twine
Luxuriant wreaths around thy forehead hoar;
And, though past pomp no changes can restore,
A soothing recompense, his gift, is thine!

["A Castle in North Wales," vv. 9–14]

At Furness Abbey he regards Nature as both beautifier and
renewer of the mouldering walls of the ancient ruin:

Here, where, of havoc tired and rash undoing,
Man left this Structure to become Time's prey,
A soothing spirit follows in the way

That Nature takes, her counter-work pursuing.
See how her Ivy clasps the sacred Ruin,
Fall to prevent or beautify decay;
And, on the mouldered walls, how bright, how gay,
The flowers in pearly dews their bloom renewing!

["Furness Abbey," vv. 1–8]

Perhaps the finest example of Wordsworth's tributes to historic ruins is his "Address to Kilchurn Castle." Dorothy in her *Recollections of a Tour Made in Scotland* tells of the impressive scene that opened to their view:

—a ruined Castle on an Island (for an Island the flood had made it) at some distance from the shore, backed by a Cove of the Mountain Cruachan, down which came a foaming stream. The Castle occupied every foot of the Island that was visible to us, appearing to rise out of the water,—mists rested upon the mountain side, with spots of sunshine; there was a mild desolation in the low grounds, a solemn grandeur in the mountains, and the Castle was wild, yet stately—not dismantled of turrets—nor the walls broken down, though obviously a ruin.

Her description records the salient features of the setting and the atmospheric conditions that render the ruin picturesque. It is a notation or sketch such as an artist might make for future use. Wordsworth's imagination kindled, and he composed the opening three lines of his poem on the spot; the remainder he wrote a number of years afterwards, no doubt after being prompted to recollection by Dorothy's journal entry. The poet does not disregard pictorial aspects of the scene, but they are transposed into the service of an imaginative vision. In his poem Wordsworth pictures the castle ruins, once a seat of ominous and honored power, now silent in age, but momentarily restored by Nature in the presence of the roaring mountain stream to the turbulence of honored defence and majesty. Even the mountain that backs the castle suspends his claims as sovereign lord in favor of the majestic ruin:

KILCHURN CASTLE at Loch Awe, Scotland
N. R. Farbman, LIFE Magazine © Time Inc.

                                                        . . . submitting
All that the God of Nature hath conferred,
All that he holds in common with the stars,
To the memorial majesty of Time
Impersonated in thy calm decay!

                                                        [vv. 17–21]

To the pomp and beauty of all Nature which pay homage to
the castle are joined the willing admiration and respect of the
two young travelers. The paradox of silence and turbulence
moves effectively through the entire poem from its arresting
opening—"Child of loud-throated War! . . . silent in thy age"
—to the muted close where "battles long ago" are as silent
now as the foaming flood beyond the castle, motionless as ice,
frozen by distance. All features of the scene are richly laid in
tribute by the poet to honor the ruined castle's honored past.

Child of loud-throated War! the mountain Stream
Roars in thy hearing; but thy hour of rest
Is come, and thou art silent in thy age;
Save when the wind sweeps by and sounds are caught
Ambiguous, neither wholly thine nor theirs.
Oh! there is life that breathes not; Powers there are
That touch each other to the quick in modes
Which the gross world no sense hath to perceive,
No soul to dream of. What art Thou, from care
Cast off—abandoned by thy rugged Sire,
Nor by soft Peace adopted; though, in place
And in dimension, such that thou might'st seem
But a mere footstool to yon sovereign Lord,
Huge Cruachan, (a thing that meaner hills
Might crush, nor know that it had suffered harm;)
Yet he, not loth, in favour of thy claims
To reverence, suspends his own; submitting
All that the God of Nature hath conferred,
All that he holds in common with the stars,
To the memorial majesty of Time

Impersonated in thy calm decay!
Take, then, thy seat, Vicegerent unreproved!
Now, while a farewell gleam of evening light
Is fondly lingering on thy shattered front,
Do thou, in turn, be paramount; and rule
Over the pomp and beauty of a scene
Whose mountains, torrents, lake, and woods, unite
To pay thee homage; and with these are joined,
In willing admiration and respect,
Two Hearts, which in thy presence might be called
Youthful as Spring.—Shade of departed Power,
Skeleton of unfleshed humanity,
The chronicle were welcome that should call
Into the compass of distinct regard
The toils and struggles of thy infant years!
Yon foaming flood seems motionless as ice;
Its dizzy turbulence eludes the eye,
Frozen by distance; so, majestic Pile,
To the perception of this Age, appear
Thy fierce beginnings, softened and subdued
And quieted in character—the strife,
The pride, the fury uncontrollable,
Lost on the aërial heights of the Crusades!

Scenes in which the Pictorial Essences of the Landscape are Drawn into a Heightened Poetic Unity

The basis for much that is illuminating in Wordsworth's poetic representation of the landscape is put forward in Coleridge's *Essay on the Fine Arts:* "The sense of beauty subsists in the simultaneous intuitive of the relation of parts each to each, and of all to the whole." Three selections from his work will show how in varying degrees this aesthetic principle is borne out. In all three we have Dorothy Wordsworth's journal entry with which to compare Wordsworth's poetic record of identical scenes. The first is a poem descriptive of the sights and sounds they saw and heard at Brother's Water on 16 April 1802. Dorothy lists them quite matter-of-factly thus:

There was the gentle flowing of the stream, the glittering, lively lake, green fields without a living creature to be seen on them; behind us a flat pasture with 42 cattle feeding. . . . The people were at work ploughing, harrowing, and sowing; lasses working, a dog barking now and then; cocks crowing, birds twittering; the snow in patches at the top of the highest hills. . . .

Contrary to his usual practice, Wordsworth set to work immediately and finished his poem before they reached the foot of Kirkstone. It is not an ambitious or profound piece, but it does successfully capture the poetic essence of "Spring is Come!" Amidst all the diversity of the scene—some parts in motion, others at rest—Wordsworth sets up an intuitive relationship of parts each to the other in the joy and life and freshness of the moment. The poetic faculty only half-creates, one might say, in this piece; but the rippling double rimes with falling accent and the spontaneous overflow of joyous spirit successfully render the scene and the feelings that it evokes. Wordsworth places it significantly with "Poems of the Imagination."

> The Cock is crowing,
> The stream is flowing,
> The small birds twitter,
> The lake doth glitter,
> The green field sleeps in the sun;
> The oldest and youngest
> Are at work with the strongest;
> The cattle are grazing,
> Their heads never raising;
> There are forty feeding like one!

> Like an army defeated
> The snow hath retreated,
> And now doth fare ill
> On the top of the bare hill;
> The Ploughboy is whooping—anon—anon:
> There's joy in the mountains;
> There's life in the fountains;
> Small clouds are sailing,
> Blue sky prevailing;
> The rain is over and gone!

A second poem is the famous one on the daffodils, which William and Dorothy saw with delight one windy day as they were passing through Gowbarrow Park along the shore of Lake Ullswater. Dorothy records the occasion as follows:

We saw a few daffodils close to the water-side. . . . But as we went along there were more and yet more; and at last, under the boughs of the trees, we saw that there was a long belt of them along the shore, about the breadth of a country turnpike road. I never saw daffodils so beautiful. They grew among the mossy stones about and about them; some rested their heads upon these stones as on a pillow for weariness; and the rest tossed and reeled and danced, and seemed as if they verily laughed with the wind, that blew upon them over the lake; they looked so gay, ever glancing, ever changing. This wind blew directly over the lake to them. There was here and there a little knot, and a few stragglers . . . higher up, but they were so few as not to disturb the simplicity, unity, and life of that one busy highway.

Grasmere Journal (15 April 1801)

Wordsworth did not compose upon their joyously shared experience until several years afterwards (c. 1804), and in 1815 he appended this note by way of explanation: "The subject of these Stanzas is rather an elementary feeling and simple impression (approaching the nature of an ocular spectrum) upon the imaginative faculty, than an *exertion* of it." In her journal passage on the daffodils Dorothy has made use of her imagination. She has endowed the daffodils with human attributes— "some rested their heads upon these stones as on a pillow for weariness; and the rest tossed and reeled and danced, and seemed as if they verily laughed with the wind." She likens the long belt of them along the shore to a busy highway of jostling people with "here and there a little knot, and a few stragglers" that in no way disturb the simplicity and unity of the show. In all of Dorothy's many recordings of the sights and sounds of Nature none surpasses the touch of creative magic she displays here. When her brother set out to make a poem on their adventure, he had his work cut out for him. What he does is to intensify the immediacy of the experience by confining it to his own person and to dramatize it by heightening the sense of sudden discovery. At the moment of revelation the wind was blowing over the lake directly on all that was before it, awakening the waves and the crowd of daffodils into agitated motion. When Wordsworth recalled the original experience, perhaps through reading Dorothy's account of it, his tranquility was stirred by the awakening of the creative spirit which, even as the wind gave life to external Nature, gave to the "forms and images" living in his memory "a breath and everlasting motion." The memory of the physical wind (which was the central driving force in the original experience) that blew upon his body as well as upon all else in the scene seems to have been the prime factor in rousing his imagination and keeping it roused during the creative act. It is the wind's action which draws all parts of the composition together and relates them to the whole. It is the breath which in the climax of recollection fills his heart with pleasure and sets it to dancing with the daffodils. There is a similar instance of the wind's creative force in the opening of *The Prelude,* where Wordsworth tells of the blessing he felt "in the gentle breeze/ That blows from the green fields and from the clouds/ And from

the sky" when he strode from the city's bondage a free
man. It seemed to him on that occasion that while the sweet
breath of heaven was blowing on his body he

> . . . felt within
> A correspondent breeze, that gently moved
> With quickening virtue, . . . a redundant energy,
> Vexing its own creation.[6]

Though the subject of the daffodil stanzas is, as Wordsworth
reminds us, rather an elementary and primarily an ocular impression, it is worth noting that the imaginative recording of
it draws upon a complex physiological response that involves
the whole of his being.

> I wandered lonely as a cloud
> That floats on high o'er vales and hills,
> When all at once I saw a crowd,
> A host, of golden daffodils;
> Beside the lake, beneath the trees,
> Fluttering and dancing in the breeze.
>
> Continuous as the stars that shine
> And twinkle on the milky way,
> They stretched in never-ending line
> Along the margin of a bay:
> Ten thousand saw I at a glance,
> Tossing their heads in sprightly dance.
>
> The waves beside them danced; but they
> Out-did the sparkling waves in glee:
> A poet could not but be gay,
> In such a jocund company:
> I gazed—and gazed—but little thought
> What wealth the show to me had brought:
>
> For oft, when on my couch I lie
> In vacant or in pensive mood,
> They flash upon that inward eye

Which is the bliss of solitude;
And then my heart with pleasure fills,
And dances with the daffodils.

Our third poem is "To a Highland Girl," which Wordsworth wrote not long after his and Dorothy's return from Scotland in 1803. He says that his sister described "this delightful creature and her demeanor particularly" in her *Journal.* Dorothy tells of two girls rather than one and of the bustling activity in and around the ferry-house on Loch Lochmond:

When beginning to descend the hill towards Loch Lomond, we overtook two girls, who told us we could not cross the ferry till evening. . . . One of the girls was exceedingly beautiful; and the figures of both of them, in grey plaids falling to their feet, their faces only being uncovered, excited our attention before we spoke to them; and they answered us so sweetly that we were quite delighted, at the same time that they stared at us with an innocent look of wonder. . . . The hut was after the Highland fashion, but without anything beautiful except its situation. . . . The peep out of the open door-place across the lake made some amends. . . . The bay . . . was all in motion with small waves, while the swoln waterfall roared in our ears. . . . At this day the innocent merriment of the girls, with their kindness to us, and the beautiful figure and face of the elder, come to my mind whenever I think of the ferry-house and waterfall of Loch Lomond, and I never think of the two girls but the whole image of that romantic spot is before me, a living image as it will be to my dying day.

Wordsworth in his poem keeps rather close to the actual conditions of the original experience as recorded by Dorothy, except that to achieve greater unity of impression he concentrates upon the elder of the two girls, the one who was remarkable for her exceeding beauty. It is perhaps stretching our categories to place "To a Highland Girl" among the landscape poems. Wordsworth does not dwell upon the scene as such; yet he does centrally associate the girl with the romantic spot of the ferry-house by the lake. She is in a very special way part of the ocular experience—she is the unifying center in a conflux of images, enlivened by merriment, mellowed by kindness, but made unforgettable and radiant through beauty. The poet has no more claim upon her as a person than as "a wave of the wild sea." Imaginative re-creation transforms the memory of her to visionary loveliness, "heavenly bright," such as one might envisage in a dream. Yet she also belongs, "in the light of common day," to that scene of grey rocks, household lawn, half-veiling trees, waterfall, silent bay, and the quiet road by the cabin. Like the skylark she is "true to the kindred points of heaven and of home."

> Sweet Highland Girl, a very shower
> Of beauty is thy earthly dower!
> Twice seven consenting years have shed
> Their utmost bounty on thy head:
> And these grey rocks; that household lawn;
> Those trees, a veil just half withdrawn;
> This fall of water that doth make
> A murmur near the silent lake;
> This little bay; a quiet road
> That holds in shelter thy Abode—
> In truth together do ye seem
> Like something fashioned in a dream;
> Such Forms as from their covert peep
> When earthly cares are laid asleep!
> But, O fair Creature! in the light
> Of common day, so heavenly bright,
> I bless Thee, Vision as thou art,
> I bless thee with a human heart;
> God shield thee to thy latest years!
> Thee, neither know I, nor thy peers;
> And yet my eyes are filled with tears.

✿   ✿   ✿

Now thanks to Heaven! that of its grace
Hath led me to this lonely place.
Joy have I had; and going hence
I bear away my recompense.
In spots like these it is we prize
Our Memory, feel that she hath eyes:
Then, why should I be loth to stir?
I feel this place was made for her;
To give new pleasure like the past,
Continued long as life shall last.
Nor am I loth, though pleased at heart,
Sweet Highland Girl! from thee to part;
For I, methinks, till I grow old,
As fair before me shall behold,
As I do now, the cabin small,
The lake, the bay, the waterfall;
And Thee, the Spirit of them all!

[vv. 1–21, 62–78]

Scenes which are Read as Symbols-Translucent of the Moral and Spiritual World

Wordsworth was ever ready to see spiritual truths mirrored in the face of Nature, to read sermons in stones. He was one with Coleridge who said: "It is the poetry of all human life, to read the book of Nature in a figurative sense, and to find therein correspondences and symbols of the spiritual world." Wordsworth felt the presence of deity in "the light of setting suns" and often recovered symbols-translucent of the creator in the glowing clouds of sunset. One evening as he traveled over the sands of Leven's estuary, he beheld and was enrapt by a celestial spectacle. He does not offer in his *Prelude* sketch a theological interpretation of the heavenly display as he was afterwards to do in *The Excursion*. Even so, the clouds in "one

inseparable glory clad" are "Creatures of one ethereal substance met/ In consistory, like a diadem/ Or crown of burning
seraphs." As de Selincourt points out, the language rings with
Miltonic echoes.

> Over the smooth sands
> Of Leven's ample estuary lay
> My journey, and beneath a genial sun
> With distant prospect among gleams of sky
> And clouds, and intermingling mountain-tops,
> In one inseparable glory clad,
> Creatures of one ethereal substance met
> In consistory, like a diadem
> Or crown of burning seraphs as they sit
> In the empyrean. Underneath that pomp
> Celestial, lay unseen the pastoral vales
> Among whose happy fields I had grown up
> From childhood. On the fulgent spectacle,
> That neither passed away nor changed, I gazed
> Enrapt.
>
> [*The Prelude*, X, 514–28]

A glorious apparition in clouds seen by Wordsworth and Sir
George Beaumont was translated into poetry in the second
book of *The Excursion* and presented there as the abode of
Spirits revealed in vision. The circumstances of the original
heavenly display and the poet's response to it are given in an
unpublished letter of Beaumont's (printed here with the kind
permission of the Trustees of Dove Cottage):

I verily think the vision near the end of the 2ᵈ book is the fairest
flower of British poesy—it perfectly fascinates me—Pray tell me if
it was not suggested by that marvellous effect we saw in returning
thro Patterdale amongst the mountains of Ullswater—Into every
crevice & hollow of the hills the clouds poured in profusion, & no
shape regular or fantastic, no colour brilliant or solemn no light
splendid or aweful, was omitted by the setting sun in that glorious

display—I remember you were struck dumb for an hour at least, &
then you told me words might do little but not much in describing
it—you have proved yourself mistaken.

(30 November 1814)

The features of the scene as they are described in *The Excursion* carry thought and feeling forward to the visionary climax.

> . . . when a step,
> A single step, that freed me from the skirts
> Of the blind vapour, opened to my view
> Glory beyond all glory ever seen
> By waking sense or by the dreaming soul!
> The appearance, instantaneously disclosed,
> Was of a mighty city—boldly say
> A wilderness of building, sinking far
> And self-withdrawn into a boundless depth,
> Far sinking into splendour—without end!
> Fabric it seemed of diamond and of gold,
> With alabaster domes, and silver spires,
> And blazing terrace upon terrace, high
> Uplifted; here, serene pavilions bright,
> In avenues disposed; there, towers begirt
> With battlements that on their restless fronts
> Bore stars—illumination of all gems!
> By earthly nature had the effect been wrought
> Upon the dark materials of the storm
> Now pacified; on them, and on the coves
> And mountain-steeps and summits, whereunto
> The vapours had receded, taking there
> Their station under a cerulean sky.
> Oh, 'twas an unimaginable sight!
> Clouds, mists, streams, watery rocks and emerald
>   turf,
> Clouds of all tincture, rocks and sapphire sky,
> Confused, commingled, mutually inflamed,
> Molten together, and composing thus,

Each lost in each, that marvellous array
Of temple, palace, citadel, and huge
Fantastic pomp of structure without name,
In fleecy folds voluminous, enwrapped.
Right in the midst, where interspace appeared
Of open court, an object like a throne
Under a shining canopy of state
Stood fixed; and fixed resemblances were seen
To implements of ordinary use,
But vast in size, in substance glorified;
Such as by Hebrew Prophets were beheld
In vision—forms uncouth of mightiest power
For admiration and mysterious awe.
This little Vale, a dwelling-place of Man,
Lay low beneath my feet; 'twas visible—
I saw not, but I felt that it was there.
That which I *saw* was the revealed abode
Of Spirits in beatitude: my heart
Swelled in my breast.—"I have been dead," I cried,
"And now I live! Oh! wherefore *do* I live?"
And with that pang I prayed to be no more!—

[II, 829–77]

Another sunset scene in *The Excursion*, Book IX, is read by
the Pastor as the "effluence" of "Eternal Spirit! universal God!"
The priest and his companions at the close of day have seated
themselves on the hillside above Grasmere Valley to enjoy the
fair prospect. The sun has dropped behind the western moun-
taintops, but its slanting rays transform "multitudes of little
floating clouds" into forms "vivid as fire" and "Scattered
through half the circle of the sky." What the heavens display,
the clear waters of the lake repeat and unify. The Pastor inter-
prets these symbols as "radiant Cherubim" who in highest
heaven fill with pomp the courts of "imperishable majesty." In
an earlier period of his career Wordsworth would have let the
metaphoric language stand by itself, without the heavy ser-

monizing of the Pastor. Such phrases as the poet uses in the descriptive passage seem wholly adequate to render its deeper meaning. In the following excerpt the theological effusions that were perhaps palatable to the Victorians are omitted in deference to the modern reader:

> Already had the sun,
> Sinking with less than ordinary state,
> Attained his western bound; but rays of light—
> Now suddenly diverging from the orb
> Retired behind the mountain-tops or veiled
> By the dense air—shot upwards to the crown
> Of the blue firmament—aloft, and wide:
> And multitudes of little floating clouds,
> Through their ethereal texture pierced—ere we,
> Who saw, of change were conscious—had become
> Vivid as fire; clouds separately poised,—
> Innumerable multitude of forms
> Scattered through half the circle of the sky;
> And giving back, and shedding each on each,
> With prodigal communion, the bright hues
> Which from the unapparent fount of glory
> They had imbibed, and ceased not to receive.
> That which the heavens displayed, the liquid deep
> Repeated; but with unity sublime! . . .
> We gazed, in silence hushed, with eyes intent
> On the refulgent spectacle, diffused
> Through earth, sky, water, and all visible space.
>
> [vv. 590–612]

Throughout his life Wordsworth was enthralled by the beauty, majesty, and antiquity of living trees. In chapter three an account was given of the poet's concern to protect from the lumberman's axe the trees that grew in the neighborhood of Rydal Mount; also, of how he assisted his neighbors in tree planting and how he himself planted many fine specimens, some of which are still standing. His affectionate attachment to trees is expressed in various places, including *A Guide to the Lakes* and in a number of poems. Several poetical accounts of trees are worthy of special comment. "Nutting" tells of the feelings he had as a boy in a grove of hazels: first luxuriating his mood in anticipation of the uncontested harvest of the tempting clusters of hazelnuts; then of his exultation in mercilessly ravaging branch and bough; finally of his sense of pain when, beholding the silent trees and intruding sky, he was awed and humbled before the living spirit in the woods. In *The Prelude* he describes a single ash tree that grew in the college yard at Cambridge, with sinuous trunk and "boughs exquisitely wreathed." From the ground almost to the top

> The trunk and every master branch were green
> With clustering ivy, and the lightsome twigs
> And outer spray profusely tipped with seeds
> That hung in yellow tassels, while the air
> Stirred them, not voiceless.

[VI, 81–85]

Wordsworth tells us that often on winter nights when he stood foot-bound looking upward at that lovely tree beaneath a frosty moon, "scarcely Spenser's self/Could have more tranquil visions in his youth" than he beheld alone beneath that "fairy work of earth." Homer in *The Odyssey* compares the wonderment Odysseus felt in beholding the beauty of the princess Nausicaa with that of seeing a fresh young palm tree shooting up by the altar of Apollo. So Wordsworth in *The Excursion* cites the mountain ash as the object in Nature whose beauty in its station is worthy by comparison to enhance the rustic youth in whom a scholar's genius shone and the spirit of a hero walked.

> The Mountain-ash
> No eye can overlook, when 'mid a grove

Of yet unfaded trees she lifts her head
Decked with autumnal berries, that outshine
Spring's richest blossoms; and ye may
    have marked,
By a brook-side or solitary tarn,
How she her station doth adorn: the pool
Glows at her feet, and all the gloomy rocks
Are brightened round her. In his native vale
Such and so glorious did this Youth appear.

                    [VII, 714–23]

But no expression of Wordsworth's response to trees is more magnificent than that found in "Yew-Trees." He begins by describing the fine old yew, the pride of Lorton Vale, of such antiquity that it could have furnished weapons for Harry Percy's army when they marched against the Scotch, or supplied bows for the archers at Agincourt nearly four hundred years before, or even earlier for the bowmen at Crécy or Poictiers. This solitary yew is "of vast circumference and gloom profound" and of form and aspect too magnificent ever to be destroyed. But of still worthier note are the fraternal Four of Borrowdale. In contemplating them Wordsworth's imagination is roused to high action, and he reads in them symbols-translucent of the spiritual world—not the spirit world of Christian faith, but the world of prehistoric pagan antiquity. Wordsworth nowhere surpassed his expression of the awesome spirit of ancient mysteries beyond that revealed in the umbrageous presence of the fraternal yews of Borrowdale. In *Modern Painters* Ruskin calls "Yew-Trees" "the most vigorous and solemn bit of forest landscape ever painted." Wordsworth himself placed it among the poems of imagination.

There is a Yew-tree, pride of Lorton Vale,
Which to this day stands single, in the midst
Of its own darkness, as it stood of yore:

Not loth to furnish weapons for the bands
Of Umfraville or Percy ere they marched
To Scotland's heaths; or those that crossed the sea
And drew their sounding bows at Azincour,
Perhaps at earlier Crecy, or Poictiers.
Of vast circumference and gloom profound
This solitary Tree! a living thing
Produced too slowly ever to decay;
Of form and aspect too magnificent
To be destroyed. But worthier still of note
Are those fraternal Four of Borrowdale,
Joined in one solemn and capacious grove;
Huge trunks! and each particular trunk a growth
Of intertwisted fibres serpentine
Up-coiling, and inveterately convolved;
Nor uninformed with Phantasy, and looks
That threaten the profane; a pillared shade,
Upon whose grassless floor of red-brown hue,
By sheddings from the pining umbrage tinged
Perennially—beneath whose sable roof
Of boughs, as if for festal purpose decked
With unrejoicing berries—ghostly Shapes
May meet at noontide; Fear and trembling Hope,
Silence and Foresight; Death the Skeleton
And Time the Shadow;—there to celebrate,
As in a natural temple scattered o'er
With altars undisturbed of mossy stone,
United worship; or in mute repose
To lie, and listen to the mountain flood
Murmuring from Glaramara's inmost caves.

Scenes in which the Landscape Acts upon Man so that the Human Interest Is Central

In his early years when Nature was sovereign in his mind
Wordsworth sometimes described the scenes before him for

their own sake. But later, having recovered from a period of depression and come into the full possession of his powers of imagination, he felt again the close relationship between the landscape and humanity. Henceforth hills and vales, streams and sounding cataracts, birds and flowers, and all the beauty of the natural world of which he wrote take on significance only as man becomes involved with them. His theme is "No other than the very heart of Man." In a letter to Wilson (June, 1802) he stated: "No human being can be utterly insensible to the natural world around him." Some who are insensible are corrected, such as Peter Bell and the Ancient Mariner. Some, like the brutish boy in *The Excursion* (VIII, 402–33), can never be shaken from their torpor. There has to be an inner response to "the fostering hand" of Nature and the "penetrating power of sun and breeze." Indeed, most of the characters in Wordsworth's poetry do respond positively to the shaping power of Nature where that power is given an opportunity to work. All readers of Wordsworth will recall the deep and irradicable influence of the landscape upon Michael:

> And grossly that man errs, who should suppose
> That the green valleys, and the streams and rocks,
> Were things indifferent to the Shepherd's thoughts.
> Fields, where with cheerful spirits he had breathed
> The common air; hills, which with vigorous step
> He had so often climbed; which had impressed
> So many incidents upon his mind
> Of hardship, skill or courage, joy or fear;
> Which, like a book, preserved the memory
> Of the dumb animals, whom he had saved,
> Had fed or sheltered, linking to such acts
> The certainty of honourable gain;
> Those fields, those hills—what could they less? had laid
> Strong hold on his affections, were to him

A pleasurable feeling of blind love,
The pleasure which there is in life itself.

[vv. 62–77]

To Lucy, Nature was "both law and impulse" and made of her
"a Lady of her own." And so with many another character and
human situation in his poetry, Wordsworth, the worshipper of
Nature, shows himself to be in reality a teacher of a saving
communion of man with Nature, a lover of his fellowmen, and
a sensitive reporter of "the still sad music of humanity."

In "The Reverie of Poor Susan" the central cluster of images
constituting the vision of Susan make up a country scene, yet
the meaning of the poem turns upon the realities of the human
situation. Through emotionally charged association with the
song of the caged thrush heard by "Poor Susan" in the silence
of the morning in London's street, the forms and images of her
country home from which she has long been separated rise in
her mind. She looks upon the beauteous scene before her restored as if by a miracle, and "her heart is in heaven." And
then as quickly as the vision has come, it fades away. Wordsworth in no way sentimentalizes upon Susan or her situation.
Yet with a deeply perceptive charity, he opens our hearts to
understanding and sympathy.

At the corner of Wood Street, when daylight appears,
Hangs a Thrush that sings loud, it has sung for
    three years:
Poor Susan has passed by the spot, and has heard
In the silence of morning the song of the Bird.

'Tis a note of enchantment; what ails her? She sees
A mountain ascending, a vision of trees;
Bright volumes of vapour through Lothbury glide,
And a river flows on through the vale of Cheapside.

Green pastures she views in the midst of the dale,
Down which she so often has tripped with her pail;

And a single small cottage, a nest like a dove's,
The one only dwelling on earth that she loves.

She looks, and her heart is in heaven: but they fade,
The mist and the river, the hill and the shade:
The stream will not flow, and the hill will not rise,
And the colours have all passed away from her eyes!

Another poem in which the human interest is central is "The Solitary Reaper," which Wordsworth composed not from a recollection of the song of the Highland girl, as might be supposed, but from reading the following sentence in Thomas Wilkinson's *Tour in Scotland*: "Passed a female who was reaping alone: she sung in Erse, as she bended over her sickle; the sweetest human voice I ever heard: her strains were tenderly melancholy, and felt delicious, long after they were heard no more." All the facts of the poem are here tersely and admirably stated. But Wilkinson was not the only begetter; his words must have awakened memories of what Wordsworth had himself seen and heard during a recent tour of Scotland with Dorothy at harvest time. They would have seen women reaping the grain and timing the strokes of the sickle to the modulation of the harvest song. And they had seen many instances of loneliness in isolated places, such as that of the Highland boy who out of the misty darkness in half-articulate Gaelic was calling the cattle home for the night.[7] Wordsworth observed to Dorothy that the solitary Highland boy and the circumstances surrounding him were "a text upon the whole history of the Highlander's life—his melancholy, his simplicity, his poverty, his superstition, and above all, that visionariness which results from a communion with the unworldliness of nature." Wordsworth made no poem upon the Highland lad and his isolation, but chose instead the simple Highland girl working and singing in the harvest field by herself. In her he captures the loneliness, melancholy, simplicity, and most of all the mysteriousness associated in his mind with the people of the Highlands. He underscores her isolation by repeating four times over in the first stanza that she is a single human figure in the landscape. The aloneness of the singer is intensified in the second stanza when she is compared to the lone nightingale singing in far-off Arabia and to the solitary cuckoo "Breaking the silence of the seas/ Among the farthest Hebrides." The melancholy tone and rhythm established in the first stanza are further developed in the third stanza. Mysteriousness is achieved by means of the reaper's song. We cannot understand her foreign tongue; hence, the theme of her "melancholy strain" is shrouded in mystery. The poet in contemplating the possible theme of the song pushes back the boundaries of time and of space. The theme, whatever it is, could be past, present, or future; it could be some personal domestic sorrow, or it could be some universal loss; it could be near at hand, at home, or it could be far off. The mystery of her plaintive song in that remote place becomes interpenetrated in our consciousness with the mystery of all human experience outside the limits of time and space. Wordsworth not only captures the whole history of the Highlander's life; he isolates for one brief moment the mystery of sorrowing humanity in the melancholy song of the reaper. He reaches the farthest limits of imaginative awareness; yet he avoids all commonplace conventionalities and falsifications of reality. The girl remains steadfastly the simple Highland lass cutting and binding the grain and singing at her work.

> Behold her, single in the field,
> Yon solitary Highland Lass!
> Reaping and singing by herself;
> Stop here, or gently pass!
> Alone she cuts and binds the grain,
> And sings a melancholy strain;

O listen! for the Vale profound
Is overflowing with the sound.

No Nightingale did ever chaunt
More welcome notes to weary bands
Of travellers in some shady haunt,
Among Arabian sands:
A voice so thrilling ne'er was heard
In spring-time from the Cuckoo-bird,
Breaking the silence of the seas
Among the farthest Hebrides.

Will no one tell me what she sings?—
Perhaps the plaintive numbers flow
For old, unhappy, far-off things,
And battles long ago:
Or is it some more humble lay,
Familiar matter of to-day?
Some natural sorrow, loss, or pain,
That has been, and may be again?

Whate'er the theme, the Maiden sang
As if her song could have no ending·
I saw her singing at her work,
And o'er the sickle bending;—
I listened, motionless and still;
And, as I mounted up the hill,
The music in my heart I bore,
Long after it was heard no more.

Wordsworth had spent many months of his young manhood in London and amidst the endless bustle and stream of men had come to know firsthand of the suffering, vice, and deformity that throng the streets of that great city. But he had also discovered steadfastness, beauty, and harmony there. In contrast to the daytime turmoil, he had beheld scenes that took "possession of the faculties":

—the peace
That comes with night; the deep solemnity
Of nature's intermediate hours of rest,
When the great tide of human life stands still;
The business of the day to come, unborn,
Of that gone by, locked up, as in the grave;
The blended calmness of the heavens and earth,
Moonlight and stars, and empty streets, and sounds
Unfrequent as in deserts.

[*The Prelude* VII, 654–62]

Initially the lift in spirit from such scenes as these came from an aesthetic delight in seeing the city in its periods of calm when Nature had arranged and blended the components of beauty. Wordsworth once told the mother of Caroline Fox that the beauty of the country opened his eyes to see beauty everywhere: "Nothing is common or devoid of beauty. . . . Wherever there is a heart to feel, there is also an eye to see; even in a city you have light and shade, reflections, probably views of water and trees, and blue sky above you, and can you want for beauty in all these?"[8] On one occasion after his return home from London, he found that some of the imagery of the city had been more present to his mind than that of his beloved vale of Grasmere. This happened after an unforgettable experience in March, 1808, which he recounts in a letter to Sir George Beaumont.[9] He had been much in Coleridge's company for over a month. Then early one Sunday morning he parted from his friend in "a very thoughtful and melancholy state of mind," greatly depressed over Coleridge's ill-health, and, as he says,

entirely occupied with my own thoughts, when, looking up, I saw before me the avenue of Fleet Street, silent, empty, and pure white, with a sprinkling of new-fallen snow, not a cart or carriage to obstruct the view, no noise, only a few soundless and dusky foot-passengers here and there. You remember the elegant line of the curve of Ludgate Hill in which this avenue would terminate, and beyond, towering above it, was the huge and majestic form of St. Paul's, solemnised by a thin veil of falling snow. I cannot say how much I was affected at this unthought-of sight in such a place, and what a blessing I felt there is in habits of exalted imagination. My sorrow was controlled, and my uneasiness of mind—not quieted and relieved altogether—seemed at once to receive the gift and anchor of security.

In the midst of what was one of London's busiest, most crowded and dirty streets, Wordsworth had been surprised by a scene of simple beauty composed as an artist might arrange and harmonize it: Fleet Street, silent, empty, and white with snow; the sweeping curve of Ludgate Hill; and the lofty majesty of St. Paul's softened by the thin veil of falling snow. Nature had worked "upon the outward face of things/ As with imaginative power" to create a scene of beauty. When Wordsworth looked up and saw the beauty before him, he was in special readiness to respond to it as an artist might; for he and Coleridge had recently visited Angerstein's great collection (later to become the nucleus of the National Gallery), and they had engaged in talk about the pictures of Michelangelo and Rembrandt. In reporting his experience to Beaumont, patron of the arts and a landscape painter, Wordsworth skilfully depicts for his friend the pictorial beauty of the scene and relates his involvement of feeling with it. From "habits of exalted imagination," he says, the beauty before him helped him to see things in a new way. What he means is that the snow storm in Fleet Street by the accidents of circumstance had created "a sudden charm . . . diffused over a known and familiar landscape." It had brought into combination "the truth of nature" with the novelty arising from "the modifying colours of imagination" which, Coleridge says, was to be exemplified in the *Lyrical Ballads*. It was natural, then, for Wordsworth to connect this scene with the imagination and to explain to Beaumont its effect on him. No truth was revealed to him, but his attitude was changed. As in other quasi-mystic experiences in the prescence of beauty, comfort seemed to touch his heart, and strength and restoration to flow in upon him. He had experienced a spiritual catharsis. Wordsworth tells us in *The Prelude* that during his residence in London amidst the blank confusion of "that spectacle," there had appeared to him, in favored moments, glimpses of beauty that made him aware of "an underpresence of greatness." Just as the mountain's outline and steady form opened "the prospect of his soul to grandeur" so, too, he felt in the great city, diffused through the press of self-destroying transitory things, "The soul of Beauty and enduring life. . . / Composure and ennobling Harmony." Above the city's roar he heard the muted music of humanity.

There was another occasion—one well known to all readers of Wordsworth—when he responded to the beauty and humanity of the great city and recorded them in his poetry. This is his sonnet "Composed upon Westminster Bridge, September 3, 1802." Dorothy gives in her *Journal* a brief account of the circumstances that lay behind the composition of the poem:

. . . we left London on Saturday morning at ½-past 5 or 6, the 31st of July. . . . We mounted the Dover Coach at Charing Cross. It was a beautiful morning. The city, St. Paul's, with the river and a multitude of little boats, made a most beautiful sight as we crossed Westminster Bridge. The houses were not overhung by their cloud of smoke, and they were spread out endlessly, yet the sun shone so brightly, with such a fierce light, that there was even something like the purity of one of nature's own grand spectacles.[10]

As Dorothy says, they saw "a most beautiful sight," and she fills in the features of it that most impressed her. To her it was a splendid spectacle, a wondrous scenic panorama; but it remained just that to her—a show of things seen, feeding the physical sight, and without touching off any intellectual response. But the poet from long, intimate acquaintance knew of the sufferings and triumphs of humanity within the city. So, although he responds at once, as Dorothy does, to the dazzling splendor spread out in the "bright and smokeless air" before them—to the pictorial beauty, that is—his deeper response is to his awareness of the human life in the city. What makes the sight before him "so touching in its majesty" are the man-made components of the scene: ships, towers, domes, theatres, temples, and houses. He emphasizes the humanness of the sight by the use of the simile in which the beauty of the morning is likened to a human garment worn by the city. The calm which he feels, as noted above, he has known before during the city's hours of rest—

> When the great tide of human life stands still;
> The business of the day to come, unborn,
> Of that gone by, locked up, as in a grave. . . .

Now once again in the early morning on Westminster Bridge he looks upon the city when all life before him seems locked in profound sleep. At this moment all objects, conditions, and moods conspire to bring Nature and humanity into "an ennobling harmony." The result of this inspiring conjunction is a memorable poem in which the landscape becomes imaginatively joined to the humanness of existence, indeed almost seems to be that existence.

> Earth has not anything to show more fair:
> Dull would he be of soul who could pass by
> A sight so touching in its majesty:
> This City now doth, like a garment, wear
> The beauty of the morning; silent, bare,
> Ships, towers, domes, theatres, and temples lie
> Open unto the fields, and to the sky;
> All bright and glittering in the smokeless air.
> Never did sun more beautifully steep

In his first splendour, valley, rock, or hill;
Ne'er saw I, never felt, a calm so deep!
The river glideth at his own sweet will:
Dear God! the very houses seem asleep;
And all that mighty heart is lying still!

There is no better poetic example of how the landscape acts upon man than "Lines Composed a Few Miles Above Tintern Abbey." In this poem Wordsworth epitomizes his philosophic faith in Nature to foster joy, to strengthen character, and to give insight into the spiritual governance of the universe. He offers a luminous record of how Nature moulded his character and how it may mould others who bring a "heart that watches and receives."

Wordsworth first visited the Wye Valley in 1793, a few months after his return from France. At that time his creative faculties were under the dominance of the analytic intellect. As solace for the impairment of his powers he then sought passionately to feed his mind with the physical forms and colors of the landscape. He "roamed from hill to hill, from rock to rock,/ Still craving combinations of new forms,/ New pleasure, wider empire for the sight"; but his wanderings brought him only temporary and fitful relief. In the period following his first visit to Tintern Abbey he again fell upon dark days: solitude, bewilderment, and depression were his portion. This state endured until his sister Dorothy joined him at Race-down in 1795. There in due course she alleviated his melancholy and led him back to his true, creative self. In June, 1797, Wordsworth and his sister went to live near Coleridge in the lovely Quantocks, where they spent a year of close intimacy. Both poets were then in constant exaltation of spirits and both were at the top of their creative powers. They were ambitious to make the world better through their poetry by sharing the secret they had discovered of a principle of joy in the universe.

The result of their joint effort was soon to be given to the world under the title *Lyrical Ballads*. It was while Wordsworth and his sister were at Bristol seeing the *Lyrical Ballads* through the press that he felt a longing to see the hills and valleys of Wales, through which he had wandered five years before, and to share with Dorothy the beauteous scenes which through a long absence he had never forgotten. They walked from Bristol to the Severn and crossed the river, probably at Aust Ferry. The details of the tour are given in a note Wordsworth wrote for his nephew, Christopher Wordsworth, to be inserted in the *Memoirs*: "We crossed the Severn Ferry and walked ten miles further to Tintern Abbey, a very beautiful ruin on the Wye. The next morning we walked along the river through Monmouth to Goodrich Castle, there slept, and returned the next day to Tintern, thence to Chepstow, and from Chepstow back again in a boat to Tintern, where we slept, and thence back in a small boat to Bristol." As they re-entered Bristol Wordsworth composed "the last 20 lines or so" of the now famous poem whose full title is "Lines Composed a Few Miles above Tintern Abbey, on revisiting the Banks of the Wye during a Tour, July 13, 1798."

"No poem of mine," he said afterwards, "was composed under circumstances more pleasant to remember than this. I began it upon leaving Tintern, after crossing the Wye, and concluded it just as I was entering Bristol in the evening, after a ramble of four or five days, with my Sister. Not a line of it was altered, and not any part of it written down until I reached Bristol." The title given to the poem is not quite accurate, for, as Wordsworth says, it was composed after leaving Tintern Abbey. But the prospect described is the one as seen a few miles above the abbey.

The travelers seem to have taken Gilpin's *Tour of the Wye* with them. In the opening stanza of "Tintern Abbey," at any rate, the landscape prospect is overtly described (in picturesque terms) from "under this dark sycamore," and the closing lines appear to owe a debt to Gilpin.[11] R. A. Aubin identifies a number of features of the poem that belong to eighteenth-century topographical poetry: the here-I-am-again-motif, the retirement theme, the intensely personal tone, the decorative hermit, the incidental meditation, the early-recollections theme, the apostrophe to the river, and the address to the person dear to the poet.[12] But in the impassioned music of Wordsworth's verse, which in his view made "Tintern Abbey" comparable to an ode, these old friends appear in shining raiment. The landscape is described with more than usual care and has many tactual images rendered with great clearness for the eye and mind to rest upon:

> Five years have past; five summers, with the length
> Of five long winters! and again I hear
> These waters, rolling from their mountain-springs
> With a soft inland murmur.—Once again
> Do I behold these steep and lofty cliffs,
> That on a wild secluded scene impress
> Thoughts of more deep seclusion; and connect
> The landscape with the quiet of the sky.
> The day is come when I again repose
> Here, under this dark sycamore, and view
> These plots of cottage-ground, these orchard-tufts,
> Which at this season, with their unripe fruits,
> Are clad in one green hue, and lose themselves
> 'Mid groves and copses. Once again I see
> These hedge-rows, hardly hedge-rows, little lines
> Of sportive wood run wild: these pastoral farms,
> Green to the very door; and wreaths of smoke
> Sent up, in silence, from among the trees!
> With some uncertain notice, as might seem
> Of vagrant dwellers in the houseless woods,

Or of some Hermit's cave, where by his fire
The Hermit sits alone.

[vv. 1–22]

There is no lack of significant pictorial detail in this opening
passage; yet there is also much that points to an inward psychi-
cal response. The waters of the river are heard "rolling from
their mountain springs," but the full impression is not of a river
seen or heard but of a river felt in its continuing entity winding
from its mountain home to its confrontation "inland" by the
tides of the sea. Wordsworth has moved from the river of the
outer physical world to a river whose existence is an inner prospect of the mind. So, too, the "steep and lofty cliffs" before him
"on a wild secluded scene" impress *"thoughts of more deep
seclusion."* Additional features of the landscape suggest a commingling of man and Nature, and this commingling becomes
significant both inwardly and symbolically. The grass of the
pastoral farms is "green to the very doors"; plots of cottage-
ground "lose themselves in groves and copses"; hedgerows and
woodlands intermingle; wreaths of smoke (man created) lose
themselves among the houseless woods where men dwell. Then
somehow the upward movement of the lofty cliffs and smoke
connect the living, inhabited landscape with the quiet of the
sky in an ascent that suggests a spiritual union of the whole.
Wordsworth has rendered a masterful landscape in these
verses, selecting and dramatizing its pictorial features as a
Constable would, but he has also endowed it with inward symbolic significance. In his landscape of the Wye, man, Nature,
and the Divine world are interfused—all exist in a mighty
unity.

The landscape before him starts the ruminative process, and
he thinks of all that the memory of this beautiful scene has
done for him during his five years of absence. He believes that

he owes to those beauteous forms three blessings; first, sensations sweet, physical and restorative, "felt in the blood," which
pass even into his innermost mind with quieting effect; sec-
ondly, feelings unperceived and unremembered which nevertheless mysteriously guide him in the performance of kind and
unselfish acts, such as the severing of the tree root for old
Simon Lee; thirdly, and crowning all, he has been lifted at intervals to a mystic vision that enabled him to "see into the life
of things":

> Nor less, I trust,
> To them I may have owed another gift,
> Of aspect more sublime; . . . that serene and
>   blessed mood,
> In which the affections gently lead us on,—
> Until, the breath of this corporeal frame
> And even the motion of our human blood
> Almost suspended, we are laid asleep
> In body, and become a living soul:
> While with an eye made quiet by the power
> Of harmony, and the deep power of joy,
> We see into the life of things.
>
> [vv. 35–37, 41–49]

It is unlikely that Wordsworth experienced this last and highest gift until perhaps a year or so before his second visit to the
Wye.[13] But restorative sensations nourished his physical and
moral being often during the years of loneliness:

> . . . when the fretful stir
> Unprofitable, and the fever of the world,
> Have hung upon the beatings of my heart—
> How oft, in spirit, have I turned to thee,
> O sylvan Wye! thou wanderer thro' the woods,
> How often has my spirit turned to thee!
>
> [vv. 52–57]

As he looks upon the "steep woods and lofty banks" he recalls the image of himself as he came that way five years before. He sees himself as one who then sought refuge from tormenting mental conflict by flinging himself into physical delight in Nature like one driven by insatiable thirst:

> The sounding cataract
> Haunted me like a passion: the tall rock,
> The mountain, and the deep and gloomy wood,
> Their colours and their forms, were then to me
> An appetite; a feeling and a love,
> That had no need of a remoter charm,
> By thought supplied, nor any interest
> Unborrowed from the eye.
>
> [vv. 76–83]

But now "that time is past/ And all its aching joys are now no more/ And all its dizzy raptures." The loss, however, is compensated by "other gifts" more precious. The sounding cataracts that haunted him on his first visit and the din and turmoil in the cities which followed it have been replaced by the "soft, inland murmur" of the river and by the silent beauty of the landscape. The new-found tranquility before him induces a quietistic response within. He now has a gentler outlook on the tragedy of humanity ("Nor harsh nor grating, though of ample power/ To chasten and subdue"). And he gains a sense of Presence deeply interfused around him and in him, illimitable and united in one joyous harmony of all existence.

> And I have felt
> A presence that disturbs me with the joy
> Of elevated thoughts; a sense sublime
> Of something far more deeply interfused,
> Whose dwelling is the light of setting suns,
> And the round ocean and the living air,
> And the blue sky, and in the mind of man.

> A motion and a spirit, that impels
> All thinking things, all objects of all thought,
> And rolls through all things. Therefore am I still
> A lover of the meadows and the woods,
> And mountains; and of all that we behold
> From this green earth; of all the mighty world
> Of eye, and ear,—both what they half create,
> And what perceive.
>
> [vv. 93–107]

Wordsworth's return to the Wye in 1798 supplied him with a montage (a superimposition of one experience upon another) that confirmed his belief in the unity of past and present as well as his belief in the unity of man and Nature. The chief human agency in the reconciling work was Dorothy, who was in the precise stage of development that the poet had been in five years before.

> For thou art with me here upon the banks
> Of this fair river; thou my dearest Friend,
> My dear, dear Friend; and in thy voice I catch
> The language of my former heart, and read
> My former pleasures in the shooting lights
> Of thy wild eyes. Oh! yet a little while
> May I behold in thee what I was once,
> My dear, dear Sister!
>
> [vv. 114–21]

To Dorothy still belonged the ecstatic, primitive delight in natural things that Wordsworth recognizes no longer can be his. He does not "murmur" at his own change, but projects his own present into his sister's future in a warmly felt and generous prayer for her as a worshipper of Nature.

> My dear, dear Sister! and this prayer I make,
> Knowing that Nature never did betray
> The heart that loved her; 'tis her privilege,

Through all the years of this our life, to lead
From joy to joy: for she can so inform
The mind that is within us, so impress
With quietness and beauty, and so feed
With lofty thoughts, that neither evil tongues,
Rash judgments, nor the sneers of selfish men,
Nor greetings where no kindness is, nor all
The dreary intercourse of daily life,
Shall e'er prevail against us, or disturb
Our cheerful faith, that all which we behold
Is full of blessings. Therefore let the moon
Shine on thee in thy solitary walk;
And let the misty mountain-winds be free
To blow against thee: and, in after years,
When these wild ecstasies shall be matured
Into a sober pleasure; when thy mind
Shall be a mansion for all lovely forms,
Thy memory be as a dwelling-place
For all sweet sounds and harmonies; oh! then,
If solitude, or fear, or pain, or grief,
Should be thy portion, with what healing
    thoughts
Of tender joy wilt thou remember me,
And these my exhortations!

                [vv. 121–46]

Nature in its beauty is a source of joy and of healing thoughts
that will minister to Dorothy in her future need as it has min-
istered to the poet in the past. Wordsworth's faith in Nature's
power to bring comfort to his sister was a complex, intuitive
belief made up of sensation, feeling, knowledge and half-
knowledge, moral awareness, and mystical insight all united in
the powerful solvent of his tenacious memory. And beautifully
intertwined with the intricate network of impressions held in
memory is the quality of hope, running forward and backward,
opening up vistas that look towards the "Uncreated."

Among the poems of moderate length "Tintern Abbey" is the supreme record of the impact of the landscape upon the innermost recesses of the human mind.[14] The poetic expression of the effects of this impact was as spontaneous as it was powerful, taking shape while the poet's feelings were still overflowing with excess of joy and his faith in the power of Nature to dispel "fear or pain or grief" was still at high tide. In later years, of course, he qualified and subdued his pronouncements in "Tintern Abbey." But he never lost his delight in sympathetic converse with Nature or his faith that all created things can bring pleasure to the sensitive person impelled by love and praise.

RETROSPECT AND CONCLUSION

As we have seen, Wordsworth had an undeviating faith in the spiritual reality of Nature.[1] He believed that it is given to man in favored moments to participate in this spiritual Power that permeates and activates all existence. At such times the landscape will open out a prospect of quiet, of solitude, or of space to soothe his being rather than excite it. The beautiful objects of Nature, impregnated with free, active power will strengthen his character, humanize his attitude towards man, and enable him "to see into the life of things." The divine light of Spirit will flow into him and give him insight into the spiritual governance of the universe. To this communion, in which all men are fitted to take profit and delight, the creative artists are best equipped to direct our attention; for they are, as Wordsworth says, "endowed with more lively sensibility, more enthusiasm and tenderness, . . . have a greater knowledge of human nature, and a more comprehensive soul, than are supposed to be common among mankind."[2] Moreover, their art will succeed in proportion as it follows Nature's lead, for Nature is permeated with the living God and shapes its beauty "from its *own* divine vitality." In any of the arts, therefore, the artist who is divinely inspired will follow the lesson that Nature teaches. "Thy Art be Nature," counsels Wordsworth; "the live spirit quaff."

"The art in seeing Nature is a thing almost as much to be acquired as the art of reading the Egyptian hieroglyphics," said

Constable in his pregnant way. This truth Wordsworth confirmed by his own experience; for highly gifted though he was, he mastered the art in poetry only after long effort and steady devotion. Like Constable he aimed at a faithful rendering of Nature. He put his trust in the senses, in the particular instance, in the concrete rather than the abstract. He was ready to follow the Man of Science in the search for truth. But he scorned the mere matter-of-fact cataloguing or positivistic view of Nature. He looked steadily at the external world with the physical eye, and the visible scene would enter his being charged with emotion and bodily substance. All the while an auxiliary light from his mind bestowed new splendor on the forms and colors of earth conceived both inwardly and outwardly. They become in his poetry a manifest creation of pure Spirit, a transparent veil for the mysteries they emblemized. In Wordsworth's imagination all the forms of Nature are linked into "one galaxy of life and joy," even though in any specific instance the vast majority are not directly apprehended. As A. N. Whitehead observes in *Science and the Modern World,* Wordsworth's theme is "Nature *in solido,* that is to say, he dwells on that mysterious presence of surrounding things, which imposes itself on any separate element which we set up as an individual for its own sake. He always grasps the whole of Nature as involved in the tonality of the particular instance. That is why he laughs with the daffodils, and finds in the primrose thoughts too deep for tears."

Wordsworth's singleness of vision as expressed in his poetry extended to all the arts. In whatever medium he was working, whether as a critic of art, gardener, viewer of the landscape, or composer of poetry, Wordsworth was guided by the single concept that all proper art is the embodiment of the Spirit of Nature imaginatively perceived. His unifying vision gives depth and meaning to all his theorizing about the art of landscape. Thus the landscape painter, like the poet, should not let the objects of a scene before him overwhelm him, but seize the essentials and through his imagination modify forms and colors and blend them into one harmonious whole. The painter, moreover, will store his mind with ideas fed by wide reading so that when he captures the poetic moment he can permeate his rendering with meaning and new splendor. The artist, said Wordsworth, cannot possibly excel in his painting "without a strong tincture of the poetic spirit." So, too, the landscape gardener will succeed, as the poet succeeds, when he has learned the lessons Nature has to teach, in so far as Nature is the art of God. Composing poetry and gardening are both "simple Nature trained by careful Art." In tree-planting the gardener will let the images of Nature be his guide. He will not allow formal art and foreign plantings to set up discordant notes. Nor will he—in the manner of "Capability" Brown—round off the landscape and shear it of its native beauty. The true servants of landscape gardening are under the direction of divine Nature conferring value on the objects of sense and paying homage to the human heart in its need for beauty and happiness. Likewise the art of scenic travel is grounded in a proper response to Nature. Inasmuch as the natural landscape is shaped into beauty by an indwelling universal Spirit, the traveler should never contemplate the scene before him without some awareness of the powers of Nature. The thoughtful man will not look upon the landscape as a superficially pretty picture, but as a portion of Nature endowed with spirit ceaselessly speaking to him and working upon him. In proportion as the traveler takes along with him a heart that watches and receives will he unlock the beauty around him.

The eighteenth-century practitioners of the art of landscape prepared the way for Wordsworth's exalted concept of the art; they also offered him a plentiful supply of models for emulation. With his predecessors, however, the landscape for the most part was viewed picturesquely in patterns made fashionable by the Italian painters. When the poets began to write about Nature, their great familiarity with Italian landscape painting led them often to describe scenes in some of the more obvious aspects of pictorial art. James Thomson, the initiator of descriptive Nature poetry, characteristically construed his scenes in the visual schemata of the painters. Still, he wrote with his eye upon the object. *The Seasons* gained a position of eminence because Thomson reported what he saw with fidelity as well as richness. In the hands of his scores of imitators, however, the descriptions of Nature became too much like catalogs or arrangements of the scene in the style of a painter. Varnished trees and verdurous meadows seem to overflow from the canvas onto the poet's landscape. Nevertheless, the scenes they described were at least British; and the better poets, like Thomson, Gray, Collins, and Cowper, did not stop merely with picturesque description: they reflected upon what they saw.

When innovations in landscape gardening were begun, early in the century, the gardeners, as the poets had done, studied the paintings of the Italian masters and applied the management of light and shade discoverable in them to the laying out of grounds. As the fashion for making gardens resemble pictures was carried forward into the second half of the century, the picturesque style of gardening was challenged by "Capability" Brown, who disregarded the pictorial approach and laid out the landscape so that it would be smooth, undulating, and open. After Brown's death, Humphrey Repton continued to emphasize plainness and general utility. Brown and his followers were vigorously opposed by three popular champions of picturesque beauty—William Gilpin, Richard Payne Knight, and Uvedale Price. But as the contest between the utilitarians and the picturesque gardeners wore on, each yielded something to the other. By the end of the century picturesque gardening as a rendering of set pictures went out of fashion, and the improvers were half converted to the formal garden near the house and to other features of the picturesque style.

The art of viewing scenery picturesquely had its beginnings in the admiration of English travelers for the paintings of Claude Lorrain and Salvator Rosa through which they learned to identify the pictorial elements in the landscape. When Thomas Gray returned from the Grand Tour, he was a confirmed enthusiast for grand scenery viewed picturesquely. His *Journal in the Lakes* became an admired pioneer in the literature of picturesque travel and did much to make the Lakes a popular touring ground. Among travel books, however, none matched the originality and influence of those by William Gilpin. It is Gilpin's special contribution to the art of travel that in his many books he identifies a great range of picturesque effects and describes them with gusto. He quickened people's interest in "the new science" of travel and sent them in droves to the countryside to analyze Nature for themselves.

The painting of English scenery by native-born artists did not properly begin until the sixth decade of the century. Before then the English landscapists had generally either painted foreign scenes or made local scenes look like something done by the Dutch or Italian masters. The break from foreign art was at last cleanly made by Richard Wilson, who turned out original landscapes sparkling in color, radiant with air and space, and with effects of light surpassing Claude's. Thomas Gainsborough, Wilson's contemporary, was fond of capturing the rustic aspects of country life in his landscape paintings—picturesque gypsies, farm groups with animals, or peasants at the cottage door. These he enlivened with glimmering freshness and richness of coloring that stimulated Constable to pay him high tribute. But after Wilson and Gainsborough English landscape painting relapsed in the hands of their successors.

In the closing decade of the eighteenth century a point was

reached where it was possible for inspired leadership to open up the way for new advances in all branches of the art of land-scape. It was this leadership that Wordsworth in a consider-able measure supplied. His belief in the spiritual reality of Nature quickened whatever he did in the arts, whether it was inspiring new techniques in landscape painting, laying out a garden, viewing scenery, or translating the landscape into a poem. In every one of the landscape arts he made notable con-tributions. It is true that because of his conservative taste he failed as a critic to recognize the advances being made in land-scape painting in his day; nevertheless, by his example he in-spired Constable to undertake his daring experiments in style that vitalized landscape painting in the nineteenth century. As a landscape gardener, Wordsworth inclined to the school of picturesque gardeners; at the same time he did not lose sight of the fact that a garden must reflect the life and character of the surrounding countryside, the personality of the owner, and his way of life. He knew that the successful gardener must bal-ance the talents of an artist with those of a plantsman; that he must be able to open the spaces of lawn to the sky and antici-pate the quiet shadow patterns of the trees as they expand across the garden. Wordsworth said that composing poetry and gardening are both but "simple Nature trained by careful Art." To substantiate his faith he did in very truth create living poe-try of the trees, shrubs, flowers, walls, and paths in the gardens that he made. As a guide to scenic travelers, Wordsworth served his generation by lifting travel to the status of an art. His own progress towards the true art of viewing the landscape was beset with problems, but he mastered these problems. And when he had done so, he taught others to experience joy in the presence of landscape beauty. He pointed out the way in *A Guide to the Lakes,* and he demonstrated the fact of joyousness in the best of his travel poems. As a practitioner of the art of travel, Wordsworth built upon the aesthetics of eighteenth-century writers on travel, notably Gilpin, but he goes far beyond all of them both in theory and practice and in prose as well as in verse. Supremely it is, of course, in his poetry that Words worth excels in the art of landscape. He moves through a great range from purely descriptive poems (though even here very few are restricted to pictorial features) to those in which the inner response and human significance are central. His images are firm and carry with them the power to open our eyes, quicken our sensibilities, and deepen our insight. With Wordsworth we do not have a prettifying of Nature (as with Cowper); nor a sentimentalizing of the scene (as with Tennyson); we have a transfiguration. In the great tradition of the poetical interpreters of landscape—from Homer, Virgil, Theocritus, through Wordsworth, Keats, and Tennyson to Frost—each has something original and refreshing to contribute. But amongst them all, none can match the breadth of interest, the depth of penetration, and the loftiness of vision of Wordsworth.

Notes

INTRODUCTION

1. Myra Reynolds in *The Treatment of Nature in English Poetry between Pope and Wordsworth* 2nd ed. (Chicago, 1909) offers supporting evidence for the generalizations in my introductory paragraph.

2. In his pioneering study on *The Picturesque* (1927), Christopher Hussey equates the picturesque with the art of landscape. But as Hipple has pointed out, Hussey distorts much of the data on the picturesque and belittles its theoreticians. See Walter J. Hipple, Jr., *The Beautiful, the Sublime, and the Picturesque* (Carbondale, Ill., 1957), p. 190. Hussey also downgrades many practitioners of the art of landscape so as to fit them into the neat formula of the picturesque.

CHAPTER ONE

1. *The Moralists*, written in 1709 and published in 1711 (quotation from 1732 ed., II, 393–94).

2. Horace Walpole, *History of Modern Gardening* (1771), in *The Works of Horace Walpole* (London, 1798), V, 535.

3. Myra Reynolds finds occasional and not ineffective expression of new attitudes towards Nature among poets (i.e., Ambrose Philips, Lady Winchelsea, Thomas Parnell, and others) during the two decades before the publication of Thomson's *Winter* (1726); but, as she says, the indications of a new attitude among this group are fugitive and usually unconscious. See *The Treatment of Nature in English Poetry*, p. 74.

4. C. V. Deane, *Aspects of Eighteenth-Century Nature Poetry* (Oxford, 1935), p. 73.

5. Jean H. Hagstrum, *The Sister Arts* (Chicago, 1958), p. 296.

6. Deane, p. 78.

7. William Mason (*The English Garden*, 1772) favored the picturesque garden with emotional appeal. William Chambers (*A Dissertation on Oriental Gardening*, 1772), also approved the picturesque approach to gardening ("Art must supply the scantiness of nature") and encouraged the use of Chinese features, such as seats, alcoves, bridges, pagodas, and the like. Horace Walpole (*History of Modern Gardening*, 1771) cautions against the imminent danger to taste in the pursuit after novelty. "If we once lose sight of the propriety of landscape in our gardens," he warns, "we shall wander into all the fantastic sharawadgis of the Chinese." But Walpole concludes his garden history with a rapturous burst of praise for the pictorial beauty of English landscapes rising in every part of the island: "How rich, how gay, how picturesque the face of the country . . . when the daily plantations that are making have attained venerable maturity."

8. *Observations on the Mountains and Lakes of Cumberland and Westmoreland*, 3rd ed. (London, 1808), I, xxi.

9. Ibid., II, 182–83.

10. *Observations on the River Wye*, 5th ed. (1800), pp. 60–61.

11. *Observations on the Mountains and Lakes*, I, xiii.

12. *Remarks on Forest Scenery*, 3rd ed. (1808), I, 226.

13. *Observations on the Mountains and Lakes*, I, 146.

14. *Remarks on Forest Scenery*, I, 1.

15. The note is quoted in Uvedale Price, *Essays on the Picturesque* (London, 1810), III, 249.

16. *An Essay on the Picturesque* (London, 1796), p. 4.

17. Ibid., p. 15.

18. Ibid., p. 335.

19. *The Works of Thomas Gray*, ed. Edmund Gosse (London, 1884), I, 244.

20. Ibid., II, 45.

21. Ibid., III, 223.

22. Arthur Young, *A Six Months Tour through the North of England* (London, 1770), III, 188.

23. Ibid., III, 155–56.

24. A plano-convex mirror in which the landscape appears with exaggerated perspective.

25. *Journal in the Lakes* in *The Works of Gray*, I, 265–66.

26. Gilpin's works on travel in order of publication are: *Observations on the River Wye and Several Parts of South Wales, etc., Relative Chiefly to Picturesque Beauty*, 1782; *Observations on . . . the Mountains and Lakes of Cumberland and Westmoreland*, 1786; *Observations on Several Parts of Great Britain particularly the Highlands of Scotland . . .*, 1789; *Three Essays: On Picturesque Beauty; On Picturesque Travel; On Sketching Landscape, to which is Added a Poem on Landscape Painting*, 1792; *Observations on the Western Parts of England . . .*, 1798; *Observations on the Coasts of Hampshire, Sussex, and Kent . . .*, 1804; *Observations on . . . the Counties of Cambridge, Norfolk, Suffolk, and Essex . . . also on Several Parts of North Wales*, 1809.

27. *Three Essays on Picturesque Beauty*, 3rd ed. (London, 1808), p. 49.

28. Ibid., p. 54.

29. *Scenery of the Mountains and the Lakes*, 3rd ed. (London, 1808), I, 184.

30. Ibid., p. 194.

31. Ibid., p. 201.

32. C.R. Leslie, R.A., *The Life of John Constable*, ed. The Hon. A. Shirley (London, 1937), p. 402.

CHAPTER TWO

1. *The Prelude*, IX, 77.

2. William Wordsworth to William Mathews, 23 May 1794. *The Early Letters of William and Dorothy Wordsworth*, ed. E. de Selincourt (Oxford, 1935), p. 116.

3. In 1796 Wordsworth wrote to William Mathews asking him to check with Basil Montagu about "Gilpin's tour into Scotland, and

his northern tour, each 2 vols.," and "very expensive," which were in his collection of books at Montagu's. Ibid., p. 155.

4. Quoted by Martha H. Shackford, *Wordsworth's Interest in Painters and Pictures* (Wellesley, Mass., 1945), p. 24.

5. William Wordsworth to Sir George Beaumont, January or February, 1808. *The Letters of William and Dorothy Wordsworth: The Middle Years*, ed. E. de Selincourt (Oxford, 1937), p 171.

6. *The Farington Dairy*, ed. James Greig (London, 1922–28), IV, 129.

7. *Letters: Middle Years*, p. 171.

8. William Wordsworth to Sir George Beaumont, 28 August 1811. *Letters: Middle Years*, pp. 467–68.

9. *A Guide to the Lakes* (Kendal, 1835), p. 67.

10. Quoted by Shackford, p. 32.

11. Wordsworth to the Bishop of Lincoln. Quoted by William A. Knight, *Life of William Wordsworth* (Edinburgh, 1889), II, 323.

12. Hussey says (*The Picturesque*, pp. 49–50) that Wordsworth is patronizing Beaumont's art. But Hussey misreads Wordsworth's intention, which he makes explicit in his prose note to the poem. See *The Poetical Works of William Wordsworth*, ed. E. de Selincourt (Oxford, 1940–49), III, 420.

13. William Wordsworth to Sir George Beaumont, 16 November 1811. *Letters: Middle Years*, p. 475.

14. Constable to John Dunthorne, 29 May 1802. *The Letters of John Constable*, ed. Peter Leslie (London, 1931), p. 21.

15. Preface to *Lyrical Ballads*, 1802.

16. Letter by Constable to John Dunthorne, 29 May 1802, quoted by C. R. Leslie, R.A., *The Life of John Constable*, Everyman ed. (London, 1912), p. 13.

17. *The Farington Dairy*, II, 207. 21 March 1804.

18. "Constable and Wordsworth," *College Art Journal*, XII (1952–53), 196–209.

19. *The Farington Diary*, IV, 239. 12 December 1807.

20. Ibid., p. 108. 1 April 1807.

21. *Victoria and Albert Museum: Catalogue of the Constable Collection* (London, 1960), I, 23.

22. Ibid., VII, 272.

23. Constable's finest work, with but few exceptions, was done between his fortieth and fiftieth years (1816–1826). Among his most successful canvases are: *Flatford Mill* (1817), *The White Horse* (1819), *Stratford Mill* (1820), *The Hay-Wain* (1821), *A View on the Stour* (1822), *Salisbury Cathedral from the Bishop's Garden* (1823), and *The Lock* (1824). *The Hay-Wain* was exhibited at the Louvre, in 1824, where it was awarded a gold medal. In 1825 he exhibited *The Leaping Horse,* his masterpiece, and in 1826 *The Cornfield,* a popular favorite. During the last twelve years of his life his manner became even more free, with spots and splashes of pure color. *Salisbury Cathedral from the Meadows, The Cenotaph,* and *Arundel Mill and Castle* show his palette-knife technique in its highest development.

24. Preface to *Lyrical Ballads.*

25. L. C. W. Bonacina of the Royal Meteorological Society, quoted by Kurt Badt, *John Constable's Clouds* (London, 1950), p. 47.

26. C. R. Leslie, *Memoirs of the Life of John Constable,* ed. J. Mayne (London, 1951), p. 73.

27. Quoted by Sir Kenneth Clark, *Landscape into Art* (London, 1949), p. 79.

28. Constable's Prospectus to *English Landscape,* 1830.

29. Ibid.

30. Quoted by Constable from Wordsworth's "Praised Be the Art."

31. *John Constable: The Hay-Wain* (London, 1944), p. 3.

32. C. R. Leslie, R.A., *The Life and Letters of John Constable, R.A.,* (London, 1896), p. 353.

33. Ibid., p. 69.

34. E. V. Lucas, *John Constable the Painter* (London, 1924), p. 1.

35. R. B. Beckett, "Correspondence and other Memorials of John Constable, R.A." (typescript in Victoria and Albert Museum), I, 117.

36. Diary entry: 26 August 1824. In a letter to Dorothy, 13 December 1824, Robinson writes: "I met with a painter who had met Mr. Wordsworth at Sir George Beaumont's some years ago: Mr. Constable." *The Correspondence of Henry Crabb Robinson with the Wordsworth Circle,* ed. Edith J. Morley (Oxford, 1927), I, 134.

37. 27 October 1823. Beckett, "Correspondence and other Memorials of John Constable," I, 119.

38. Leslie, *Memoirs of John Constable,* p. 73.

39. Beckett, IV, 233.

40. Paul M. Zall, "Wordsworth on Constable," *Modern Language Notes,* LXXI (1956), 338.

41. Beckett, I, 120–21.

42. Now in the Bodleian Library.

43. J. R. Watson, "Wordsworth and Constable," *Review of English Studies,* XIII (1962), 367.

44. Leslie, *Memoirs of Constable,* p. 273.

45. Henry Crabb Robinson, *Diary, Reminiscences, and Correspondence,* ed. T. Sadler (Boston, 1877), II, 41.

46. William Wordsworth to C. R. Leslie, 2 September 1837 (MS).

47. From a record kept by Mary Wordsworth, quoted by Shackford, *Wordsworth's Interest in Painters and Pictures,* p. 46.

48. T. Landseer, *Life and Letters of William Bewick,* quoted in Shackford, p. 20.

49. William Hazlitt, "The Spirit of the Age," *The Complete Works of William Hazlitt,* ed. P. P. Howe (London, 1932), XI, 93.

50. William Wordsworth to Sir George Beaumont, 20 September 1824. *Letters: Middle Years,* p. 155.

51. Knight, *Life of Wordsworth,* III, 296.

52. William Wordsworth to Lord Lonsdale, 7 October 1820. *Letters: Middle Years,* p. 902.

53. "The new things gave us but little pleasure, though not uninteresting as shewing the present state of French art which really does not seem to have much to boast of." William Wordsworth to Isabella Fenwick, 24 March 1837. *The Letters of William and*

Dorothy Wordsworth: The Later Years, ed. E. de Selincourt (London, 1939), p. 841.

CHAPTER THREE

1. Knight, *Life of Wordsworth,* II, 328.

2. Edna Shearer, "Wordsworth's Marginalia in Knight's *Inquiry into Principles of Taste," Huntington Library Quarterly,* I (October, 1937), 63–99.

3. Grasmere *Journal,* 27 June 1800. *The Journals of Dorothy Wordsworth,* ed. E. de Selincourt (London, 1952), I, 52.

4. Dorothy Wordsworth to Lady Beaumont, 19 January 1806. *Letters: Middle Years,* p. 3.

5. William Wordsworth to Sir George Beaumont, 28 August 1811. Ibid., p. 467.

6. "Kendal and Windermere Railway," *The Prose Works of William Wordsworth,* ed. A. B. Grosart (London, 1876), II, 329.

7. The poet's grandson Gordon Wordsworth reported this to Frederika Beatty; see *William Wordsworth of Rydal Mount* (New York, 1939), p. 18.

8. Quoted by Marian Mead, *Four Studies in Wordsworth* (Menasha, Wisc., 1929), p. 252.

9. *Early Letters,* p. 522.

10. Dorothy Wordsworth in her *Recollections of a Tour Made in Scotland (Journals,* ed. de Selincourt, I, 349) describes the ell-wide gravel walk on the Duke of Athol's estate "conducted at the top of the banks, on each side, at nearly equal height and equal distance from the stream." She tells also of her and William's astonishment, when they were looking at a painting of Ossian, of suddenly being startled by the theatric display in a splendid room of waterfalls "reflected in innumerable mirrors upon the ceiling and against the walls." Wordsworth in an "Effusion in the Pleasure-Ground on the Banks of the Bran" (1814) condemns the bad taste of such devices.

> Vain pleasures of luxurious life,
> For ever with yourselves at strife;
> Through town and country both deranged

By affectations interchanged,
And all the perishable gauds
That heaven-deserted man applauds;
When will your hapless patrons learn
To watch and ponder—to discern
The freshness, the everlasting youth,
Of admiration sprung from truth;
From beauty infinitely growing
Upon a mind with love o'erflowing—
To sound the depths of every Art
That seeks its wisdom through the heart?

11. On this latter point Ruskin's attitude is similar: "Only natural phenomena in their direct relation to humanity—these are to be your subjects in landscape. Rocks and water and air may no more be painted for their own sakes than the armour carved without the warrior." "Lectures on Landscape" in *The Works of Ruskin* (London, 1906), XXII, 17.

12. *A Guide Through the District of the Lakes,* p. 78.

13. Ibid., p. 85.

14. Alfoxden *Journal,* 15 April 1798. *Journals of Dorothy Wordsworth,* I, 15.

15. Grasmere *Journal,* 8 June 1802. Ibid., p. 155.

16. Dorothy Wordsworth, *Recollections of a Tour Made in Scotland,* ibid., pp. 297–98. De Selincourt wrongfully identifies Mr. Brown in this passage as John Brown, D.D. (1715–66), author of *Estimate of the Manners and Principles of the Times* (1757). Dorothy has in mind, of course, the creator of the famous artificial river and lake at Blenheim, who when he beheld his wonder cried out, "Thames, will you ever forgive me!"

17. William quotes in a note to "Bothwell Castle" from Dorothy's *Recollections.* See *The Poetical Works of William Wordsworth,* III, 532–33.

18. William Wordsworth to John Taylor Coleridge, 28 November 1840. *Letters: Later Years,* p. 1056.

19. William Wordsworth to Mrs. Howley, 20 November 1837. London *Times Literary Supplement,* August 10, 1962, p. 614.

20. "A Tour of the Isle of Man" (1828), *Journals of Dorothy Wordsworth*, II, 407.

21. Dorothy Wordsworth to Jane Marshall, 10 September 1800. *Early Letters*, p. 248.

22. Grasmere *Journal*, passim.

23. Ibid., I, 144.

24. Ibid., p. 168.

25. See Wordsworth's sonnet, "Admonition." *Poetical Works*, III, 2.

26. William Wordsworth to Sir George Beaumont, 10 November 1806. *Letters: Middle Years*, p. 76.

27. William Wordsworth to Lady Beaumont, 23 December 1806. *Letters: Middle Years*, pp. 90–99.

28. Sir George Beaumont to William Wordsworth, 28 October 1811. Autograph letter in Dove Cottage Library, quoted by permission.

29. Sir George Beaumont to William Wordsworth, 1 May 1808. Autograph letter in Dove Cottage Library.

30. William Wordsworth to Lady Beaumont, 3 February 1807. *Letters: Middle Years*, p. 112.

31. Ibid., p. 113.

32. Daughter of the Archbishop of Canterbury and Mrs. Howley.

33. William Wordsworth to Isabella Fenwick, 24 July 1841. *Letters: Later Years*, p. 1082.

34. William Wordsworth to Mrs. Howley, 23 August 1841. London *TLS*, August 10, 1962, p. 612.

35. Knight, *The Life of William Wordsworth*, II, 82.

36. When Scott visited Coleorton, he often retired to this sandstone seat where he composed a good part of *Ivanhoe*.

37. Autograph letter in Dove Cottage Library.

38. *Letters: Middle Years*, pp. 472–76.

39. William Wordsworth to Sir George Beaumont, 27 November 1811. *Letters: Middle Years*, p. 478.

40. Fenwick note on "This Lawn, Carpet All Alive," *Poetical Works*, IV, 424.

41. William Wordsworth to Dora Wordsworth, Spring, 1830. *Letters: Later Years*, p. 467.

42. Letter by Ellis Yarnall to Prof. Henry Reed, quoted by Christopher Wordsworth in *Memoirs of William Wordsworth,* ed. H. Reed (London, 1851), II, 498.

43. Ibid., p. 505.

44. "English Note-Books," in *The Complete Works of Nathaniel Hawthorne* (Boston, 1899), VIII, 27.

45. Philip Kempferhausen, *Letters from the Lakes* (Ambleside, 1889), p. 87.

46. Quoted by Knight, *Life of Wordsworth,* II, 328.

47. Fenwick note to "Poor Robin," *Poetical Works,* IV, 438.

48. H. D. Rawnsley, *Lake Country Sketches* (Glasgow, 1903), p. 38.

49. Recalled by George Middleton, *Some Old Trees and Travel-Tracks of Wordsworth's Parish* (Ambleside, 1918), p. 42.

50. Ibid., p. 43.

51. Eliza Fletcher, *Autobiography* (Edinburgh, 1875), p. 243.

52. Quoted by Knight, *Life of Wordsworth,* III, 419–20.

53. Dorothy Wordsworth to Catherine Clarkson, 30 August 1807. *Letters: Middle Years,* p. 141.

54. Rawnsley, *Lake Country Sketches,* p. 31.

55. Ibid., p. 33.

56. Ibid., p. 53.

57. Vera Wheatley, *The Life and Work of Harriet Martineau* (London, 1957), p. 247.

58. William Wordsworth to Isabella Fenwick, early 1840. *Letters: Later Years,* p. 1020.

59. Rawnsley, p. 32.

CHAPTER FOUR

1. Wordsworth's intimacy with travel literature (both loco-descriptive poetry and Lake District guide books and "surveys") began when he was a schoolboy at Hawkshead, as we know from entries in his brother Christopher's notebook. (See Z. S. Fink, *The Early Wordsworthian Milieu* [New York, 1958].) Among books of

travel accumulated during a lifetime and listed for sale from the poet's library are many pertaining to touring in countries that he visited: James Boswell's *Journal of a Tour of the Hebrides;* Gilbert Burnet's *Travels in France, Italy, Germany, and Switzerland;* William Coxe's works of history and travel in Switzerland; *Guide to Perthshire* and four other topographical works on Scotland; two bundles of various guide books, English and Continental, with maps; John Ray's travel books on the Low Countries; tour books of western Europe by Seth A. Stevenson; several tour books on the Alps; M. Valéry's guide to Italy; Thomas West's *Antiquities of Furness,* 1805, and *Guide to the Lakes,* 1807; W. Bennett's *Six Weeks in Ireland, Guide to the Isle of Man,* Hastings' Guide, Oxford Guide, etc.; *Guide to the English Lakes* by Ford; J. N. Wright's *Guide through Scotland; Wye Tour* by J. D. Fosbroke, *Teignmouth and Torquay Guide* by Carrington, *Guide to the Lakes,* 1819; William Gilpin's tour books on the River Wye, Scotland, and northern England and the Lakes.

2. William Wordsworth to G. H. Gordon, 1 December 1829. *Letters: Later Years,* p. 433.

3.   . . . for I had an eye
Which in my strongest workings, evermore
Was looking for the shades of difference
As they lie hid in all exterior forms.

[*The Prelude,* III, 157–60]

4. This passage was written in Goslar in 1799 and originally intended as part of Book II of *The Prelude.* It was revised later and included as part of Book VIII. (See *The Prelude,* ed. de Selincourt, Notes, p. 564.)

5. Fenwick note, *Poems,* I, 319.

6. William Wordsworth to Dorothy Wordsworth, 6 September 1790. *Early Letters,* p. 30.

7. See G. H. Hartman, "Wordsworth's *Descriptive Sketches* and the Growth of the Poet's Mind," *PMLA,* LXXVI (1961), 519–27. I am indebted to this excellent article for insight into the poet's intellectual crisis as represented in *Descriptive Sketches.*

8. Ibid., p. 522.

9. *The Prelude*, XII, 144–45.

10. R. A. Aubin, *Topographical Poetry in XVIII-Century England* (New York, 1936), p. 255.

11. Wordsworth's prose note (part of which has been quoted in the text) shows that he was conscious of what he was doing: "Had I wished to make a picture of this scene I had thrown much less light into it. But I consulted nature and my feelings. The ideas excited by the stormy sunset I am here describing owed their sublimity to that deluge of light, or rather of fire, in which nature had wrapped the immense forms around me; any intrusion of shade, by destroying the unity of the impression, had necessarily diminished its grandeur." According to the formula of picturesque composition, the rules of proportionate light and shadow should be applied, but Wordsworth sensed that they should not be applied here.

12. Generally assumed to be derived from William Godwin's *Political Justice*.

13. By "picturesque" Wordsworth also approvingly means those features that would add interest and liveliness to the landscape, whether or not they were recorded in words or painted on canvas, or those features when they were so recorded. Thus the quality of "roughness" is attractively "picturesque"—what he calls Dutch details—achieved by the action of time on a temple, a tree, or a man.

14. Op. cit., p. 525.

15. *Journals of Dorothy Wordsworth*, I, 78, 80, 104, 116, 134, 180, 184.

16. *Letters: Middle Years*, p. 351.

17. *Journals of Dorothy Wordsworth*, I, 86.

18. Ibid., pp. 126–27.

19. Ibid., p. 133.

20. *Collected Letters*, ed. E. L. Griggs (Oxford, 1956), I, 92–93.

21. Rev. G. H. B. Coleridge, "Samuel Taylor Coleridge Discovers the Lake Country," in *Studies in Honor of G. M. Harper*, ed. E. L. Griggs (New York, 1939), pp. 143–44.

22. Ibid., p. 149.

23. Ibid., p. 163.

24. *Journals of Dorothy Wordsworth*, I, 245.

25. Ibid., p. 246.

26. Ibid., pp. 251–52.

27. Ibid., p. 271.

28. Ibid., p. 371.

29. Ibid., p. 390.

30. Ibid., p. 272.

31. Ibid., pp. 299–300.

32. Ibid., p. 286.

33. Wordsworth's *Guide to the Lakes* was first published anonymously in 1810 as an introduction to the Rev. Joseph Wilkinson's *Select Views in Cumberland, Westmoreland, and Lancashire*. In 1820 it appeared in a volume of his own verse, *The River Duddon . . . and Other Poems*, and was entitled *A Topographical Description of the Country of the Lakes*. Two years later it appeared separately under the title *A Description of the Scenery of the Lakes in the North of England*. In 1823 a fourth, enlarged edition was issued, and in 1835 the final form of the work appeared under the title *A Guide through the District of the Lakes in the North of England*.

34. Such as Gray's *Journal* (1769), Young's *Tours* (1774), West's *Guide to the Lakes* (1778), Gilpin's *Observations on the Several Parts of Great Britain* (1789), and Mrs. Radcliffe's *Observations during a Tour of the Lakes* (1795).

35. William Wordsworth to Jacob Fletcher, 17 January 1825. *Letters: Later Years*, p. 173.

36. *A Guide Through the District of the Lakes*, p. 95.

37. Dorothy Wordsworth to Lady Beaumont, 7 November 1805. *Early Letters*, pp. 538–39.

38. *A Guide Through the District of the Lakes*, p. 102.

39. Ibid., p. 32.

40. Ibid., p. 94.

41. Ibid., p. 95.

42. Ibid., p. 7.

43. Ibid., p. 98.

44. Ibid., p. 52.

45. Ibid., p. 31.

46. Ibid., pp. 33–34.

47. Aubin, *Topographical Poetry*, p. 241.

48. S. C. Wilcox, "Wordsworth's River Duddon Sonnets," *PMLA*, LXIX (1954), 136.

49. "Most Sweet It Is with Unuplifted Eyes."

50. Dorothy Wordsworth to Lady Beaumont, 14 August 1810. *Letters: Middle Years*, p. 387.

51. *Journals of Dorothy Wordsworth*, II, 21.

52. 6 January 1821. *Letters: Later Years*, p. 7.

53. Ibid., p. 6.

54. 20 September 1824. *Letters: Later Years*, p. 152.

55. *Letters: Later Years*, pp. 416–17.

56. January 1820. *Letters: Middle Years*, p. 861.

57. Christopher Wordsworth, *Memoirs of William Wordsworth*, II, 428.

58. William Wordsworth to R. P. Gillies, 25 April 1815. *Letters: Middle Years*, pp. 666–67.

59. Fenwick note, *Poetical Works*, I, 329.

60. "Kendal and Windermere Railway," *The Prose Works of William Wordsworth*, II, 330.

61. Christopher Wordsworth, *Memoirs*, II, 301.

CHAPTER FIVE

1. Quoted by Eric Robertson, *Wordsworthshire* (London, 1911), p. 170.

2. *Memorials of a Tour on the Continent*, 1820.

3. 16 April 1822. *Letters: Later Years*, p. 65.

4. Colin C. Clarke, *Romantic Paradox: An Essay on the Poetry of Wordsworth* (New York, 1963), p. 25. Clarke has persuasively argued that Wordsworth's power in landscape description in large measure is related to the ambivalent status of "the image in Vision."

5. Ibid., p. 66.

6. For additional examples in Wordsworth's poetry of the breeze of nature stirring the creative spirit see M. H. Abrams, "The

Correspondent Breeze: A Romantic Metaphor," *Kenyon Review,* XIX (1957), 116–18.

7. See above, p. 173 of this book.

8. Journals of Caroline Fox in *Memories of Old Friends* (London, 1883), p. 197.

9. *Letters: Middle Years,* p. 186.

10. *Journals of Dorothy Wordsworth,* I, 172–73.

11. The following passage from Gilpin should be compared with "Tintern Abbey" vv. 8–18: "Many of the furnaces, on the banks of the river, consume charcoal, which is manufactured on the spot; and the smoke, issuing from the sides of the hills; and spreading its thin veil over part of them, beautifully breaks their lines, and unites them with the sky."

12. *Topographical Poetry in XVIII-Century England,* p. 238.

13. Mary Moorman notes that a few months preceding his second visit Wordsworth had written a passage for "The Ruined Cottage" afterwards, slightly altered and incorporated into the "poem of his own life," which shows a close kinship to the lines in "Tintern Abbey."

> . . . with bliss ineffable
> I felt the sentiment of Being spread
> O'er all that moves and all that seemeth still;
> O'er all that, lost beyond the reach of thought
> And human knowledge, to the human eye
> Invisible, yet liveth to the heart. . . . Wonder not
> If high the transport, great the joy I felt
> Communing in this sort through earth and heaven
> With every form of creature, . . .
> One song they sang, and it was audible,
> Most audible, then, when the fleshly ear,
> O'ercome by humblest prelude of that strain,
> Forgot her functions, and slept undisturbed.
> [*The Prelude,* II, 400–18]

Though this passage describes an experience of boyhood, its similarity to the one in "Tintern Abbey" shows that the experience was continually repeated in adult life and was probably especially strong during the preceding happy year.

14. *The Prelude* is, of course, the full and detailed record of how the poetic imagination is nourished and shaped by the external world of Nature.

RETROSPECT AND CONCLUSION

1. Classic utterance of this belief is to be found in the opening lines of *The Excursion,* Book IX:

> To every Form of being is assigned . . .
> An *active* Principle:—howe'er removed
> From sense and observation, it subsists
> In all things, in all natures; in the stars
> Of azure heaven, the unenduring clouds,
> In flower and tree, in every pebbly stone
> That paves the brooks, the stationary rocks,
> The moving waters, and the invisible air.
> Whate'er exists hath properties that spread
> Beyond itself, . . .
> Spirit that knows no insulated spot,
> No chasm, no solitude; from link to link
> It circulates, the Soul of all the worlds.
> This is the freedom of the universe;
> Unfolded still the more, more visible,
> The more we know.

2. Wordsworth is here referring, of course, to the superior endownment of poets; but Picasso has even more forceful language for those who would place the artist in anything less than a superior role: "What do you think an artist is—an imbecile with a brush or pen? An artist is a man who must see more widely, think more deeply, feel more strongly than the others of his time."

INDEX

Addison, Joseph: advocate of naturalness, 5–6; Italy opened up landscape to, 9, 11; responded to wildness in Nature, 35

"Address to Kilchurn Castle," 215–7

"Airey-Force Valley," 210, 213

The Alps: awakened a taste for grand scenery, 34–6; compared to English scenery, 179, 193

Antiquity: co-partner to Nature, 60, 96, 97, 214

Art: is of divine origin, 60–1; will follow Nature, 251; is embodiment of the Spirit of Nature, 252

Beattie, James, *The Minstrel*, 15

Beaumont, Sir George: influence upon Wordsworth, 55; had wide circle of artist friends, 55; private collection accessible to Wordsworth, 55–8; introduces Constable to Wordsworth's poetry, 67; urged Constable to imitate paintings, 75, 84, 86; Constable's *The Cenotaph* honors, 81; with Wordsworth sees glorious apparition, 226–7; Wordsworth's letter on St. Paul's to, 238; 78–81, 111–26, *passim*

Bewick, Thomas, 88

Bowles, William Lisle, 15–6

Bridgeman, Charles: natural garden design, 8; introduced the ha-ha, 8

Brown, "Capability": his method of landscape design, 21; most popular from mid-century until 1783, 21; creator of river at Blenheim, 266

"Brownists," 33, 95

Burns, Robert, 196

Chimneys of Lake District, 182

Claudian elements, 8–34 *passim*

"Cock is crowing, The," 219–20

Coleridge, Samuel Taylor: walking tour of Wales, 45; exposed Wordsworth to his ideas on art, 59; opinion of the Winter Garden, 118; scene-hunting in Wales and the Lake Country, 169–71; toured with Wordsworth, 189; his landscape poetry usually pictorial, 199; quoted, 199

Collins, William; nature pictures shadowy, 13

Combe, William, 45–8

"Composed by . . . Grasmere Lake," 212